UTAH'S LAWLESS FRINGE

UTAH'S LAWLESS FRINGE

Stories of True Crime

Edited by Stanford J. Layton

Favorite readings from the
UTAH HISTORICAL QUARTERLY

SIGNATURE BOOKS • SALT LAKE CITY

Cover design by Ron Stucki

∞ *Utah's Lawless Fringe: Stories of True Crime*
was printed on acid free paper and was composed, printed,
and bound in the United States of America.

06 05 04 03 02 2001 6 5 4 3 2 1

Library of Congress Cataloging-in-Publication Data
Utah's lawless fringe : stories of true crime—favorite readings
from the Utah historical quarterly / edited by Stanford J. Layton.
p. cm.
Includes bibliographical references.
ISBN l-56085-148-1 (pbk.)
1. Crime—Utah—History. 2. Criminals—Utah—History.
3. Criminal justice, Administration of—Utah—History. I. Layton,
Stanford J. II. Utah historical quarterly.

HV6793.U8 U73 2000
364.9792—dc21
00-055616

Contents

Illustrations

Editor's Introduction

It was at least twenty years ago that the idea of a favorite essays book first popped up within the editorial offices of Utah Historical Quarterly. The thought emerged from the always fertile imagination of Miriam Murphy, associate editor. At the time our venerable journal was nearing its 50th volume year. We lamented the fact that most of the back issues were out of print and that their trove of articles was inaccessible to and largely forgotten by many contemporary readers.

Unfortunately the Bicentennial era was just ending and so were the flush times for our publications program. True, we would always have sufficient funds to produce the *Quarterly* and other membership publications, but the days were past when we could plan on producing a book or two a year. In fact, by the early 1980s we had suspended book publication for the indefinite future. A "favorite articles" anthology came to be thought of less and less frequently and then only as an angel dead in heaven.

Imagine the elation in the office upon receiving an invitation from Signature Books in the summer of 1999 for just such an anthology! Miriam had recently retired, but her idea still inspired the staff. We responded with alacrity and went to work. It was a special thrill to me to be named series editor. Yes, *series.* Signature had outlined the prospect of more than one volume—perhaps as many as five or more over the coming years.

It did not take long to frame the first five general themes. Selecting a dozen or more articles for each took a little longer, but not much. I knew the field of candidates pretty well. Those articles published in the *Utah Historical Quarterly* during my twenty-seven years as managing editor were as familiar to me as individual students to an elementary school teacher by year's end. I had been the first to read them as submissions, had managed the evaluation process, had guided the authors through revisions, had copy-edited many of the articles, and proofread them all at least three times. But I was tolerably well acquainted with the articles published even before 1973 when I took on my editorial duties, having been a subscriber and reader of *UHQ* since early graduate school days in 1967 and having read earlier volumes that go back to 1928.

Understandably my favorite articles come from the last twenty-seven years. Had I not liked them in the first place, they would not have made the printed page in "my journal." (I have often said that editors generally thrive on anonymity but that this does not prevent us from having a tyrannical streak!) I also think that historical research and writing need to be up to date.

Good scholarship, polished writing—two clearly defined criteria for an anthology. Beyond that, my decisions were strictly personal. These were articles that I especially enjoyed—those I never tired of proofreading and to which I have returned again and again for one reason or another since their initial publication.

Here, then, are fourteen considerations of some aspect of lawlessness in Utah history. They come from fifteen authors who together represent the amazing array of professions, interests, ages, and backgrounds that has characterized our contributors generally. Graduate students, high school teachers, professors, archivists, attorneys, retired businessmen, elected officials, and others—both professional and lay—are here. At least one is now deceased and another is lost to us, but all have helped to make my job one of the most enjoyable that a person could ever hope for.

The first essay begins with two high-profile murders in 1851 just after territorial status had come to Utah. The cases were similar in that each suspect was a respected member of his community and each acted from the same motive, avenging his honor by killing the man who had seduced his wife. The counsel for the defense argued a very simple proposition: "The principle, the only one, that beats and throbs through the heart of the entire inhabitants of this territory, is simply this: The man who seduces his neighbor's wife must die, and her nearest relative must kill him!" Both defendants were acquitted under the tenets of this "mountain common law." They would not be the only ones. Other trials of avenging husbands and fathers were to follow, with the precedent of justifiable homicide holding sway. Although these types of trials were not unique to Utah, extraordinary factors were at play here as values and procedures were impacted by that most ubiquitous Utah peculiarity, polygamy.

Arthur Pratt, lawman and son of one of Utah's most respected couples, is the subject of the second selection. Showing little deference to Brigham Young, the territory's most revered citizen and highest ecclesiastical leader, Pratt served him with a subpoena and roughed up his gatekeeper for good measure. Though a Mormon himself, Pratt wore his religion uneasily and at first glance seemed the type who could easily abuse his law enforcement auspices. The biographical analysis that unfolds, however, portrays a complex man with a personality actually well suited to his time, place, and circumstances, holding ideas that proved worthy and progressive.

Southeastern Utah is the setting for the next essay as "murder and mayhem" loomed large in that rugged, sparsely populated region for twenty years. Unlike every other corner of the territory of that time, this one was already occupied by white settlers, cattlemen from Colorado, when Mormons first sent their colonizers. The two groups did not mesh well; additionally, neither cared much for the Native Americans of the area (and vice versa). Effective law enforcement replaced vigilantism and chaos only slowly and not before a raucous chapter in Western history had been stamped indelibly into the record.

Utah Historical Quarterly has never specialized in blood-and- guts stories, but it could not purport to be a credible source for Utah history without an occasional article of that genre. Here come five in a row. The first zeroes in on the murder of a man who was already at some risk just for being black in a predominately white society during the racist years of the Gilded Age. But as a sheepman in cattlemen's country, he seemed almost doomed. Gobo Fango's death is better understood now, upon being subjected to this historian-turned-detective analysis. The next two articles deal with sensational robberies and murders in Salt Lake City at the turn of the twentieth century. In both instances the writers found something more than a blood-spattered crime scene and a dramatic trial. Both cases provided spectacular histrionics. One—the Lynch and King case—seems right out of Hollywood as the climax followed quickly upon the heels of an action-packed, bullet-whizzing breakout at the state penitentiary. In contrast, the high drama of the Peter Mortensen case came during the trial when issues regarding the admissibility of evidence turned on the question of divine revelation.

The final two essays within this sanguinary quintet focus on lynching in Utah, one being a descriptive analysis of the event, the other a personal essay, both by the same author and both eminently enlightening as we come face to face with the baser instincts that help define the historical record. The author reminds us that "history is cumulative, for good and for ill" and that the historian has an obligation to self and to society that transcends the discipline itself. It is good to be reminded that the historian's task goes beyond that of researcher, interpreter of facts, and storyteller. He or she is also charged with moral and ethical judgments, with serving as a clarion voice in the collective conscience of a people.

The most omnipresent of all vices, prostitution, was not long in coming to Utah Territory. It trailed behind Johnston's Army in the 1850s, positioned itself outside their garrison in Cedar Valley, and thrived for three years until the outbreak of the Civil War scuttled the troops in 1861. At the end of that decade, it returned, this time following the transcontinental railroad. For a time it confined itself to railroad and mining towns, but as Salt Lake City grew in size and diversity the ladies of the night gravitated there. By the 1870s they had ensconced themselves on Commercial (now Regent) Street, within hailing distance of city hall and Temple Square. A generation later, acting on the Progressive impulses of the time, city fathers launched a daring experiment in prostitution management that may seem quite incredible to the modern reader.

Next are three articles dealing with Prohibition. The first treats the unlikely attempt to prohibit the sale of tobacco products in Utah in 1921. Generally conceded to have failed, the law was repealed two years later but not before adumbrating many of the social, political, economic, and cultural issues that have attended debates on tobacco since. The essay also reveals the difficulties of enforcement in matters of Prohibition generally, a theme carried on in the succeeding article on the bootlegging of liquor. Here one of Utah's premier historians guides us through the back roads, back alleys, and back yards where the "good stuff" was illegally distilled, brewed, pressed, and sold. Clever bootleggers and wiley law officers matched wits and resources from one end of the state to the other during the late 1910s, 1920s, and early 1930s in this fast-paced narrative.

The third Prohibition-related piece, "The Night before Doomsday," is of a type seen only infrequently in the *Quarterly* and almost never in other scholarly journals: the first-person reminiscence. Yet, if well done, as this one is, such essays are illuminating and entertaining, and our readership likes them. So do I, and so does my editorial advisory board. "A marvelous memoir—publish as is!" was the message written in half-inch block letters on a critique sheet for this submission. Little wonder that the article won the Morris S. Rosenblatt Award (best general interest article published in *UHQ*) for 1983. Its haunting images of dissipation, worry, fear, and torment are not soon forgotten.

We end this volume with a look at penal reform. In the first of two such articles, we again encounter our old friend Arthur Pratt, by now warden of the state penitentiary. Embracing the Progressive tenets of the time, he advocated and implemented a road-building program for certain of his inmates. Not without some frustration and occasional disappointments, the road-gang experience boasted many successes, and the statistics touted by Warden Pratt will intrigue today's reader. Similarly the concluding selection on juvenile detention, 1888-1910, is full of information, human interest, and ideas. Though conditions, scale, and sociological concepts have changed significantly over the past century, both essays project a certain utilitarianism. This is a dimension we do not always see in history, but how nice when we do.

These, then, are a few of my very favorite articles from my favorite journal. I am delighted beyond words to be able to share them with readers who may have missed them the first time around or who, like me, simply enjoy revisiting old treasures.

1.

"Mountain Common Law"

The Extralegal Punishment of Seducers in Early Utah

Kenneth L. Cannon II

Violence was widespread in nineteenth-century America. White caps, regulators, vigilantes, Ku Klux Klansmen, lynchers, and various other extralegal groups carried out their own distinctive brands of justice, generally through violent means, all around the country. Though older parts of the continent were not unaffected, most of these vigilante groups appeared in frontier areas where legal justice systems were often ineffective. The West was especially impacted.[1]

Utah was an enigma within the nineteenth-century American West. It was settled largely by a closely knit religious group that frowned on lawlessness for the most part and put a high premium on living together peacefully. It thus differed markedly from most of the Old West. As late as 1868 George Q. Cannon, a Mormon apostle and editor of the *Deseret Evening News,* proudly reported that Utahns had not yet had to resort to vigilante justice.[2] Cannon's assertion that it never occurred in Utah seems to be largely accurate in the sense that organized vigilance committees were not formed; there were, however, lynchings during the last half of the nineteenth century and other instances of extralegal "justice,"[3] and Utah's Mormon majority condoned extralegal measures in at least one area: the punishment of

Howard Egan, a prominent early settler of Utah and one of the original pioneer company. When he learned that his wife Tamson had an affair, he shot and killed the "seducer." Church attorneys defended Egan's action based on what they called "mountain common law" and thereby won his acquittal. *Utah State Historical Society, all rights reserved*

seducers. Insights into the social and legal views of early Utahns are provided by examining the "unwritten law" surrounding this issue and the reasons for societal approval of such punishment, and by comparing the Utah experience with the American experience generally.

Two cases of extralegal punishment occurred in 1851. In that year Madison D. Hambleton killed Dr. John M. Vaughn, and Howard Egan killed James Monroe.

The first of these occurred in Manti in February 1851. Dr. John M. Vaughn had apparently been having an adulterous affair[4] with Madison Hambleton's wife while Hambleton was in another geographic locale working. Dr. Vaughn was warned that his life would be in danger if he continued carrying on with Mrs. Hambleton, but he persisted, secretly meeting with her even after her husband returned home. One Sunday afternoon after attending church meetings, Hambleton shot and killed Vaughn, then immediately surrendered himself to his bishop and was escorted to Great Salt Lake City. There a court of inquiry was convened to investigate his act. Brigham Young, who had only recently been sworn in as territorial governor, represented him. Hosea Stout acted as attorney for the prosecution. The supreme court of the territory heard the case and acquitted Hambleton. Those in attendance enthusiastically voiced their approval of the court decision.[5]

The Egan case was more widely publicized, and transcripts of portions of the trial appeared in the local newspaper. Probably because of this greater public exposure and notoriety, later Mormon jurists and journalists looked to the case as a precedent rather than to the earlier Hambleton case. Because of this status, it is perhaps important to review the facts of the case.

Howard Egan was a Mormon convert who came west with the larger body of Latter-day Saints in 1848. In 1849 he guided a group of would-be gold miners to California. When he returned to the Salt Lake valley, he learned that Tamson, the first of his three wives, had been seduced by James Monroe and had given birth to a child by him.[6] There is no evidence that Mrs. Egan's consent to the relationship was obtained through coercion or fraud. Monroe was forewarned that the enraged husband might try to kill him and, unlike Vaughn, left town before Egan returned.[7]

Egan went after Monroe. When, in September 1851, he found him in the company of a wagon train somewhere near the territorial border, he shot and killed him. News of this soon reached Great Salt Lake City, and a church investigation was convened. The avenged elder was quickly exonerated in the church proceedings.[8] Then on October 17 he was arraigned in First District Court in Utah.[9] Egan's defense was handled by W. W. Phelps, a prominent Mormon, and George A. Smith, a Mormon apostle.[10]

The prosecutor in the case was Seth M. Blair, another prominent Mormon. His closing arguments to the jury have apparently not survived. However, from references by defense counsel George A. Smith whose closing statement is extant, it is clear that Blair admitted that Monroe had fathered a child by Egan's wife but then argued that such an act did not warrant the killing. For procedural reasons Blair probably also held that the homicide had been committed outside the boundaries of Utah, in unorganized territory, where the federal government had sole jurisdiction.[11]

Smith, who rendered the final statement to the jury for the defense, admitted he was a "new member of the bar" who was arguing his first case. His words constitute an extremely important piece of oratory because they display the sentiments of Mormon Utah society at the time. Smith stated he would not refer the jury "to authorities on legal points" but would "simply talk the common mountain English, without reference to anything technical." He expressed a view commonly held at the time that the jury would be interested in "looking for justice instead of some dark, sly, or technical course" by which they might be prejudiced. He admitted that the English common law had been enacted to some extent in Utah by the Territorial Organic Act, but asserted that "if a law is to be in force upon us, it must be plain and simple to the understanding, and applicable to our situation."[12]

Smith was outraged that seduction in England gave rise only to a civil suit for damages. He argued that "in this territory it is a principle of mountain common law, that no man can seduce the wife of another without endangering his own life." Rephrasing this, he continued: "The principle, the only one, that beats and throbs through the heart of the entire inhabitants of this territory, is simply this: The man who seduces his neighbor's wife must die, and her nearest relative must kill him!" Smith then attempted to show that such a principle had numerous adherents in other parts of the country, referring to several obscure American cases in which such avengers had been acquitted. He reiterated his position on "mountain common law" several times and concluded by stating, for the same procedural reasons that motivated Blair, that the act was committed within the confines of Utah Territory.

Following the closing statements, Judge Zerubbabel Snow addressed the jury. He reviewed the law pertaining to murder, rejecting Smith's argument that killing a seducer was proper justice that could be formally countenanced: "Though the deceased may have seduced the defendant's wife, as he now alleges, still he had no right to take the remedy into his own hands." It mattered not at all that Egan believed "he killed Monroe in the name of the Lord." If he had hunted down Monroe and killed him, it was murder.[13]

Turning to the procedural question of jurisdiction, which he found to be "the most difficult part of the case," Judge Snow explained that the territorial courts held "a mixed jurisdiction." The court was presently sitting as a United States court; it would thus look to federal statutes "for our authority of law." Sitting in its role of federal court, the tribunal had no jurisdiction over crimes committed within Utah Territory. Because the United States had criminal jurisdiction only in cases "said to be national in their character" or when the alleged crime was committed where the federal government had "sole and exclusive jurisdiction," as in unorganized territory, the place where Monroe was killed was crucial. If the jury found that the act was committed within the territory of Utah, the verdict would have to be not guilty irrespective of the substantive merits of the case because of the court's lack of jurisdiction.

Following Judge Snow's charge, the jury left the courtroom to deliberate. Fifteen minutes later it returned a verdict of not guilty.[14] There is no indication whether this turned on the jurisdictional question, whether jury members believed that Egan had actually not killed Monroe (a highly unlikely possibility because Egan relied on his affirmative defense of justifiable homicide), or whether members of the jury preferred Smith's "mountain common law" concept to the better informed legal analysis of Judge Snow, in essence disregarding the judge's instructions concerning the applicable law. It is possible that the decision turned on jurisdiction, but given the apparent contemporary sentiments of most Utahns, the jury almost certainly would have returned a similar verdict even if it determined that the crime was committed within the court's jurisdiction—at least, if subsequent cases are any indication.

An interesting point is that James Monroe did not commit criminal seduction or even actionable civil seduction; that is, no criminal action against him could have been brought and Tamson Egan would not have had a civil cause of action against him. This is so for several reasons. Seduction is always a difficult thing to prove, and under almost all statutes, including the one enacted by the Utah Territorial Legislature in 1852 after the killing of Monroe, the woman seduced had to be unmarried and of a previously chaste nature.[15] Furthermore, as already stated, Mrs. Egan had evidently not been an unwilling party to the sexual relationship.

Something significant that followed the Egan case has been largely ignored by historians. That is the publicity given the case, not only by non-Mormons, many of whom saw the case as a further manifestation of extralegal Mormon "justice,"[16] but also by the Latter-day Saints themselves. For example, George A. Smith's closing statement in the case was published in full by the *Deseret Evening News* and then published by Mormons in pamphlet form at least twice in England in 1852.[17] This seems puzzling in light of rumors of "Danites" and other supposed extralegal Mormon groups that the gentile (non-Mormon) press in America seized upon. Two questions thus arise from the Egan case, and from similar cases that followed: Why would Mormons countenance the extralegal "execution" of Monroe and others in similar circumstances and why would they publicize the radical statements of George A. Smith?

Definitive answers to both questions are elusive, but the historical record and legal theory provide some hints. First, Mormons were not unanimous in their opinion of the case, and some were privately troubled about the precedent it set. Mormon lawyer Hosea Stout, for example, confided to his diary his worry that the case might prove to be a very dangerous "precident for any one who has his wife, sister, or daughter seduced to take the law into his own hands and slay the seducer."[18]

But the criminal legal theory of Herbert L. Packer aids modern observers in understanding why the majority of early Utahns seem to have had few qualms about the outcome of the case. Rather than approaching the question of justice from a legal-extralegal standpoint, Packer formulated two models of criminal process. These he called the "Due Process Model" which he perceived as placing emphasis on courts and law enforcement and its rival in what he called the "Control of Crime Model," emphasizing repression of crime through either legal or extralegal measures.[19]

Applying these models to the Egan case, it becomes evident that Judge Snow's instructions to the jury incorporated the idea of due process. One simply could not justifiably take the law into one's own hands and kill another in the circumstances under consideration. Taken further, Snow probably believed that if Utah society felt that the punishment assigned to a crime was not commensurate with the severity of the crime, it should alter the statutory punishment through normal legislative processes.[20]

On the other hand, it is also evident that many early Mormons, following George A. Smith's logic, believed that the punishment accorded to a conviction of seduction was not equal to the seriousness of the crime, that it was insufficient to control the crime. A criminal statute enacted by the Utah legislature in 1852 called for a minimum prison term of one year and maximum sentence of twenty years. It allowed for a minimum fine of $100 and a maximum fine of $1,000.[21] Most Utahns evidently did not believe that this was sufficient to protect women in the territory, especially in circumstances such as Monroe's "seduction" of Mrs. Egan where no punishment would have been available under the statute or the common law. According to this view, a home had perhaps been ruined by the sexual relationship with Tamson Egan and yet the law offered no remedy (or scapegoat) at the time other than an adultery charge against both parties.

Perhaps even more perplexing than the question of why Mormon Utah countenanced Monroe's murder is the question of why the case was so widely publicized by the Mormons in 1851 and 1852. The answer seems to be at least twofold. On the local front, outsiders were made aware of the opinion Mormons had of seducers. An editorial afterword to the *Deseret Evening News* transcript of defense attorney Smith's famous closing statement noted that the case should "prove a sufficient warning to all unchaste reprobates, that they are not wanted in our community."[22] In regard to the world outside of Utah, the answer seems to lie in the fact that widespread reports of Mormon immorality preceded and followed the public announcement of plural marriage in 1852. Publication of the Egan case beyond Utah's borders was partially in response to such reports. It served to advertise the church's position that while gentile society condoned extramarital encounters, Mormons limited their sexual relationships to the marriage state, albeit one man might have several wives.

As noted earlier, some Mormons such as Hosea Stout were concerned about the dangerous precedent. An extensive search of newspapers between the time of the Egan trial in 1851 and the late 1860s failed to reveal any similar cases, indicating that Stout's fears may have been exaggerated. In the late 1860s and early 1870s, however, several cases arose with factual circumstances similar to those found in the Egan case, and the term "mountain common law" once again found its way into local newspapers.[23] The cases and the editorial comment that accompanied them attest to the continued support for such extralegal measures, at least among Mormons who still greatly outnumbered gentiles in the territory.

The first incident from this period publicized by Utah newspapers came in 1868. William Hughes's daughter was working in a restaurant in Salt Lake City. The proprietor, a man named Campbell, reportedly seduced the daughter by promising to marry her. Hughes learned of his daughter's seduction and contacted the local police. A policeman accompanied Hughes to Campbell's residence, and there they found Campbell and the daughter in bed together. Campbell asserted that the two were married, but it was soon established that they were not, and he was arrested on a charge of seduction. The next morning a preliminary examination was held. The evidence convinced Hughes that his daughter had in fact been seduced. According to the newspaper account, he "looked upon his child as she stood there the victim of a scoundrel's lust, and saw all the bright future that had been before her, forever darkened by the villain's hellish arts, and in his roused indignation he drew a revolver and shot him down in the court room."

Hughes was, of course, arrested. Although Campbell was severely wounded, the *Deseret Evening News* reported that the wound was "not necessarily fatal." However, the report continued, "The prevailing feeling is that it is a pity the shot did not do its work as effectually as it could be done." The *News* article continued by presenting the first of a series of editorial comments: "Will not such men as this never [*sic*] learn that this community will not tolerate such damnable and villainous deeds in their midst? That the atmosphere of this Territory is most uncongenial to those who wish to introduce anything in the shape of 'pretty waiter girls,' and everything in the shape of illicit intercourse? Public opinion in these mountains declares that a man who seduces a woman ought to pay the penalty with his life; and her nearest of kindred should bring him to account."[24]

Hughes was tried for assault with intent to kill and found not guilty.[25] None of the hoopla that surrounded Campbell's preliminary hearing was evident in the publicity of the Hughes trial. A brief line in the locals column of the *News* was all that publicly announced the verdict. The acquittal and prior editorial comments both indicate that the sentiment first expressed by George A. Smith continued and had become perhaps embedded as a common social belief.

More editorial comment came a few weeks later, following another incident when a father found a man trying to seduce his daughter. The *News,* on February 25, 1868, advised the "oily tongued scoundrel" who had escaped the father by running away, to "keep running, lest he should run against a bullet." It then published a long lead editorial on the "inviolability of virtue." The column, almost certainly authored by editor George Q. Cannon, supported the view that homicides and shootings of seducers were publicized to counter charges of immorality against Mormons: "Because we believe in and practice polygamy, there are many people, who, for the want of correct information, imagine that we are licentious and corrupt, and think of nothing but the gratification of passion. All the pulpit eloquence which finds vent against us, has this view of our character for its basis." However, he countered, "It is time that the world should know what we have been endeavoring to impress upon it for years, that the people of this Territory are determined, by every means in their power, to check vice and foster virtue." The editor-apostle then reaffirmed the "unwritten law": "The people of this Territory have long ago resolved that the chastity of their daughters, sisters and wives shall be sacredly maintained, and that one man who seeks to seduce them from the path of virtue, or makes them the victim of unbridled lust, shall receive the penalty of his crime. If a farmer or shepherd catches a wolf preying upon his flocks, he kills it, if he can. Shall a wild beast in human form, who with hellish duplicity seeks to mislead and destroy the innocent members of his family, be any more leniently dealt with?"[26]

Apparently no seducers were shot during 1869, but a related brand of extralegal violence was carried out and editorially condoned. As he was being escorted to prison, a man convicted of rape and sentenced to fifteen years in the territorial penitentiary was shot five times and killed by the husband of the woman he had raped. Here was a clear case of a husband believing that the law was too lenient. The local probate jury evidently agreed because the man was found not guilty of the murder charge, the jury classifying his act as justifiable homicide.[27]

In 1871 at least two men were killed by relatives of the women they seduced. Editorial comment on the incidents indicates that, while not recorded on a statute book, certain procedures were to be followed in carrying out the responsibilities of "mountain common law." Richard Brown, a Provo resident, was killed. Henry Davis was accused of committing the murder. During Davis's trial, John J. Baum rose in the courtroom and admitted killing him, defending his action on the ground that Brown had seduced his (Baum's) niece after promising to marry her. Davis was immediately acquitted, and it soon became clear that public sentiment supported Baum's act.[28] The only reservations people had, according to the *Salt Lake Daily Herald,* were that Brown had been killed during the night and that Baum had not openly admitted committing the act earlier: "What we object to, and object to in the most emphatic terms, is the hour at which it was done. We are most strenuously opposed to deeds done in the dark. Let a man's actions be open and above board; done in the face of day and of his fellow man. There is no jury of honest honorable men ...

that would convict a man for slaying the slayer of a young, trusting, confiding girl's peace, happiness and life-long reputation, that girl being his near relative." Thus, if Baum had confronted and killed Brown during the day, there would have been no question that he would have been acquitted. Nevertheless, having killed him at night and delayed turning himself in, he was still acquitted.[29]

Appearing in a *Herald* editorial that both condemned and condoned Baum's act was a comment generally opposing extralegal measures, except when formal legal processes did not provide a sufficient remedy: "We are opposed to any man attempting to administer what he may deem justice, where the courts are open and the law provides a proper punishment for the crime. But unfortunately there are some crimes for which, the sense of the great public declares, no adequate punishment is provided by statutory enactment. Among these, seduction is preeminent. And although the statute books declare it murder to kill a seducer, there is an unwritten law ... which calls it justice and acquits the person who kills a heartless seducer."[30]

The gentile *Salt Lake Daily Tribune* emphatically raised its journalistic voice against such extralegal punishment. It is difficult to gauge just how genuine such criticism was, however, because the *Tribune* at the time opposed practically anything the *News* and the *Herald* supported and was especially interested in publicizing anything that might put the Mormon church in an unfavorable light. With these considerations in mind, the comments of the *Tribune* still offer some insights: "Again we enter our protest against irresponsible killing in Utah. The daily papers record the killing of a young man at Provo named Brown, upon the suspicion of illicit intercourse. The judge acquitted the prisoner upon the ground of justifiable homicide. Efforts have been made by the Orthodox to justify the killing, based on the assumption of the impure life of the slain man. Our position is, that if seduction is worthy of death, it should be executed by the officers of justice alone and not by an irresponsible individual. ... This doctrine that killing seducers is justified is more dangerous in Utah, and needs more attention here than elsewhere, because it has been publicly taught."[31]

Still another killing during this period occurred in September 1871. James Hendry had "shown attention" to James Hall's daughter who was married but estranged from her husband and living with her parents. Hall told Hendry to stay away from his daughter. The latter secured work for the daughter away from home and then seduced her. When Hall and his son Ezra learned of this, they killed Hendry with two blasts from a shotgun and several rounds from a pistol. The Halls were arrested but escaped.[32] The *Ogden Junction,* a Mormon paper edited by Charles Penrose, and the *Deseret Evening News* agreed that "the universal feeling among the community is that Hendry richly deserved his fate. Death to the seducer is mountain law, let libertines understand it and govern themselves accordingly."[33]

After 1874 major criminal actions were taken from the jurisdiction of the local probate courts in Utah, primarily to facilitate enforcement of the antipolygamy statutes. This had the effect of removing cases involving extralegal punishment of seducers from Mormon-controlled courts.[34] Utahns found another way to relieve punishers of seducers from criminal liability, however, in at least one case in 1877.

When William Hobbs shot Con Sullivan on June 25, 1877, on the Eagle Emporium corner in Salt Lake City, all three of the major Salt Lake newspapers had an opportunity once again to air their opinions. Hobbs, who ran a boarding house in West Jordan, suspected that his fifteen-year-old daughter and a local saloon keeper were engaged in an illicit relationship. According to what Hobbs told a *Herald* reporter, one Sunday night after he had ordered his daughter to stay home, she stole away when he stepped out for a moment. He reported that he went to the Sullivan residence and knocked on the door but received no answer. He then returned home and fetched an implement to break his way into the house. He did so and found Sullivan and his young daughter "*flagrante delicto*." He returned home, this time for a weapon, but by the time he again reached Sullivan's house the couple had fled.[35]

Hobbs hunted all night for the two. On the following day, June 25, he heard that they were in Salt Lake, so he took the train into town and found them near the Eagle Emporium. Sullivan began to run. Hobbs fired four shots at the fleeing man and hit him with two. The wounded Sullivan was taken to the Townsend House and later to St. Mark's Hospital.

All three newspapers carried rather extensive coverage of the sensational shooting. The *News* avoided much of the editorial comment that it had endorsed in earlier cases. The paper's position, however, was implicitly stated in its description of Hobbs's attempt to "annihilate the destroyer of the virtue of his daughter." The *Herald* maintained its earlier position by calling the shooting one of "genuine merit," headlining the news article with "The Seducer's Portion."[36] So neither the official Mormon paper nor the morning paper owned and operated by Mormons engaged in the radical editorial rhetoric of the early 1870s. The greatest amount of editorial comment this time came from the gentile *Tribune.*

The non-Mormon paper was much more willing to let a legal tribunal determine whether or not there had been a criminally intimate relationship between the young girl and the saloon keeper. The precedent of the Egan case hung heavily over the present situation: "We think we see a manifest determination on the part of the priests to acquit Hobbs on the ground of the alleged seduction. Such a proceeding would be based on the 'mountain common law,' as laid down by George A. Smith, in his plea for Howard Egan who murdered James Monroe for the offense of seduction." The writer continued by stating that Smith's "great speech ... contains more blood and thunder than any other sermon in the Journal of Discourses." He accused the "Mountain Meadows press" of "endeavoring to create public sympathy in favor of Hobbs, regardless of the bottom facts of the case." Finally the editorial stated that the only established fact was that a deliberate attempt had been made upon the life of one man by another.[37]

Hobbs was examined by a local police court over which Alexander Pyper presided. The *Herald* simply reported that Hobbs was discharged because "Justice" Pyper held "that the shooting was justifiable."[38] The *Tribune* took a less dispassionate approach. The paper once again criticized "the late George A. Smith's 'Mountain law,'" and "Bishop" Pyper's decision, whereby "the progress made by the world during three thousand years in restraining the untamed passions of man, and subordinating all to the impartial decrees of the law, [now] by the divinely-inspired legislation of this modern Israel is set aside."[39] Even though criminal jurisdiction had been removed from local probate courts in 1874, Mormon sentiments still won out in this Salt Lake City police court.

It is evident that the Egan case was viewed as a precedent in these later decisions. While the term "mountain common law" probably did not originate with George A. Smith, he certainly popularized the term and gave it significance in pioneer Utah. The term symbolized something that was apparently representative of more general sentiments around Utah and became almost a watchword among many. The reliance that Judge Snow placed on due process was apparently waylaid, at least in regard to seduction, in local probate courts where all these murder charges, except the one against Hobbs, were brought. No case of a man being convicted in Utah of extralegally punishing a relative's seducer or rapist has been found during the years between 1851 and 1877.

Not all cases of seduction ended in the extralegal option, however. For example, under the law of Utah Territory, criminal action was barred where the seduced and the seducer entered into matrimony. In 1873 a woman accused a man of seduction and an action was about to be brought against him when the two were married. The charge was dropped, and it is clear that the man was thought to have assumed "the better part of valor" in the case.[40]

In 1888 Chief Justice Charles Zane of the Utah Supreme Court rendered an opinion in a case similar to those described above. Wilford H. Halliday killed a man, Reeves, twenty-four hours after learning that the latter had committed adultery with his wife. Halliday argued that he acted "in a sudden heat of passion" after learning of his wife's "defilement." The trial court and the higher Utah court rejected the argument: "The law will not permit the husband to say that he slew the defiler in a sudden heat of passion after deliberating upon the defilement 24 hours. ... The law is that if the husband after learning of the defilement of his wife waits and deliberates, and then kills the defiler, in so doing he commits the crime of murder."[41]

That the relatives of a seduced woman bore responsibility for punishing a seducer was clearly condoned by early Utah society, which also felt that it was not alone in supporting this practice. For example, in editorializing on the Baum case in Provo, the *Salt Lake Daily Herald* stated that the "unwritten law" of killing seducers was "recognized everywhere throughout this great Republic."[42] Writing in the twentieth century, Mormon historian and leader B. H. Roberts agreed. He found justification:

> where a father or a brother personally avenges the outraged chastity of a daughter or sister; or a wronged husband slays the despoiler of his domestic peace and home. Such cases are not peculiar to communities of Latter-day Saints in the United States, they are recognized as appeals to the "*unwritten law of the land*," and trial juries quite generally in the United States refuse to convict, either for manslaughter or murder those who take the law into their own hands in such cases. Granting that the severity of the denunciations against violations of chastity and the purity of the home encouraged appeals to "the unwritten law," and hence that such appeals were made more frequently in Utah than elsewhere, —if they were more frequently in Utah than elsewhere in western America—it still remains to be determined whether or not that is a reproach to the community, or a tribute to the high sense of honor, the virility, the strength, and the courage of the community's manhood.

Obviously Roberts believed that it was a moral right to avenge a woman's honor. His words might be interpreted to refer primarily to cases involving the slaying of a rapist, except that the reference he gives is to the Egan case.[43]

There are, in fact, indications that such extralegal actions were countenanced in other parts of the country. One such homicide of a "seducer" brought sadness to Mormon Utah in 1857. This was the death of Mormon apostle Parley P. Pratt who had married Eleanor McLean. Since Mrs. McLean had not obtained a divorce from her first husband, Hector, he (McLean) viewed Pratt's plural marriage to his wife as no marriage at all. He hunted for Pratt throughout the eastern United States until he found him in Arkansas and killed him. McLean escaped and never faced trial.[44] Under the tenets of the "mountain common law" and from his own perspective, McLean had simply done that which the law probably would not do, and his act was condoned by many.

Although the two cases cited by George A. Smith before the jury have not been located, it is very possible that the two did involve the acquittal of killers of seducers.[45] There were other cases. In the same issue of the *Salt Lake Daily Herald* that discussed the Baum case, an account of such a homicide in San Francisco was published. Citizens there reportedly approved the act.[46]

Even as late as 1906, in an American Bar Association report prepared by prominent Louisiana attorney Thomas J. Kernan, it was asserted that a number of extralegal acts were countenanced by the public. Two of these were the killing of an adulterous man by the wronged husband and the slaying of a seducer of a virgin.[47]

Almost contemporaneous with Kernan's report was one of the most famous murder trials of the twentieth century. Harry K. Thaw, heir to a huge fortune and playboy husband of Evelyn Nesbitt, a famous stage actress, killed Stanford White on the roof of Madison Square Garden in New York City, a building White had designed. The reason Thaw gave was that the man had approached his wife, hoping to continue a sexual liaison they had had before she married. Thaw relied on the "unwritten law"—or what he called *Dementia Americana*—that held that such a man deserved death. Thaw wanted to fight the case on the merits, feeling that "White was a villain who had met his just desserts" and that "on such an issue no jury in the world would ever convict me."[48]

Placing the Utah experience into historical perspective, it is evident that it was in some ways similar to the experience of other parts of the country. Though by no means universally approved of in nineteenth-century America, extralegal violence was clearly condoned by many Americans, especially those living in the southern and western parts of the country. In fact, the scale of extralegal measures is quite staggering. Vigilantes and supporters of vigilante movements included U.S. presidents Andrew Jackson and Theodore Roosevelt, senators, congressmen, governors, literary luminaries, legal scholars, prominent lawyers, and businessmen, as well as representatives from practically every class of American society.[49] It is from this perspective that the relatively few instances of extralegal violence in early Utah must be viewed.

While Herbert Packer's theory goes far in helping explain the appeal of extralegal justice, and while it certainly applies to Utah, as well as to the broader society, there were subtly different reasons in Utah for allowing a man to kill his relative's seducer. Most vigilantes were intent primarily on bringing order to society and on controlling crime. The Mormons were certainly interested in controlling seduction and publicized these cases partly for that reason, but they also used the cases for propaganda purposes. They hoped by publicizing the Egan matter and similar cases that followed to indicate to the country and world that they were not lax in morals. The extent to which they succeeded is an interesting question that still awaits a definitive answer.[50]

Notes

1. For analyses of lawlessness in the Old West, see W. Eugene Hollon, *Frontier Violence: Another Look* (New York: Oxford University Press, 1974), and Wayne Gard, *Frontier Justice* (Norman: University of Oklahoma Press, 1949). On vigilantism, see Richard Maxwell Brown, "Historical Patterns of Violence in America," in Hugh Davis Graham and Ted Robert Gurr, eds., *The History of Violence in America: Historical and Comparative Perspectives* (New York: Bantam Books, 1969), 45-83, and "Legal and Behavioral Perspectives on American Vigilantism," in Donald Fleming and Bernard Bailyn, eds., *Law in American History* (Boston: Little, Brown & Co., 1971), 95-144.

2. *Deseret Evening News,* January 22, 1868.

3. Larry R. Gerlach, "Ogden's 'Horrible Tragedy': The Lynching of George Segal," *Utah Historical Quarterly* 49 (1981): 157, and reprinted in this volume. Gerlach has found evidence of at least twelve lynchings in Utah.

4. Vaughn was said to have seduced Mrs. Hambleton even though there is no indication that the relationship was anything but consensual. This emphasizes the then-current notion of male dominance over women. Seduction has become almost entirely archaic as a legal concept in the twentieth century.

5. Brigham D. Madsen, ed., *A Forty-niner in Utah with the Stansbury Exploration of Great Salt Lake: Letters and Journal of John Hudson, 1848-1850* (Salt Lake City: Tanner Trust Fund, University of Utah Library, 1981), 107-109. Vaughn had apparently had another illicit affair in Great Salt Lake City and had been indicted for adultery there. Some residents of the capital city believed Vaughn was lucky not to have been shot on that occasion (ibid., 107).

6. Earlier historical works dealing with the case do not list which of Egan's wives was involved in the seduction. See Orson F. Whitney, *The*

History of Utah, 4 vols. (Salt Lake City: George Q. Cannon & Sons, 1892-1904), 1:480-82, and B. H. Roberts, *A Comprehensive History of the Church of Jesus Christ of Latter-day Saints, Century One,* 6 vols. (Salt Lake City: Deseret News Press, 1930), 4:135-36. An order issued by Zerubbabel Snow in the proceedings of *United States v. Egan* makes it clear that it was Tamson, Egan's first wife. Order of the Hon. Z. Snow, October 18, 1851, First District Court Records, TJ103.18, Box 1, Document 61, Utah State Archives, Salt Lake City.

7. *Deseret Evening News,* November 15, 1851.

8. Journal History of the Church of Jesus Christ of Latter-day Saints, October 3, 1851, archives, Historical Department, Church of Jesus Christ of Latter-day Saints, Salt Lake City, Utah.

9. Whitney, *History of Utah,* 1:481.

10. Andrew Jenson, *L.D.S. Biographical Encyclopedia,* 4 vols. (Salt Lake City: Andrew Jenson History Company, 1888-1936), 1:37-42, 3:692-97.

11. *Deseret Evening News,* November 15, 1851; Whitney, *History of Utah,* 1:481; Clair T. Kilts, "A History of the Federal and Territorial Court Conflicts in Utah, 1851-1874" (M.A. thesis, Brigham Young University, 1959), 50.

12. *Deseret Evening News,* November 15, 1851. On early Mormon attitudes critical of lawyers and the formal legal system in the United States, see James H. Backman, "Attitudes within the Church toward the Study of Law, Lawyers, and Litigation—The Brigham Young Era Compared to the Present" (unpublished paper in the possession of the author).

13. *Deseret Evening News,* November 15, 1851. Judge Snow did not entirely ignore the importance of the seduction, and took an affidavit from Tamson Egan in which the following questions were put to her: "1. Was you seduced in the year A.D. 1850 by one James Monroe, if so under what circumstances, how often, where, in what month and day of the month, if not positive, as near as possible. 2. Did you by reason of such seduction have a child by the said James Monroe, if so, how long after such seduction. Order of the Hon. Z. Snow, October 18, 1851."

14. *Deseret Evening News,* November 15, 1851.

15. "An Act in Relation to Crimes and Punishments," Title 2, Section 21 (1851-52 Utah Territorial Laws).

16. See, e.g., *National Intelligencer,* February 15, 1852. The so-called runaway judges also reported critically on the Egan and Hambleton affairs. (See Norman F. Furniss, *The Mormon Conflict, 1850-1859* [New Haven, CT: Yale University Press, 1960], 28-29; Whitney, *History of Utah,* 1:480-81.)

17. *Deseret Evening News,* November 15, 1851. The two pamphlets were published by Franklin D. Richards and an undisclosed person who had his edition printed by R. James. A more readily available source for Smith's statement is *Journal of Discourses,* 26 vols. (London: Latter-day Saints' Book Depot, 1854-86), 1:95.

18. Juanita Brooks, ed., *On the Mormon Frontier: The Diary of Hosea Stout, 1844-1861,* 2 vols. (Salt Lake City: University of Utah Press and Utah State Historical Society, 1964), 2:407-408. Interestingly Stout believed Hambleton was justified in killing Vaughn (ibid., 2:396). He may have been concerned that two such incidents within a short period of time would set a precedent and cause widespread lawlessness.

19. Herbert L. Packer, *The Limits of the Criminal Sanction* (Stanford, CA: Stanford University Press, 1968), 153, 149-73.

20. In fact, the 1852 legislature provided for a judgment of justifiable homicide when a person killed another who had defiled the first person's "wife, daughter, mother, sister, or any other female relative or dependent," as long as such killing was "in a sudden heat of passion." "An Act in Relation to Crimes and Punishments," Title XI, Section 112 (1851-52 Utah Territorial Laws). Egan's deliberate stalking of James Monroe more than a year after the "defilement" of his wife would hardly qualify as justifiable homicide under the 1852 statute. It is interesting to note that Utah was one of the few states that, as late as the early 1970s, still considered such a homicide justifiable and not criminal (Utah Code Ann. Section 76-30-10[4] [repealed 1973]).

21. "An Act in Relation to Crimes and Punishments," Title 2, Section 21 (1851-52 Utah Territorial Laws).

22. *Deseret Evening News,* November 15, 1851.

23. It is possible that there had been such extralegal acts between 1851 and 1868 and that these were publicized beginning in the later year as fair warning to gentiles who would be riding the soon-to-be-completed transcontinental railroad. Or perhaps the rate of incidence increased due to collateral tensions caused by the influx of "outsiders."

24. *Deseret Evening News,* February 4, 1868.

25. *People v. Wm. Hughes*, Salt Lake County Probate Records, Docket Number 1585, March 8, 11, 1868, 21800001801, Box 24, Utah State Archives; *Deseret Evening News,* March 11, 1868.

26. *Deseret Evening News*, February 26, 1868.

27. Ibid., March 27, 1869.

28. *Salt Lake Daily Herald,* January 1, 1871.

29. Ibid., January 4, 1871.

30. Ibid.

31. *Salt Lake Daily Tribune,* January 1, 1871.

32. *Deseret Evening News,* September 28, 1871.

33. *Ogden Junction,* September 27, 1871; *Deseret Evening News,* September 28, 1871. The *News* merely copied the *Junction's comments approvingly into its own columns. The Tribune,* of course, viewed the act quite differently (see September 27, 1871).

34. Poland Act, 18 Stat., 254. On the jurisdiction and fairness of the local probate courts, see James B. Allen, "The Unusual Jurisdiction of the County Probate Courts in the Territory of Utah," *Utah Historical Quarterly* 36 (1968): 132-42; Jay E. Powell, "Fairness in the Salt Lake County Probate Court," *Utah Historical Quarterly* 38 (1970): 256-62; and Elizabeth D. Gee, "Justice for All or for the 'Elect'? The Utah County Probate Court, 1855-72," *Utah Historical Quarterly* 48 (1980): 129-47.

35. *Salt Lake Daily Herald,* June 26, 1877. The *Deseret Evening News* article, also purportedly based on the personal account of Hobbs, varied slightly from the *Herald* account.

36. *Salt Lake Daily Herald,* June 26, 1877; *Salt Lake Daily Tribune,* June 26, 27, 1877; *Deseret Evening News,* June 26, 1877.

37. *Salt Lake Daily Tribune,* June 27, 1877.

38. *Salt Lake Daily Herald,* June 28, 1877.

39. *Salt Lake Daily Tribune,* June 29, 1877.

40. Ibid., July 14, 1873. The two were, in fact, married by the judge in the courtroom just before the action was to have been introduced in court. There were also cases of men who were tried and convicted of seduction (see *Salt Lake Daily Tribune,* May 12, July 14, 1873).

41. *People v. Halliday,* 5 Utah 467, 474 (1888).

42. *Salt Lake Daily Herald,* January 4, 1871.

43. Roberts, *A Comprehensive History of the Church,* 4:135.

44. Steven Pratt, "Eleanor McLean and the Murder of Parley P. Pratt," *BYU Studies* 15 (Winter 1975): 225, 245-48.

45. The two cases Smith referred to were *Louisiana v. Horton* and *New Jersey v. Mercer* (*Deseret Evening News,* November 15, 1851.

46. *Salt Lake Daily Herald,* January 4, 1871. The acceptance of such extralegal action was not universal. In a similar case in Pennsylvania in 1854, the judge roundly criticized adherents of such a view and described how much wiser the law is (*Commonwealth v. Moore,* 2 Pittsburgh 502, 509 [1864]).

47. As quoted in Brown, *Perspectives on American Vigilantism,* 134.

48. Harry K. Thaw, *The Traitor; Being the Untampered with, Unrevised Account of the Trial and All that Led to It* (Philadelphia: Dorrance & Co., 1926), 149, 163. Some legal commentators found Thaw's defense lacking, noting that there was "no place" in the laws of New York for the so-called "unwritten" or "higher" law. See "The Thaw Case," *Canadian Law Review* 6 (1907): 101.

49. Brown, *Perspectives on American Vigilantism,* 106–44.

50. American society apparently did not receive this message entirely as the Mormons might have hoped. Roberts points out that enemies of the Latter-day Saints identified the homicides of seducers as examples of "blood atonement" practiced by the Mormons (*A Comprehensive History of the Church,* 4:135).

2.

Arthur Pratt, Utah Lawman

Richard S. Van Wagoner and

Mary Van Wagoner

In the late afternoon of 11 October 1874, Deputy U.S. Marshal Arthur Pratt approached the gate of Brigham Young's Lion House office to serve a subpoena on the Mormon church president. Pratt was told that Young was ill and could not be disturbed. The gatekeeper, Joseph Shaw, advised that the papers could be served when Young's secretary returned. But the twenty-one-year-old lawman refused to accept this arrangement and left briefly, only to return with fellow marshal George R. Maxwell. Shaw still refused entrance, and a scuffle ensued. Pratt wrestled Shaw to the ground, subdued and arrested him, and took him to the penitentiary. The two lawmen, with a contingent of deputies, then returned to Young's office where they were met by Salt Lake City mayor Daniel H. Wells who assured them that President Young would now accept the subpoena.

The Mormon community was used to seeing Brigham Young treated with imperial respect and was incensed by these actions. Deputy Pratt was particularly singled out in a 13 October *Deseret Evening News* editorial: "There is a disposition manifest by some persons in this community," the piece began, "to do their utmost to create excitement, and not only excitement but real trouble." The chief concern of the *News* was how the eastern press would respond to the incident. "Nobody was hurt," the editor argued, "and, with a little

The exterior wall of the Utah State Penitentiary where executions were conducted by firing squad. Arthur Pratt, son of LDS apostle Orson Pratt, was warden for nineteen years and oversaw the execution of labor-union activist Joe Hill at this spot in 1915. *Photo taken November 1903, Shipler Collection, Utah State Historical Society, all rights reserved*

coolness, civility, and consideration on both sides, but especially on that of the deputy who gave the original offence, there would have been nothing at all amiss. It adds nothing to the dignity of the Federal Government when any one of its officers conducts himself with gratuitous offensiveness, and there are few Americans of any kind, or men of any nationality, who have the spirit of men within them, who would not resent the overbearing and hectoring arrogance and insolence of men clothed with a little brief authority."

Had Arthur Pratt been a boozing, womanizing non-Mormon, appointed to his position by eastern political hacks, perhaps it would have been easier to understand his determination to serve the papers. But Pratt was the son of one of Mormonism's best-known couples, Apostle Orson Pratt and his first wife, Sarah M. Bates. Born in Salt Lake City on 12 March 1853, Arthur was educated in the city school system and graduated from the University of Deseret. In early 1870 he served as foreman of the Nineteenth Utah Territorial Legislature of which his father was Speaker. After a stint as director of a stage line from Salt Lake City to Pioche, Nevada, he married Agnes E. Caine[1] on 25 December 1872, moved in with his father, and began new employment as an agent for the Salt Lake Furniture Company.

Pratt had just begun his new job as a deputy U.S. marshal in the fall of 1874 when smoldering family difficulties with Mormon leaders came to a head. Arthur's mother, who experienced polygamy-related trouble with Joseph Smith in the early 1840s, became rabidly antipolygamous and secretly raised her children to disbelieve in Mormonism. Sarah's 1868 refusal to accept Orson's other wives on equal grounds resulted in the couple's separation. Brigham Young, who had taken a dim view of Sarah beginning in the 1840s, had her evicted from the Pratt family home south of the temple block on the claim that he owned the land. Sarah disputed Young's assertion and sued him in court. Though the case was ultimately resolved in Sarah's favor in the summer of 1876, it was not without great trauma to the Pratt family. In the midst of the lawsuit, Sarah was excommunicated on 4 October 1874 for apostasy. The next day Arthur suffered the same fate. His determination to serve Young with the subpoena becomes more understandable when it is known that the incident occurred only one week after he and his mother had been excommunicated.[2]

Arthur's law enforcement encounter with Brigham did not end in 1874. One year later on 30 October the church president was ordered imprisoned for refusal to pay $9,500 in alimony to his divorced wife, Ann Eliza Young. Judge Boreman deemed it best to place the church president under house arrest, and for three weeks Arthur Pratt and Boman Cannon served as his guards.

Despite Pratt's seemingly anti-Mormon posture, his long-term career in law enforcement proved him to be a man of integrity and unflinching honesty—a well respected officer determined to fight injustice wherever found. Unfortunately law enforcement officials usually retain their positions through the good graces of their political superiors. Pratt experienced the first of several political shake-ups in February 1876 when, according to his own account, "I attempted to expose what I believe to be corruption in the marshal's office."[3] When the administration changed hands, however, Pratt was rehired and was quickly back in the saddle again.

The Silver Reef area of southern Utah experienced a boom period during the late 1870s when silver soared to $1.20 per ounce. By the early 1880s, however, plummeting prices plus production difficulties in the Stormont, Buckeye, and California mines resulted in financial losses for eastern stockholders. On 1 February 1881 Silver Reef miners were ordered to take a pay cut from $4.00 to $3.50 per day. The miner's union refused to accept the measure and a strike resulted. A month later sixty union miners gathered at the Stormont office of W. I. Allen and forced the company boss out of the camp. After being "escorted" from the area by strikers, Allen rode to Beaver, the seat of the federal district court, where he requested an investigation.

The federal grand jury was insensitive to the miners' concerns and found indictments against forty of them. The warrants were placed in the hands of Deputy U.S. Marshal Arthur Pratt, who ordered Sheriff A. P. Hardy of Washington County to raise a posse of some twenty-five men. Pratt deputized the men, and under cover of a snowstorm the group rode to Silver Reef where they took the camp completely by surprise. Thirty-six men were placed in irons and taken to Beaver for trial, where twenty of them were convicted of riot, and on April 11 Marshal Pratt arrived in Salt Lake with these men and ten others, all of whom were incarcerated in the territorial penitentiary at Sugarhouse.[4]

In the late 1870s and 1880s, Pratt's efforts in carrying out the government's antipolygamy campaign frequently pushed him to the forefront of the news. Stories, publicly denied by Orson Pratt in the 23 March 1878 *Deseret Evening News,* even rumored that Arthur had arrested his father on polygamy charges. Despite Apostle Pratt's spirited public defenses of Mormon beliefs, Arthur, like his mother, was very much opposed to polygamy.[5] In an 1882 newspaper interview, he was asked why he was not a Mormon. "I will tell you why," he replied; "I am the son of my father's first wife, and had a mother who taught me the evils of the system."[6] The fact that he was no longer of the faith improved his chances for advancement in the federal government after the March 1882 passage of the Edmunds Bill. This amendment to the anti-bigamy law of 1862, among other things, barred those guilty of polygamy or unlawful cohabitation from holding any civic office or position of public trust. All registration and elective offices were declared vacant in Utah Territory, and provisions were made for placing their duties upon "proper persons" to be appointed by a bipartisan commission of five members chosen by the president with advice and consent of the Senate. On 22 September 1882 Arthur Pratt called on Judge Elias Smith with a commission from the governor and demanded possession of the office of sheriff, together with the keys of the county jail. He was denied access to the position. It was March 1885 before the Edmunds Bill was declared constitutional by the U.S. Supreme Court. During this interval Pratt found employment as a bookkeeper for McCormick & Company. On 13 March 1886 Governor Eli H. Murray appointed both Pratt and Bolivar Roberts to territorial positions. But Mormons James Jack and Nephi Clayton would not vacate their offices. Six days later Pratt and Roberts entered suit in the Third District Court for possession of the territorial positions of auditor of public accounts and librarian-recorder of marks and brands (Pratt) and treasurer (Roberts).

Federal officials, recognizing that the issue would not be resolved in court for some time, sought temporary positions for their men.

"Arthur Pratt has resigned his position as a bookkeeper," the 16 October *Salt Lake Herald* reported, and "he will devote his energies to aiding Marshal Dyer in running down offending Mormons. The average deputy's salary is understood not to be an extremely fat thing, so that to induce Mr. Pratt to leave as good a position as he had, Marshal Dyer must have offered something tempting. Mr. Pratt's obvious experience in that line, and more than all, his wide acquaintance among the people, constitute his value in the Marshal's eye."

Pratt wasted no time adjusting to his new assignment. On 5 December as the *Herald's* associate editor Brigham H. Roberts was preparing the daily dispatches, Deputy Pratt arrested him for "unlawful cohabitation." And on 11 February 1887 Pratt accompanied Marshal Frank H. Dyer on a well coordinated raid on Mormon church property, including the tithing office, the historian's office, and the Gardo House. However, church president John Taylor and George Q. Cannon, the main objects of the search, were not apprehended. Apostle Pratt, the husband of ten wives, had died five years earlier, and young Pratt was never faced with having to arrest his father. But the deputy had a special interest in proving a case against boyhood friend Abraham H. Cannon, a member of the First Council of the Seventy. Cannon noted in his journal on 10 May 1886 that Arthur Pratt told the governor: "Cannon is the one who when asked if he had broken the law answered, 'Yes, thank God, I have.'"[7] Though he claimed that Pratt misrepresented his words, Cannon worried about the deputy's intentions. On 27 July Cannon noted that one of his wives sent her brother to say that "Deputy Marshal Pratt had told Alfales Young that I [Cannon] was married to M[ary] E. C[roxall]. She therefore thinks it best to remain concealed for a time, in which decision I agreed with her." Three days later, after the funeral of President John Taylor, Cannon recorded: "Arthur Pratt is trying to work up a polygamy case against me, and the remark is attributed to him that he knew I had married Mamie Croxall since I was released from prison. I sent word that the officers might pull at that string as long as they liked. I saw M. E. C. in the evening and told her of the rumor. She will endeavor to avoid a subpoena. Her health is good and she is comfortably situated."

Despite his devotion to arresting Cannon and other polygamists, Deputy Pratt's intensity was apparently only job-related. On 30 January 1888 he was appointed warden of the Utah Territorial Penitentiary (Sugarhouse) where most Mormon "cohabs" were imprisoned. When George Q. Cannon gave himself up to serve his time, he was treated remarkably well by Warden Pratt, even to the extent of allowing his cell door to remain open. On one occasion when a guard was abusive, Pratt immediately transferred the employee elsewhere. And Abraham H. Cannon, on a visit to his father, was permitted a guided tour of a new part of the prison. Abraham noted in his journal on 23 January 1889 that Pratt had taken the elder Cannon into his confidence on at least one occasion. "The one great secret of all this present [polygamy] raid," Pratt told Cannon, "was the fees obtained for every arrest. $8.00 per day was allowed for a team in going to make an arrest and $5.00 per day for feed for a team and man, all of which was charged to expense acc't. Then there is a fee for each man captured. [Marshal] Exum has charge of affairs in the northern part of the Territory, and he has made $4500.00 at the business within a short time, in addition to which he has paid Dyer 40% of all fees. If the fees were removed considerable of our persecution would cease."

Joseph Amos became prison warden on 27 July 1889, and Arthur Pratt was appointed deputy marshal in charge of the First Judicial District (Ogden). Some Mormons hated to see Pratt leave. Abraham Cannon noted on 29 July that Pratt had "won for himself many friends because of his firm yet kind discipline while in charge of the 'Pen,' and many will be sorry at his removal." Illustrating Pratt's respect for "those imprisoned for conscience' sake," he reportedly said, "I could plow a furrow around a hundred acre field of such men, and tell them to stay within the boundary, and I would feel perfectly safe that not one of them would disobey instructions."

Pratt did not live in Ogden long. On 6 January 1890 the U.S. Supreme Court ruled that he and Bolivar Roberts could assume their positions as territorial auditor and recorder, respectively. The Pratt family returned to Salt Lake and took up residence at 164 East South Temple. In addition to his territorial position, Pratt served as secretary of the Salt Lake City Gas Company and assisted in the organization of the Republican party.

The 19 February 1892 *Deseret Evening News* reported assault charges brought against Pratt by D. A. Sullivan. The incident was the result of an election day fracas when Sullivan, an unregistered voter, was refused voting rights by election judge Rulon S. Wells. In his anger Sullivan struck Wells. Pratt, who was in the vicinity, immediately came to Wells's aid and "dealt Sullivan a blow over the head with a walking stick." Pratt's acquittal was noted in the 24 February *News*.

Despite satisfaction with his territorial position, Pratt's heart was in law enforcement. In late 1893 he was elected Salt Lake City chief of police. Prior to taking command on 1 January 1894, he visited the San Francisco police department. Speculation ran high that Pratt would make significant changes to lessen the frequent charges of police brutality. "A good many members of the police force will stop twirling their ebony, cherry and mahogany clubs early in January," the 28 December 1893 *News* editorialized; "others will also be retired to private life as soon as the new men become initiated."

But Chief Pratt's first year on the job was rife with difficulties. California was rampant with unemployment and hundreds of men unable to find jobs were given free passage to Ogden, Weber County, Utah, by Southern Pacific Railroad. As the first group of the "Industrial Army" arrived in Utah, they began to drift south through neighboring Davis County looking for food, shelter, work, or a passage elsewhere. Within a three-day period in late May, more than 200 of these Industrialists, or "wealers" as they were called, reached Salt Lake City. Officials viewed them as a "menace to the peace and quietude" of the city; Pratt was assigned to "feed and watch this indigent horde."[8] Industrialists informed Pratt that not only had they been given free passage on the railroad to Ogden but that there were 15,000 more men in California waiting to catch Southern Pacific freight trains. If matters were not complicated enough for Chief Pratt, on 24 May Davis County officials telephoned Salt Lake mayor Robert Baskin requesting his assistance in combating the depredations of transients in that part of the state.

Baskin, perhaps recognizing that it was best to keep the unemployed men farther north where they would be more likely to catch a train out of the state, ordered Pratt and a force of policemen to "proceed to any point which the Davis County authorities might designate in order to check the pillage." On 25 May Pratt and twenty-two Salt Lake policemen, armed with a court injunction to prevent the drifters from crossing the Davis-Weber County line, arrived on watch.

Though the problems with the Industrial Army dissipated, Pratt continued to experience difficulties as he began upgrading the Salt Lake City police department. On 10 August he met with the entire police force behind closed doors. "Bickering, distrust, suspicion, [and] unrest" were undermining the efficiency of the force, he was quoted in the 10 August *News,* and all such behavior "must be stopped no matter how great the cost." He also warned against conveying information to newspapermen who were "often apprised of matters of importance" before the chief was. "In regard to tale bearing to the commissioners," Pratt added, "that too must be done away with if every man had to be suspended." Two weeks later nine policemen were retired from the force under the chief's "retrenchment order." Though grumbling was heard in the ranks, the 29 August *News* was quick to point out that Pratt's measure saved $815 a month without impairing efficiency.

Late 1894 again found Chief Pratt in the forefront of controversy. Headlines of the 6 December *News* announced his and two officers' arrests for contempt of court in the "Midnight Assignation Case." This involved an unmarried couple who were found engaged in "criminal relations" in a hack near Holy Cross Hospital. When the matter was brought to Pratt's attention by the investigating policemen, he ordered them to remain silent on the matter. He had interviewed the lady—a family woman who "begged that she not be exposed" and gave her his word that her identity would be kept secret. But rumors began to spread throughout the city and a grand jury was convened for the purpose of discovering the couple's identity to "remove suspicion from those who were not deserving of it." When Pratt was called, he refused to provide names. He argued that if he were to violate his word to the lady in question "it would ruin an entire well-known family of this city, and he was satisfied also that the exposure would very likely provoke bloodshed." He was arrested for contempt.

The city was divided on Pratt's adamant position. Some argued that since he had given his word it should be honored. But the 11 December *News*, "after recognizing his ethics in the situation," argued that "the fact remains that the law makes no such exceptions in favor of the scruples of recusant witnesses, as does also the further fact that a serious precedent would be set if any witness, even a chief of police, were given the prerogative of refusing to testify because, forsooth, in his judgment, no evidence to warrant a conviction could be secured. A decision of that kind is not left to the witness under any circumstances; if it were, legal investigations and trials would in thousands of cases be nothing but a farce."

Having become something of a political hot potato for the Salt Lake City Board of Police and Fire Commissioners, Pratt tendered his resignation on 31 December, but was unanimously reappointed. Two years later, however, on 7 December 1896, he was dismissed "for the good of the service" without benefit of a hearing. Believing that he was "illegally deprived of his rights," Pratt applied to the Third District Court for a peremptory writ of mandate, a measure designed to compel the board to restore him to office. During a 14 July 1897 board meeting, he was reinstated to his position. But the *Herald* on 3 September assailed Chief Pratt with such charges as "fraud" and that he "gambled at poker." Pratt filed a $30,000 libel suit against the paper, arguing that "by means of said publication [he] had been greatly injured in his standing and reputation in Salt Lake City, where he lives, and in other places where he is known." The situation was so tempestuous that when Mayor John Clark renominated Pratt at the beginning of 1898, the new board refused to ratify the appointment. In a letter to the city council, reported in the 8 February *News,* the mayor appealed the decision. "In selecting a man for chief of police," he wrote:

> I sought for a man of large experience, of conceded honesty, who could not be corrupted by bribes, of courage, discretion, executive ability, and one who would see that the laws and ordinances were strictly and uniformly enforced, without fear or favor, and yet without radicalism. Such a man I believe I found in Arthur Pratt. While out of courtesy to your honorable body, I have carefully reconsidered the nomination. I have seen nothing to change my opinion relative to him, but still believe he

> is the proper man for the chief of police. There are no charges against him of malfeasance or maladministration in office in all the years he has held the office in this community.
>
> Believing that the appointment of Arthur Pratt as chief of police will "conserve the best interests of the police department," I again submit his name and ask your "advice and consent" to his appointment.

Mayor Clark was of the opinion that though a majority of the councilmen may not have wanted Pratt, the majority of city taxpayers did. He noted in his letter that opposition to the appointment likely came from "personal prejudice, political differences, [and] dislikes imbibed from a strict enforcement of the laws and ordinances of the city in the past." But the city council was not swayed by the mayor's appeal. Another vote rejected Pratt by a count of six to nine. The 9 February *News* charged that the negative-voting councilmen were representatives of the "saloon people."

Chief Pratt commenced mandamus proceedings before Third District Court judge Cherry on 12 February. The intent was to compel the city to issue a pay voucher of $750 representing his salary for September 1897 through January 1898. A Utah State Supreme Court decision in late March ultimately vindicated Pratt. The 25 March *News* advised that no motion for a rehearing be filed and that Pratt be reinstated, that the "de jure chief of police [be] allowed to enter upon the actual performance of the duties of his office without delay." After a lengthy discussion of the merits of the court's decision, the paper further urged, "Now let wrangling cease. Let the City Council hold up the Mayor's hands in his efforts to give the city a good government. Let meddlesome schemers who were not placed in office by the people be no longer permitted to dominate the men who were. Again the 'News' says let us have peace."

The police department continued to be a hotbed of political meddling. Pratt remained its chief for a time but eventually found another law enforcement position with fewer political strings attached. In 1904 he again became warden of the Utah State Prison at Sugarhouse, a position he had held in territorial Utah.

During Warden Pratt's subsequent thirteen-year tenure, the Utah State Prison became recognized as a model institution. He abolished "locksteps," striped clothing, the shaving of heads, "dark cells," and bread and water diets. An avid baseball fan, he encouraged the sport at the prison. Prisoners who maintained good behavior throughout the week were allowed to play or watch the Saturday games. During inclement weather, musicals, literary programs, and lectures were sponsored. Vaudeville and "moving pictures" were also scheduled. And the prisoners were allowed to make use of newspapers, magazines, and books. Utah had insufficient funds for employing laborers to build new state roads during the early 1900s, so Pratt, under the guidance of Governor William Spry, advocated convict labor for state highways. Prisoners were motivated by the deduction of ten days from their sentence for each day worked on the roads. The program was a resounding success. In 1915 the system employed a daily average of 54.5 men. In 1916 that number increased to 66.5. By Pratt's own estimation the 1915 convict work force alone saved the state $44,278. In addition to the financial advantages to the state, Pratt was convinced that the work benefitted the inmates immensely. "It not only adds to their health," he was quoted, "but it gives them a better outlook on life in general and makes better men of them." As evidence of the success of the program, he noted that "of all the men we have had working on the roads only three have come back to the prison, after their termination of sentence to serve for other crimes."[9]

One of the less desirable, though necessary aspects of Pratt's duties was presiding over executions at the prison grounds or elsewhere in isolated parts of Salt Lake County. The most notorious of these was the 19 November 1915 execution of convicted murderer Joel Hagglund—alias Joseph Hillstrom, or Joe Hill as he was known in International Workers of the World circles. The "Songbird of the IWW," or the "Wobblies' Troubadour," as admirers dubbed him, drifted to Salt Lake City in the summer of 1913. On the evening of 10 January 1914, he and an accomplice fatally shot Salt Lake grocer John G. Morrison and his seventeen-year-old son Arling during an apparent robbery attempt. Hillstrom was apprehended while seeking medical help for the chest wound he had received in the shootout with the Morrisons.

Hillstrom's lawyers, hired by the IWW, tried to prove that because he had written many of the organization's revolutionary songs, he was the victim of a capitalistic conspiracy. The defense was futile and he was convicted of the double murder on 27 June 1914. Judge Morris L. Ritchie turned Hillstrom over to Pratt to be "taken to the state prison and there be kept by the warden until September 4, 1914, and that on September 4 within the exterior walls of the state prison between the hours of sunrise and sunset you be shot until you are dead by the Sheriff of Salt Lake County."[10]

The seventeen months needed to exhaust the appeals process were dramatic. IWW propagandists, through their journal *Solidarity,* charged that Hillstrom was the victim of a conspiracy of "the Utah Construction Company, the Utah Copper Company, and the Mormon Church."[11] The "Joe Hill Case" became an international symbol of labor unions. Thousands of protest letters, including a 30 September 1915 telegram from U.S. president Woodrow Wilson, were sent to Governor Spry. In early October the governor granted Hillstrom a brief reprieve, but after the 16 October meeting of the Board of Pardons his execution was rescheduled for 19 November. As that date drew ever closer, intense lobbying to postpone the execution continued. Wilson sent another telegram to Spry requesting a "thorough reconsideration of the case of Joseph Hillstrom." But Utahns were even more shocked at the presidential intervention in Utah affairs when Wilson wired labor leader Samuel Gompers that "I have telegraphed Governor Spry of Utah urging justice and a thorough reconsideration of the case."[12] Angry at the president's suggestion that justice had not already been served, Spry wired: "With a full knowledge of all the facts and circumstances submitted, I feel that a further postponement at this time would be an unwarranted interference with the course of justice. Mindful of the obligations of my oath of office to see to it that the laws are enforced, I cannot and will not lend myself or my office to such interference. Tangible facts must be presented before I will further interfere in this case."[13]

Those facts were not forthcoming and Pratt began the final preparations for the execution. On the afternoon of 18 November, he allowed newspaper reporters to interview the condemned man. Despite Hillstrom's air of bravado, he lost his nerve at 4:00 the next morning and began pounding on his cell doors, screaming with rage. Prison officials tried unsuccessfully to calm the hysterical inmate, then left him alone. When they arrived at 7:00 a.m. to escort him to the prison yard for execution, he had tied his cell doors shut with strips torn from a blanket. When the entrance was finally opened, the desperate prisoner attacked the guards with a broom handle. Deputy Sheriff Corless verbally disarmed him by saying: "Joe, this is all nonsense. What do you mean? You promised to die like a man." Hillstrom then laid down the weapon saying, "Well, I'm through. But you can't blame a man for fighting for his life."[14]

Shortly before the prisoner was strapped into a chair with his back to the prison wall, the warden received a communication from the governor to question Hillstrom regarding a William Busky. The man had sworn out an affidavit that he was with Hillstrom the night the Morrisons were murdered and that Hillstrom was innocent. But the condemned told Pratt he did not know anyone by that name, and the execution was carried out at 7:42 a.m.

As a prison reformer, Arthur Pratt was well respected by his peers. Active in national law enforcement circles, he was chosen president of the American Prison Association for 1916-17. At the conclusion of his term, he retired from the state prison and began new employment as Chief Special Agent of the Oregon Short Line with headquarters at Pocatello, Idaho. But this was to be a short-term employment. In early 1919 he fell ill and traveled to California to see if a climate change would improve his health. The vacation was short and he returned to Salt Lake City. Though not considered to be in serious condition, he nevertheless died on 20 March 1919, bringing to a close one of the most remarkable law enforcement careers in the history of Utah.

Notes

1. Agnes E. Caine was a daughter of John T. Caine, Utah territorial secretary and for many years a delegate to Congress.

2. For a complete discussion of Sarah M. Pratt's life, see Richard S. Van Wagoner, "Sarah M. Pratt: The Shaping of an Apostate," *Dialogue: A Journal of Mormon Thought* 19 (Summer 1986): 69-99.

3. Journal History, February 8, 1876, archives, Historical Department, Church of Jesus Christ of Latter-day Saints, Salt Lake City, Utah (hereafter LDS archives).

4. Andrew Karl Larson, *"I Was Called to Dixie"—The Virgin River Basin: Unique Experience in Mormon Pioneering* (Salt Lake City: Deseret News Press, 1961), 319-21.

5. Arthur Pratt, Orson Pratt, Jr., and Harmel Pratt were all antipolygamous. Only one of Sarah's children remained faithful to Mormonism: her deaf son, Laron, an avowed monogamist.

6. *Anti-Polygamy Standard,* 11 (February 1882): 81.

7. The Abraham H. Cannon Journal is in Special Collections, Harold B. Lee Library, Brigham Young University, Provo, Utah. Microfilms of the journal are also available in LDS archives and the Utah State Historical Society Library, Salt Lake City.

8. Mayor Robert Baskin to Utah Governor Caleb West, May 24, 1894, *Deseret Evening News.*

9. Undated *Deseret Evening News* clipping in Chester Pratt collection; copy in Richard S. Van Wagoner Collection, Special Collections, Marriott Library, University of Utah, Salt Lake City.

10. *Deseret Evening News,* July 8, 1914.

11. Vernon H. Jensen, "The Legend and the Case of Joe Hill," *Dialogue: A Journal of Mormon Thought* 2 (Spring 1967): 108.

12. William L. Roper and Leonard J. Arrington, *William Spry, Man of Firmness, Governor of Utah* (Salt Lake City: Utah State Historical Society and University of Utah Press, 1971), 151.

13. Ibid., 152-53.

14. *New York World*, November 20, 1915, as cited in Roper and Arrington, *William Spry*, 158.

3.

Murder, Mayhem, and Mormons

The Evolution of Law Enforcement on the San Juan Frontier, 1880–1900

Thomas E. Austin and Robert S. McPherson

Southeastern Utah is a study in marked contrast. In some areas there is beauty in lush green alpine meadows, while only a few miles removed lie stark red landscapes of sand and slickrock desert. Mountain drainages have cut deep canyons, many of which are impassable. This country literally stands on edge. In many instances it is little changed since 1879 when the Latter-day Saints (Mormons) called a colonizing mission to the Four Corners area. The diverse reasons for this expansion, the original exploration, and the actual journey by pioneer families are well chronicled in several writings, including David E. Miller's book, *Hole-in-the-Rock.*

The Mormons were not, however, the first to establish themselves in the San Juan country. They were preceded not only by a number of Native American groups but also by several gentile (non-Mormon) settlers from Colorado, various small cattle outfits, and an assortment of transient white men.[1] The area that these settlers moved into had the unsavory reputation of being a haven for renegade Indians and white outlaws. Morgan A. Barton, a son of one of the Mormon

Lemuel H. Redd, Jr., had the unenviable assignment of collecting taxes from unwilling cattlemen. The town of Bluff—the most remote settlement in the territory—was a favorite for outlaws and tax evaders who were willing to test their wills against men like Redd. *Utah State Historical Society, all rights reserved*

pioneers, explained one purpose of the San Juan mission as follows: "And why were these people called to settle San Juan? Perhaps not specifically stated or publicly announced, but definitely apparent, for in settling this part of the country they were an established outpost, detracting marauding Indians from interior southern settlements of Utah Territory as well as being a point of interception of bank robbers, horse thieves, cattle rustlers, jail breakers, train robbers, and general desperadic criminals, reducing to a minimum a continuation of their terrorizing and plundering inland settlements in their manner of living while out of reach of law and justice and into which country U.S. officers didn't care to penetrate. These people were to be a shock absorber of premeditated plots of Caucasian outlaws and Indian renegades and if they failed in tact, diplomacy, mental ingenuity and patience in handling this phase of their mission they would fall into the category of what we term today as expendables, and they performed this part of their mission as any other. Many times I have seen my father, with other men, rushing home and at times out of religious services, for their horses and guns to take up the chase of outlaws."[2]

Obviously this Mormon colony was charged with bringing law and order to an area that had not yet experienced it. This segment of their mission call was one of the hardest to accomplish since there were so many factors that made the region attractive to lawless elements. The extremely remote location, the nature of the topography, the lack of any governmental organization, and the sparse population created an excellent hideout for those "on the run." In establishing a settlement, Mormons could do little about the difficulties that nature provided, but they did do something about the sparse population along the river in installing a county government, which included law enforcement. But during the first ten years there was another type of enforcement through a type of church vigilance committee, with civil authorities participating under the direction of church officials.[3]

The pioneers arrived at the future site of Bluff on April 6, 1880, where they elected to form their settlement, having neither the provisions nor the heart to continue the fifteen miles to Montezuma as originally planned. That same day they explored the area, selected a town site, and later in the evening held a meeting in which committees were formed to lay out an irrigation ditch and to survey both town lots and agricultural fields.[4] That the meeting was held immediately after completing such an arduous trek demonstrates how these people felt about establishing order as soon as possible.

On April 26 the settlers received word that the territorial legislature favored a new county in the southeastern corner of the state—to be called San Juan County—and that the governor had appointed Silas S. Smith as probate judge. Even before the judge reached Bluff, the new selectmen called a meeting to organize the county government.[5] In addition to Smith as judge, the same act appointed Platte D. Lyman, Zechariah B. Decker, and Jens Nielson as selectmen and Charles E. Walton as clerk.[6]

As in the rest of the United States, taxes shortly followed the formation of government in San Juan. The June 7 meeting of the county court provided for taxation at six mills on every dollar of assessed property value.[7] This probably came as a blow to the Colorado cattlemen who grazed their herds in Utah to avoid taxation in their home state. The general feeling of the gentile residents of the county was that the Mormon government could levy all the taxes it wanted, but it would not be as easy to collect them.[8] Lemuel H. Redd, Jr., received the tough job of assessment and collection, and the August 4 minutes of the county court show that he had already begun to assess and collect in earnest.[9] He had a great hunger to become a wealthy man,[10] and since his wages were fixed at 12.5 percent of the total assessed taxes for the year, it benefitted him directly to ferret out every piece of taxable property.[11] He is said to have refused a bodyguard, but records show that he did have a paid escort.[12] He was steadfast in his refusal to carry a weapon into the armed camps of the cattle companies, insisting that being unarmed was the only way to avoid confrontation. On one occasion he identified himself, only to come under the guns of the cowboys. He looked at them calmly and said, "I am going to assess all the livestock and every taxable thing belonging to this company and its employees, and when the time comes, I'm going to collect every cent of tax due."[13] The county records show that he not only collected those taxes but did so efficiently for the five years that he held the position.

Another big step in creating a lawful community was the election of select county officials. In the June 7 meeting of the San Juan

Court, the election districts were established and preparations made for an August vote.[14] Accounts do not reveal when it was held, but since there was a change of selectmen on August 4, it is reasonable to assume that it was prior to that date.[15] Little was said about the outcome of the balloting, but sources indicate that Platte D. Lyman was elected to the office of prosecuting attorney, and James B. Decker was elected as sheriff.[16] Mention was also made of an appropriation of twelve dollars for the purchase of law books.[17] Thus the Mormons gave every indication that they were serious about enforcing laws since they now had a prosecutor, a sheriff, and positive knowledge of what the letter of the law was.

Though they were serious in spirit, the realities of living in such a remote area and the difficulties of raising crops the first year slowed their efforts. The prosecutor left Bluff on June 14, 1880, to try to earn a living in Colorado by cutting railroad ties and freighting supplies to the mining camps.[18] He was not even present for his election and wrote little of it in his diary, apparently attaching no great importance to the office.[19] He and most of the able-bodied men were elsewhere trying to make enough money to supply their families with the basics of life. One local historian had enthusiastically said "that the machinery had been put in order to establish and preserve law in this erstwhile lawless region."[20] The machinery might have been there, but the men were not; and, as a result, the first winter for the people left in Bluff was one of constant theft, pursuit, and recovery of their property.

The first mention of law enforcement is dated January 11, 1881. Platte D. Lyman in his diary states that "six of the boys who have been out 5 or 6 days after stolen horses returned today with 5 head for which they paid the Navajos $2.00 apiece. They found them in Comb Wash 10 miles above the road."[21] The Bluff settlers chose to ransom their stolen stock rather than implicate Indians in a criminal investigation, partly because they followed the advice to feed and placate their Indian neighbors rather than fight them. Another reason for not prosecuting Indian thieves was that it would have involved representatives of the federal government, possibly U.S. marshals, who were, at that time, actively pursuing Mormon polygamists.

The community of Bluff had at least six families structured around plural marriage.[22]

Late in March 1881 an Indian named Navajo Frank, who was especially large in stature, surly in attitude, abusive towards Bluff women, and suspected of thievery, was caught stealing horses. He escaped, leaving the horses behind, and the Mormons decided to take no action against him. A few weeks later, however, Kumen Jones caught Navajo Frank with a favorite horse on the south side of the river. The Mormon retrieved his animal and recrossed the river to Bluff, telling Bishop Nielson of the incident. A few days later the settlers found more horses missing. Nielson suggested that Thales Haskel and Kumen Jones follow Frank and try to recover the missing stock. After several days and some help from friendly Navajos, the Mormons located Frank. Haskel looked at him and said that if he persisted in stealing from the Mormons that he would "take sick and die." Frank laughed but gave them back a horse. It was several months before Frank was seen again. Jones said, "[Y]ou could scarcely believe he was the healthy, rugged Indian we had known some months before. He was thin and haggard. His full chest was all sunken in."[23] Frank had come to Bluff to plead with Haskel to write to God telling him that Frank would never again steal from the Mormons if his life would be spared. Haskel replied that he couldn't promise what God would do, but if Frank would stop stealing and encourage other Navajos to do the same, he could live. He was still alive in 1919 when Kumen Jones wrote this account.[24]

The incident with Navajo Frank was the first to involve community police action. The strategy was conceived at the highest level of Mormon church leadership, initiated by local church authority, carried out by members of the church as a religious undertaking, and played on compatible religious beliefs of the Indians. These settlers involved their theology in every facet of their lives, and the precedent pointed to future church-inspired law enforcement.[25]

The economic predicament had not improved by spring 1881 for the people of Bluff. Most of the men were forced to take jobs in Colorado, and by the middle of May very few were left in the area. These were the circumstances that greeted two young men, heavily armed, when they rode into town in September, asking to trade horses. During the conversation that ensued, one of the settlers remarked that trading would be difficult since the Bluff horse herd was grazing ten miles away in Butler Wash. Acting on this information, the two men helped themselves to the herd. Once again people turned to Bishop Nielson for direction. He selected L. H. Redd, Jr., Hyrum Perkins, and Joseph Lyman to pursue the thieves, but not to overtake them until close enough to other Mormon settlements in southwestern Utah to solicit help. The posse inadvertently overtook the bandits at Hall's Crossing on the Colorado River, where a gunfight ensued, leaving one outlaw dead and Joseph Lyman so seriously wounded that only the timely intervention of a Navajo man saved his life.[26]

This event appears to have been the first time that Mormons were pitted against truly desperate men who had little or no scruples about killing. It was an action that was initiated by church authority, with no civil officials taking part in the affair. The posse was, by closest definition, a church vigilance committee.[27]

During the first six or eight years of the 1880s, the big cattle outfits located in San Juan County flourished.[28] The cattle industry attracted men who were wanted by authorities in the eastern states for crimes committed in their jurisdictions. One account states that many of the riders for the cattle companies refused to go east of Dolores, Colorado, because they were afraid of being arrested.[29] Four such men drifted into the McElmo area during the winter of 1886 and got jobs with the L. C. Cattle Company in the spring. They worked for a few weeks and then left, taking with them some of the best horses of the company. The men headed southwest toward Bluff. On a Sunday morning they were seen by a Bluff man in Butler Wash, who approached them but was warned off by their guns. The man rode to town and interrupted the Sunday meeting with the news. Bishop Nielson again advised the Bluff men to go in pursuit and overtake these individuals. Just as they were preparing to leave, the foreman of the L. C. cattle outfit, Bill Ball, rode into town with some of his cowboys. He asked for, and received help from, the settlers in forming a posse comprised of fourteen men who elected him as leader. Then pursued a long chase, after which they overtook the rustlers several miles west of town, where the thieves ambushed them from the shelter of an old Indian ruin. Ball was mortally wounded. Even yet, the incredible drama was not complete. As the man lay dying, the killers robbed him of his pistol and spurs and then escaped across the Colorado River by a secret trail.[30]

Although this incident reads like a Wild West novel, it serves to illustrate that the Mormons, six years after the formation of the county government, still did not separate the powers of church and state. Their first instinct was to form a posse under the direction of their bishop instead of the sheriff. They then deferred to the cowboys, rather than to county law enforcement, electing Ball as leader of the posse. The investigation and pursuit that followed two weeks after the murder were initiated by friends of the murdered man, not the sheriff. When the investigation finally began, the peace officer's only function was to act as a guide to an eighteen-man posse. Amasa Barton, the sheriff, and Kumen Jones went with the posse at Bishop Nielson's direction. Ordinarily one would think that Barton would have started an investigation immediately after the killing, yet it took him two weeks, eighteen cowboys, and a bishop's directive to prompt him to action. Obviously law enforcement practiced a hands-off policy unless it involved Bluff Mormons or unless a specific request for assistance was received—and then only after approval of a church leader.

An event in 1886 that affected the county government and law enforcement again involved the Mormon settlers. Tired of fighting the river at Bluff, they began to look for an area where they could dry-farm and raise livestock. Fredrick I. Jones was called by church authorities to settle in the area of Blue Mountain where he chose the site of present-day Monticello. He surveyed an irrigation ditch, planted and cultivated a small crop, and put a fence around 300 acres of prime farm land.

By June 1887 some of the Mormons had moved families to the new town site and were established in temporary shelters. Work was proceeding on the irrigation ditch and crops had been planted. However, Edmund and Harold Carlisle, who claimed this grazing area for their New Mexico and Kansas Land and Cattle Company, saw this as a direct affront. The two Englishmen resented the encroachment of Mormon farmers and told them in blunt terms that if they did not abandon the irrigation ditch there would be trouble. Mormons sought legal aid and received it in the form of a quit claim deed that gave them possession of the land. Though an apparent victory, this was only the start of their problems with the Carlisle Cattle Company.

The following spring the Mormons erected buildings with lumber that they had cut and hauled the previous fall. With all of the planting, building, hauling logs, construction of the irrigation ditch, and fencing going on, it became obvious to the cattle companies that these settlers meant to stay. On July 9, 1888, the Carlisle company turned the water out of the Monticello irrigation ditch. An injunction served on the Mormons by U.S. Marshal Pratt indicated that the water of North Fork belonged to the cattle company, not to them. But after lengthy litigation, the courts decided that the water should be shared equally between the Carlisles and the Mormons. This decision solidified the Monticello farmers' hold on their land.[31]

By 1889 law enforcement had evolved from the vigilante mode to a more traditional form. As the county population increased, with settlements at Bluff, Monticello, and in the Bueno district, the power structure became more diverse. Officials were needed to cover these different areas, and even though most of the new appointees were Mormons, they had to represent a growing gentile population which viewed direct church involvement in government differently. As the population increased, so did crime, and so did the demand for good law enforcement.[32]

Two characters illustrate how things changed from 1889 to 1900. Elsewhere these two individuals may have been diametrically opposed, one a federal marshal during a period of federal opposition to polygamy and the other a Hole-in-the-Rock Mormon. Although information is vague, it appears that Marshal Joe Bush and Sheriff Willard "Dick" Butt worked cooperatively to make the justice system a viable force in San Juan. Marshal Bush was considered something of a hero to the people of San Juan County because he did not bother the Mormons and he usually caught the men he went after.[33] He carried a very short, sawed-off shotgun that had a tendency to make outlaws take notice. Yet Bush must have been an individual who felt that a professional image was not essential to his job, since he was arrested three or four different times in Salt Lake City for frequenting a house of ill repute, being drunk and disorderly, and discharging a firearm in a public building.[34]

Conversely Sheriff Butt was a man of personal integrity and the first sheriff of San Juan County to take his position seriously.[35] He was also the first sheriff to receive a wage, $100 a year independent of fees.[36]

Relations between the Carlisle outfit and the Monticello Mormons verged on open warfare by 1890. The cowboys viewed the Mormons as farmers, which was next to sheepmen on their scale of dislikes. Mormons felt that the employees of the cattle companies were uncivilized and uncontrolled. The cowboys tried regularly to prove that they were exactly what the Mormons claimed, occasionally riding through the streets of town shooting at buildings and terrorizing the population. One incident in 1890 brought the tension to a head.

The problem started when Mons Peterson got his freight wagon stuck in the mud some distance north of Monticello. While he was in the process of getting another team to pull it out, the cowboys found the bogged wagon and looted it. They located, among the store goods, some liquor that was being brought in for "medicinal purposes." The alcohol proved to be a great temptation for the wranglers who disposed of it in a few moments and then went on to Monticello for a night of terrorizing the locals. As the evening progressed one cowboy, John Gibson, managed to shoot himself in the foot. They finished off the evening by sacking Peterson's store and then stabling themselves and their horses within.[37]

The townspeople were outraged. Some of the community leaders went to the territorial district court in Beaver, Utah, where they filed a complaint against John Gibson, Robert Kelly, and William Johnson for the crime of riot and received warrants for the three men's arrest.[38] Marshal Bush came to Monticello only to find that Gibson was recovering from his wounded foot at his sister's house, so Bush went there to make the arrest. Apparently no one was home but Gibson. Having no desire to be taken into custody, he decided to fight it out with Bush and hid behind a curtain waiting for the marshal to come into the room. The lawman entered the house, saw a pistol protruding from the curtain, and placed a well-aimed shotgun blast into it. The shot spoiled not only the curtains but Gibson's arm and side, which were shredded "all to rags."[39] The shot served notice on cowboys that lawlessness would no longer be tolerated in Monticello. Although the justice system had been slow to mature, it was beginning to assert its authority in the San Juan country.

Ironically the feud between the Mormons and the Carlisles ended in a marriage between the two. There were again two colorful characters, the first being William "Latigo" Gordon. As foreman of the cattle company and stepson to Harold Carlisle, he was well versed in the harassment tactics that cattlemen used against the farmers. The second actor was D. H. "King" Dalton, a county commissioner who fancied himself the ultimate power figure in the region.[40] Latigo took exception to the fact that Commissioner Dalton appointed William E. Hyde as sheriff, since the cattlemen had experienced difficulties with Hyde in the past. In fact, Hyde had threatened to burn Latigo's hay, barns, sheds, and house. Latigo went to Dalton's place to encourage the new sheriff's removal, the two men argued, and Latigo shot his "44 caliber Colt's Frontier Six Shooter" in the general direction of the commissioner's son Henry. Latigo was charged, on a complaint by the commissioner, with assault to commit murder.[41] A warrant was issued and he was arrested by the sheriff.

In the court action that followed, the Monticello Mormons made an important show of support in Latigo's behalf. They filed a petition with the prosecutor requesting the charge be dropped from a felony to a misdemeanor: "[W]e are acquainted with the defendant above named, and fully appreciate the charge against him of assault with a deadly weapon with intent to kill and murder. ... We have known the defendant for years, as a kind hearted and industrious citizen and neighbour and we have never known anything bad about him, except his excessive use of liquor, which alone we are satisfied, is the responsible agency which caused him to do the act complained of. ... We know that his heart is not that of a murderer, for no man ever left his cabin hungry, or in distress. ... We solicit you not to prosecute him for Felony, but that you change the charge against him to 'Assault' to which charge, we are told he will plead guilty. We have talked to him and know that he feels the shame and senses the disgrace and wrong of his conduct." Sixty-three Monticello people, probably a good portion of the community, signed the petition. Among the signatures were those of a county commissioner, county attorney, sheriff, ex-sheriff, the justice of the peace, and other officers in the government.[42]

A few years later Latigo married one of the Mormon girls, submitting to an interview by a Mormon bishop prior to the marriage. The bishop asked if he had ever killed a man, to which Latigo replied that he did not think so, unless one counted the black man that he and some of his friends had found bathing in a water hole and had pushed under the water a few times until he did not come up again. He thought that incident would probably not count because it was more of a joke than intent to do harm.[43] Despite having such a checkered past, Latigo gradually managed through the force of his personality to win over a substantial part of the Mormon community and to bridge the gap between the settlers and the cattle company.

The Dalton/Latigo incident illustrates the progress that the justice system in San Juan County had made. In this criminal action the constituted state court requirements were met. There was a regular complaint filed; attorneys represented both sides; a petition, in correct form, was submitted; and a four-page continuance affidavit was supplied to the court.

By 1901 the final shift from church- to state-controlled law enforcement had been completed. There were still problems with lawbreakers thereafter, and it should be noted that the county officials were still primarily Mormons. However, the church and church leaders did not seem to have the degree of influence on governmental function that they had had in the early days of the county.

What caused the Church of Jesus Christ of Latter-day Saints to actively engage in law enforcement in San Juan County? Perhaps church leaders were such dynamic individuals that their followers looked to them for guidance in any difficulty. Education was a rare commodity on the frontier and certainly affected the reading and understanding of law, and may have subsequently determined who participated in its enforcement. It is also possible that church--initiated enforcement was not done by choice but by necessity. Regardless of the reasons, the facts clearly show that Bishop Nielson and other leaders of the "Hole-in-the-Rock Mormons" in Bluff supported a vigilance committee that enforced the law for the settlement's first eight years.

Notes

1. Robert McPherson, "Navajos, Mormons, and Henry L. Mitchell," *Utah Historical Quarterly* (Winter 1987), mentions there were eighteen families at McElmo when the Mormons arrived at Bluff.

2. Morgan Amasa Barton, "Back Door to San Juan," 9, as cited in David E. Miller, *Hole-in-the-Rock* (Salt Lake City: University of Utah Press, 1959), 8-9.

3. The terms *vigilante* and *vigilance* often invoke thoughts of well organized, highly structured groups who chase down and execute lawbreakers where they catch them. These terms, as used in this essay, have quite a different meaning. Most instances of church/citizen-initiated law enforcement by the Bluff area settlers were disorganized and "spur of the moment" reactions to the immediate need of recovering stolen property. The Mormon posses had no intention to execute anyone, and did, in fact, dissuade a posse of cowboys from hanging Cass Hite for ferrying some outlaws across the San Juan River.

4. Platte D. Lyman, Journal, 12, Special Collections, Harold B. Lee Library, Brigham Young University, Provo, Utah. Lyman indicates that he arrived at the site of the settlement on April 5, but the main body of the wagon train did not arrive until April 6.

5. Ibid., 16. The May 8, 1880, entry says that Lyman met S. S. Smith and a small company bound for San Juan. See also "Minutes of San Juan County Court, 1880-1900," 7, San Juan County Courthouse, Monticello, Utah. The entry for April 26, 1880, shows the selectmen were in attendance but Smith was not.

6. Ibid., 7.

7. Ibid., June 7, 1880, 8.

8. "San Juan Stake History," 93, Special Collections, Lee Library, cites an alleged eyewitness as the authority for this sentiment. It is not hard to imagine the lack of enthusiasm among gentile residents being taxed by Mormons. In addition, they were previously unaccustomed to being taxed at all.

9. Minutes ... County Court, August 4, 1880, 9.

10. Amasa J. Redd, ed., *Lemuel Hardison Redd, Jr., 1856-1923* (Salt Lake City, 1967). Redd makes the following comment: "Father remarked

many years ago that while a young man he had a great desire to have wealth and said he made it a matter of earnest prayer."

11. Minutes ... County Court, August 4, 1880, 9.

12. Ibid., December 28, 1881, 12.

13. Redd, *Lemuel Hardison Redd*, 8.

14. Minutes ... County Court, August 4, 1880, 9.

15. Ibid.

16. Albert R. Lyman, "History of San Juan County, 1879-1917," 19, San Juan County Library, Blanding, Utah.

17. Minutes ... County Court, August 4, 1880, 9.

18. Lyman Journal, June 14, 1880, 18.

19. Ibid., 26. Lyman says, "Yesterday I qualified as Prosecuting Attorney for this county having been elected to that office at the August election."

20. "San Juan Stake History," 92.

21. Lyman Journal, 33.

22. Ibid.

23. Kumen Jones, "Writings of Kumen Jones," 42, Special Collections, Lee Library.

24. Ibid.

25. Ibid., 42-43. Jones states that LDS apostle Erastus Snow told the Bluff settlers that if they would live their religion, hostile Indians would be destroyed by the hand of the Lord.

26. Albert R. Lyman, *Indians and Outlaws* (Salt Lake City: Bookcraft, 1962), 45-51; Lyman Journal, 44-45, the October 13, 1881, entry, gives a narrative of this event.

27. No mention is made in any account, including county records, that affords the three Mormon men any law enforcement authority.

28. Charles S. Peterson, "San Juan in Controversy: American Livestock Frontier vs. Mormon Cattle Pool," in Thomas G. Alexander, ed., *Essays on the American West, 1972-1973* (Provo, UT: Brigham Young University Press, 1974), Charles Redd Monographs in Western History, no. 3, page 45. See also Don D. Walker, "The Carlisles: Cattle Barons of the Upper Basin," *Utah Historical Quarterly* 32 (1964): 270.

29. Cornelia A. Perkins, Marion G. Nielson, and Lenora B. Jones, *Saga of San Juan* (Salt Lake City: Mercury Publishing Company, 1968), 94.

30. The Bill Ball killing is one of the best known of the San Juan stories. The most accurate account seems to be Albert R. Lyman's unpublished "History of San Juan County." Much of the information was

extracted from interviews with participants in the events. Since it was written in 1918, it is logical to assume that the resources he used were more accurate than later renditions. For example, Lyman's 1918 account says that J. B. Decker had a horse killed in the ambush. Minutes ... County Court, December 8, 1886, substantiate this: "A petition was presented by James B. Decker, asking for an appropriation of one hundred dollars to reimburse him for losses sustained while following horse thieves."

31. Perkins et al., *Saga*, 90.

32. From the Minutes of the County Court, it is obvious that the region was marching to a faster tempo by 1888-89. The entries prior to those years were short and show that at times no meetings were held at all. Between 1880 and 1889 there are only four entries that make direct reference to criminal cases. There are that many references in 1890 alone.

33. Frank Silvey, "Noted Characters in the Pioneer Settlement of San Juan County—Joe Bush," 4, Microfilm 920, #94, Genealogy Library, Brigham Young University.

34. From various accounts in the *Deseret News*.

35. For complete treatment of Willard Butt as sheriff of San Juan County, see Albert R. Lyman, "Dick Butt, Sheriff of San Juan," Microfilm 920, #94, Genealogy Library, Brigham Young University.

36. Minutes ... County Court, December 30, 1891, 113.

37. Perkins et al., *Saga,* 107-108; also Lyman's "History," 68-69.

38. *The People v. Robert Kelly, William Johnson and John Gibson; Indictment for Riot* (15 March 1890), San Juan County Courthouse, Monticello, Utah.

39. Silvey, "Bush," 5; also Lyman, "History," 69.

40. An interview with a direct descendant of Dalton who prefers to remain unnamed indicates that King's egotism earned him the epithet.

41. *The State of Utah v. W. E. Gordon; Indictment for Assault with Intent to Murder* (27 June 1901), San Juan County Courthouse.

42. *The State of Utah v. W. E. Gordon; Petition by Citizens ... in San Juan County* (August 1901), San Juan County Courthouse.

43. Redd, *Lemuel Hardison Redd,* 154-55.

4.

The Controversial Death of Gobo Fango

H. Dean Garrett

When the first pioneers entered the Salt Lake Valley in 1847, there were several blacks in the group. Later, pioneer blacks came as free people or in some instances as slaves of southern converts to the Latter-day Saint church. Together with others of African descent who came as workers on the railroad, these soon constituted a small black community in nineteenth-century Utah. One of them was Gobo Fango who left South Africa as a child and settled in the Salt Lake Valley. He lived in the Tooele, Utah, area and eventually moved to near Oakley, Idaho, where he was killed in 1886. His life is a fascinating, yet sad story—and it remains controversial in Idaho and Utah today.

Gobo Fango was born in the Cape of Good Hope in South Africa about 1855. He was a member of a tribe ruled by Chief Creile. His early life was shaped by the events of the Kaffir wars that raged around him. As a result of the wars and a concurrent famine, his young mother left her tribal home with her three-year-old son and a baby daughter and fled to a nearby farm owned by Henry Talbot.[1] Her weakened condition made it impossible for her to complete the journey with both children, so she kept the baby with her and left Gobo in the crotch of a tree out of the reach of wild animals.[2] After she arrived at the farm, Henry's boys rescued Gobo. He would soon become an indentured member of the family.[3]

The Talbots' lives changed dramatically when a friend introduced Henry to the Mormon religion. On December 28, 1857, he was baptized into the church. Six months later his wife Ruth and their children were also baptized; however, no records indicate that Gobo was ever baptized a Mormon. Soon, upon the encouragement of church leaders, the Talbots sold their farm and moved to Port Elizabeth to await the opportunity of traveling to Zion in America. That opportunity came on February 20, 1861, when they boarded the ship *Race Horse* and set sail for Boston. They had intended to leave Gobo behind with friends, but he complained so much they allowed him to accompany them. The family at that time consisted of Henry and Ruth, their fourteen unmarried children, and their married son Henry James Talbot and his wife and child.[4] One account indicates that Gobo was hidden in a blanket and remained undetected until they were at sea.[5]

Except for a heavy gale in the Caribbean and a collision with another vessel in Boston harbor, in which the *Race Horse* lost its bow, the trip was uneventful. However, the Talbots' arrival in Boston came at an exciting moment in history, for five days earlier shots had been fired at Fort Sumter and the Civil War had begun. President Abraham Lincoln had issued a call for volunteers, and many men were enlisting in the army. Flags were flying, martial music was playing, and great excitement was felt everywhere.

In Boston the Talbot family and Gobo boarded a train, traveling through New York and then on to Chicago. They met their first challenge to Gobo's presence in Chicago where certain people, undoubtedly influenced by the excitement of the war, accused the Talbots of owning a slave. Apparently they set about to give Gobo his freedom. According to one account Gobo, greatly frightened by the uproar, "fled inside the train and one of the ladies of the company hid him beneath her crinolines while the angry emancipationist searched the train without success. To avoid a recurrence of the trouble, Gobo was dressed in girl's clothing and his head was covered with a huge sun bonnet. At awkward times a veil was added to make sure his black face was completely hidden."[6] The railroad ended at Joseph,

Edward Hunter, Presiding Bishop of the Latter-day Saints church, purchased a black slave named Gobo Fango sometime after 1865. Fango was fond of his employer, who helped the former slave become an independent sheepherder, and he included the bishop in his will. Fango was murdered by a neighbor in 1886 in a dispute over range rights. *Engraving by H. B. Hall and Sons, New York, Utah State Historical Society, *

Iowa. The immigrants then traveled to Florence, Nebraska, where they outfitted wagons and undertook their journey west to the Salt Lake Valley, joining the company led by Homer Duncan. They arrived in Salt Lake in the fall of 1861 and wintered there. The following spring they moved to Kaysville, Utah, about twenty miles north of Salt Lake, and settled on a farm. Gobo remained with the Talbots and worked on their farm as an indentured slave.

Slavery was at this time still practiced by some Mormons from the South. In 1860 there were twenty-nine reported slaves in Utah.[7] There was also a group of free blacks who had joined the Mormon church or who had settled in Utah for employment purposes. Between 1860 and 1870 the black population of Utah grew from 59 to 113. Some of this increase was due to the arrival of the transcontinental railroad.

Gobo was expected to work for the Talbots as a laborer and sheepherder, and life was apparently hard for him. He lived in a shed in back of the Talbots' house. One cold winter his feet froze, and he lost part of the heel on one foot. An acquaintance reported: "When he [Gobo] came to our place, his feet were badly frozen, and he was a cripple until his death. My first recollection was always seeing him wrapping his feet with cloths, and later I remember he had boots."[8] She also remembered seeing Gobo take off his boot to show her brother his foot: "The heel was all gone, and he had wool in his boot so his foot would fit better."[9] Gobo remained with the Talbot family until he was in his teens.[10] Eventually the Talbots either gave or sold Gobo to the Lewis Whitesides family in Kaysville.[11]

A daughter, Ruth Whitesides Hunter, had a herd of sheep in Grantsville, Utah, and she was finding that her daughters were spending all of their time with the sheep and not learning the domestic sciences. When she remembered that Gobo was with her family in Kaysville, she asked her husband, Edward Hunter,[12] if he would obtain Gobo for her. According to Hunter's biographer, "Edward paid for Gobo, then immediately put him on the payroll, just as he did all the hired hands. Gobo regarded Edward as his benefactor and was very fond of him. ..."[13]

The legal sanction for slavery in Utah ended in the spring of 1862. President Lincoln issued the Emancipation Proclamation in

1863. Some slave owners waited to release their slaves until 1865 when involuntary servitude was abolished throughout the United States.[14] For instance, it appears that Gobo was sold to the Hunters after 1865.[15]

The Hunters took Gobo to Grantsville where he helped herd sheep in Utah's western desert through the 1870s. During this time he was able to develop a sheep herd of his own.

A group of Mormon settlers moved from Tooele and Grantsville to Goose Creek Valley, Idaho, as early as 1880[16] and began to irrigate and farm the land there and to raise sheep. About that same time, Gobo, two of the Hunter brothers, and Walter Matthews went to Goose Creek to run their sheep on the desert. Gobo and Matthews also leased a band of sheep from Thomas Poulton and his sons.[17]

At that time Cassia County, Idaho, which included Goose Creek, was a "huge expanse of lush range lands and high mountains."[18] This area had already attracted the attention of cattlemen from the Midwest and Texas who had moved into the area with large herds. The first arrived in 1871, and when sheepmen began moving into the same area, tension between the cattlemen and sheepmen arose. One report complained that "the sheep are getting so thick that they are eating the range out."[19] This problem was compounded by the drought that began in the summer of 1885 and continued for several years. "It was dry and hot," a local history states. "Snow did not pile up in the mountains. The grass turned brown, and the cattle and horses cropped it to the ground."[20] Due to the combination of overstocking and drought, the range was overgrazed. The cattlemen claimed first rights, the sheepmen disagreed, and a range war developed. Under pressure from the powerful cattlemen, Idaho's territorial legislature passed an act known as the Two-mile Limit which prohibited "sheep grazing within two miles of any possessory claim."[21] The range rivalry continued to grow and the cattlemen issued their own edict that all sheepmen must leave.

In this setting early in the winter of 1886, Gobo Fango was herding his sheep in the Goose Creek Valley beyond the cattlemen's deadline for leaving. Apparently he was close to the two-mile limit of a claim of Frank Bedke. Early one day Bedke and a companion rode into Gobo's camp and told him to leave immediately. The *Idaho*

Tri-Weekly Statesman reported that Gobo challenged Bedke to produce evidence of ownership of the land on which he was herding. Bedke indicated that he did not want to have trouble but wanted rather to be a friend. He dismounted his horse, caught Gobo off guard, and commenced shooting.[22] The *Deseret News* account of the incident indicated that Bedke fired the first shot which "must have been aimed at his temple and carried away his eyebrow." The report continued that Gobo was beaten about the head with the pistol and was then shot again, "the bullet entering at the back part of the head and ranging to the neck, where it stopped close to the jugular vein and not very deep from the skin." A third time Bedke fired, "the bullet entering Gobo's side from the back and coming out near the navel."[23] The newspaper indicated that Gobo recovered consciousness and overheard a conversation concerning disposition of Gobo's gun which Bedke had taken. Gobo was eventually able to "crawl about four and a half miles to the Walter Matthews home east of Oakley, holding his intestines with one hand."[24] A doctor from Albion was summoned to take care of him, but Gobo survived only four or five days, during which time he made out a will providing for amounts of money to be given to acquaintances and friends, especially to the Hunter family. The rest was bequeathed to the Salt Lake temple fund and the Grantsville City "needy, poor people." Mrs. Solomon E. Hale indicated that "he left me $125 in his will before he died, as also some of my other sisters. He left $50 to one of them. ..."[25]

Gobo was buried in the Oakley, Idaho, cemetery. Marking his final resting place is a headstone with the simple inscription:

Gobo Fango
died February 10, 1886
30 years old

Frank Bedke and his companion rode to Albion, Idaho, where Bedke reported the shooting to the sheriff. A trial was held, and Bedke pleaded "not guilty due to self-defense." His companion backed his story, and the first trial ended in a hung jury. Bedke was brought to trial again one year later. This time the jury's decision was "not guilty." The events of that trial were reported in the newspaper: "Frank Bedke, who was tried at Albion a year ago on a charge of killing Gobo Fango, colored, the trial resulting in a 'hung' jury, eleven voting for a conviction and one for an acquittal, has again been tried and acquitted, the first ballot of the jury showing 10 for an acquittal and 2 for conviction. Three ballots only were taken before an agreement to acquit was reached. The dying declaration of Fango was the most serious testimony offered. Judge Waters of Bellerue, Charles Cobb of Albion, and Ransford Smith of Ogden, defended Bedke."[26]

The man who killed Gobo Fango had traveled the world over as a seaman and then settled in the Goose Creek Basin to raise cattle. Frank Carl Bedke was born in Rieth, Prussia, Germany, on November 22, 1844. He had limited schooling in Germany, and at the age of sixteen became a sailor on a ship bound for New York. He did not return to Germany, deciding instead to remain in the States. A family history states, "Near the end of the Civil War Frank Carl boarded a ship in Boston Harbor for San Francisco, sailing around Cape Horn."[27] He spent about a year sailing the West Coast and then worked on mining claims. In 1868 he traveled to Montana on a prospecting tour and wintered in Bozeman. In 1870 he went to Cottonwood, Utah, and joined the gold hunt, remaining there until 1877. After a short stay in Nevada, he moved to Park City, Utah, and sold milk to the miners. Then in 1878 he traveled to Grouse Creek, Utah, to winter 97 head of cattle. In the spring he took the cattle to Goose Creek Basin, Idaho, to a place now called Bedke Spring. He lived in a dugout and rode range for other operations until he was able to fully establish his own.

When he arrived in the Oakley area, it was about the same time the Mormons from Grantsville, Utah, appeared there. A close-knit group, the Mormons were not particularly open to outsiders. Bedke felt that he was an outsider, but he was intent on staying in the area. When an Indian uprising occurred, he remained and co-existed with the Indians while most of the other settlers fled to Kenton, Utah, for safety.

He married Polly Ann McIntosh on January 2, 1882.[28] Polly Ann was born in Grantsville, Utah, in March 1863 to Solomon P. and Mary Harper McIntosh. At the age of seventeen, she drove a team and wagon from Grantsville to Idaho. Her marriage to Bedke was not viewed favorably by her family or the Mormon church, and this eventually led to her estrangement from both.

During the early years of their marriage, the Bedkes and their Mormon neighbors found themselves in conflict. One cause was the fact that Polly's husband was not Mormon. A second was the strong anti-Mormon feeling among other settlers in southern Idaho at that time. A third and perhaps more important source of conflict between the Bedkes and their neighbors was the dispute between the cattlemen and the sheepmen. The natural animosity between these two groups was amplified during the drought.

Despite these early difficulties, following his acquittal in the second jury trial Bedke became a successful and respected member of his community. One biographical volume stated that he was "active and forceful in the affairs of the community and aided in promoting its welfare both as a private citizen and as a useful public official, serving faithfully as a school trustee for nine years [and was] a firm and zealous working Democrat in political faith, giving loyal and serviceable support to the candidates and policies of his party."[29] During the latter part of his life, he was described as a man "well prepared to meet all emergencies and perform every duty of citizenship with readiness and ability. He [was] a valuable element in the progress and development of Cassia County, giving substantial and helpful aid to every commendable undertaking for its improvement and the comfort and convenience of its people. Among the enterprising and public-spirited citizens of the county, he is in the front rank, and is secure in the esteem of all classes of the people."[30]

The death of Gobo Fango has inspired a voluminous amount of folklore and conflicting stories. The nature of the homicide is disputed by the descendants of Frank Bedke who feel that their grandfather was justified in killing Gobo Fango. This is based on several factors. They view Frank as an independent, self-sufficient man who reacted to any challenge to his rights or livelihood. In the eyes of his family, his reaction to the sheepmen, and especially Gobo, was right and justified because, according to their claims, Gobo was within the two-mile limit and refused to respect the lawful owner of the land. Second, the Bedke family finds it hard to believe that Gobo, so severely wounded, could have traveled 4.5 miles to Walter Matthews's home and still be in a condition to testify to what happened. Gobo's account was given secondhand at the trial by those who claimed to have heard him speak it. Frank and his companion gave firsthand accounts. The Bedke family also feels that contemporary newspaper reports reflected the sheepmen's side of the story rather than what actually took place. Some believe that Gobo arrived at the Matthews home with $200 on his person[31] and ask how a black man at that time could have had that much money when many in the area were struggling for survival. One of the Bedke family has suggested that it could have been blood money paid to Gobo to kill Frank.[32] In fact, the Bedkes are proud that their grandfather killed Gobo rather than possibly allowing his own life to be taken. They feel his actions reflected the reality of survival on the frontier. The family points to his acquittal in the second jury trial as ample evidence of his innocence and the rightness of his actions.[33]

Many questions remain unanswered and are indeed unanswerable. The problem for a modern researcher is being able to look back a hundred years where records of an event are sparse. Much folklore and family tradition exist, but only a few newspaper articles and a secretarial account of the two Bedke trials are currently available. All of the original court records have been misplaced or lost.[34] The probate records of Gobo Fango's estate indicate that the medical care rendered to him by the doctor was extensive.[35] Yet, despite his injuries, he was able to recount the details of his shooting and draw up a will.

Why was there such a dynamic change between the first trial, in which there was a strong sentiment to convict Bedke, and the second trial just one year later in which the jury acquitted him? Did the emotions of the times, generated by the sheepmen versus the cattlemen conflict, dictate the outcome of the court cases? We know that Gobo Fango was killed and that Frank Bedke did it. The question remains, why? Was it murder or could it have been self-defense?

This frontier episode illustrates the conflicts between segments of society in the West at that period of time. Gobo Fango was a black man in a white world. He was identified with Mormon sheepmen from Utah when they came head to head with strong-willed, non-Mormon cattlemen from the Midwest and Texas. This was compounded by a pre-existing animosity between Mormons and non-Mormons in southern Idaho in the 1880s. Regardless of why Frank Bedke pulled the trigger, Gobo Fango was a victim of the times in which he lived.[36]

Notes

1. "The Life of Henry James Talbot in South Africa," typescript, photocopy in archives, Historical Department, Church of Jesus Christ of Latter-day Saints, Salt Lake City, Utah. The Talbot family migrated from England to South Africa in 1820, eventually settling in the Winterburg area where they cultivated a large farm. For his service during the Kaffir War, Talbot received a farm at Thorn River from the government. Gobo was found on this farm.

2. Some accounts say the girl was left with her brother and both found by the Talbot brothers.

3. Alan K. Makin, *The 1820 Settlers of Salem Hezekiah Sephton's Party* (Wynberg, South Africa: Juta & Co., 1971), 112.

4. Ibid., 115-16.

5. S. Austin Hunter to Edward C. Talbot, August 7, 1934, Grantsville, Utah, in Historical Data of the Talbot Family, Special Collections, Harold B. Lee Library, Brigham Young University (hereafter BYU Library).

6. Makin, *The 1820 Settlers,* 115-16.

7. Ronald G. Coleman, "A History of Blacks in Utah, 1825-1910" (Ph.D. dissertation, University of Utah, 1980), 54.

8. Mrs. Solomon E. Hale to Kenneth Larson, August 31, 1934, BYU Library.

9. Ibid.

10. "Henry James Talbot and Descendants," BYU Library. See also Martha Anderson, *Black Pioneers of the Northwest, 1800-1918* (Seattle: Author, 1980), 219; Makin, *The 1820 Settlers*, 117.

11. Kate B. Carter, ed., *Our Pioneer Heritage,* 20 vols. (Salt Lake City: Daughters of Utah Pioneers, 1958-77), 8:544.

12. At that time Hunter was presiding bishop of the LDS church.

13. William Hunter, *Edward Hunter, Faithful Steward* (Salt Lake City, 1970), 244.

14. Coleman, "A History of Blacks," 54.

15. Gobo was born in 1855. If he was in his teens when he went to the Whitesides family, then he was sold to the Hunters after 1865.

16. Wayne R. Boothe, "A History of the Latter-day Saint Settlement of Oakley, Idaho" (Master's thesis, Brigham Young University, 1963), 30-31.

17. Virginia Estes, ed., *A Pause for Reflection* (Burley, ID: Daughters of Utah Pioneers, 1977), 158.

18. David H. Grover, *Diamondfield Jack: A Study in Frontier Justice* (Norman: University of Oklahoma Press, 1986), 9.

19. Edward Hunter, Jr., to his uncle, Edward Hunter Collection, BYU Library.

20. Boothe, "A History of ... Oakley, Idaho," 37.

21. Grover, *Diamondfield Jack*, 12.

22. *Idaho Tri-Weekly Statesman*, March 31, 1887, 3.

23. *Deseret News,* February 12, 1886, 3.

24. Estes, *A Pause*, 158.

25. Mrs. Solomon E. Hale to Kenneth Larson.

26. *Salt Lake Tribune,* April 3, 1887, 2; *Idaho Tri-Weekly Statesman,* March 31, 1887, 1.

27. *They Called Me Bedke* (Salt Lake City: Bedke Family Association, 1975), 16.

28. Ibid.

29. *Progressive Men of Southern Idaho* (Chicago, 1904), 57.

30. Ibid.

31. No documents indicate that $200 was found on Gobo.

32. Interview with Bruce Bedke and Ann Bedke Woodhouse, Oakley, Idaho, July 7, 1987.

33. Ibid.

34. *They Called Me Bedke*, 294.

35. Probate Records of Gobo Fango, Cassia County Courthouse, Burley, Idaho.

36. For an account of a later conflict between the cattlemen and Mormon sheepmen, see Grover, *Diamondfield Jack,* which details the murder of two Mormons and the trial, conviction, and eventual acquittal of Diamondfield Jack Davis.

5.

The Peculiar Case of James Lynch and Robert King

David L. Buhler

At 2:00 a.m. on Tuesday, September 11, 1900, three men, revolvers in hand and handkerchiefs pulled snugly over their faces, entered the upstairs Sheep Ranch,[1] a gambling house located on Salt Lake City's notorious Commercial Street. Two of the three masked men stayed near the door with their guns drawn. The third approached Colonel George Prowse,[2] the proprietor, who was seated at the Ranch's "bank." As the man approached, Prowse pulled a gun from the table's drawer and rose to his feet. They exchanged shots—witnesses could not say who fired first. The robber fell to the floor unconscious. The two remaining masked men fired five times, hitting Prowse at least once, and then bolted downstairs to the alley below. Simultaneously Prowse fired four more shots. In the exchange a Sheep Ranch employee, Ernest Sidell, was wounded as a bullet grazed his ear and shoulder.

Salt Lake City police sergeant John B. Burbidge heard the shots and arrived shortly after two of the bandits had fled. What he saw was Prowse "sitting in a chair, his head dropped forward" and Sidell "staggering around the room in a dazed manner, while the [third] robber lay on the floor in a pool of blood and to all appearances dead." Prowse was taken to St. Mark's Hospital for treatment. Sidell was examined at a neighborhood drugstore. The robber was taken to

Commercial Street in Salt Lake City in 1903 where gambling, drinking, and prostitution were the rule. It was here in September 1900 that the proprietor of the Sheep Ranch gambling hall was murdered in a botched robbery attempt. The ensuing trial was full of surprises. *Shipler Collection, Utah State Historical Society, all rights reserved*

jail where his wound was treated by a physician and determined to be superficial.

Later that morning the prisoner identified himself as James Lynch. He said he was twenty-six years old, from Albany, New York, and had worked in mines and smelters in the West and British Columbia before coming to Salt Lake three days earlier. Asked by a reporter if he had done any of the shooting at the Sheep Ranch, Lynch replied, "Damn if I know."

Newspaper reporters, jailers, and policemen all endeavored to persuade Lynch to name his still at-large accomplices. At one point Detective George Sheets brought him a pint of whiskey, hoping this "friendly gesture" would prompt the prisoner to become more cooperative, but Lynch steadfastly refused to identify partners, saying only that he did not know their names.

The police were not entirely without leads. Several witnesses said they had seen Lynch's accomplices. One witness was Frank Lyon, a Sheep Ranch employee who said he saw three men, including Lynch, at the establishment for several nights before the shooting. Lyon finished his shift about an hour before the attempted robbery. Prior to leaving that night, he saw the men unlock the back doors. One of the three was Lynch, Lyon said, and he was positive he could identify the other two if he saw them again.

A second witness was a seventeen-year-old messenger boy, William Wittenberg, who saw two men run from the Sheep Ranch down an alley and into the nearby Headquarters Saloon. He followed them, talked with one of them, and got a good look at both. The Headquarters bartender told police that he had noticed the two men, and provided a similar description.

A clue left near the scene of the crime—a new-looking leather valise found at the foot of the Sheep Ranch stairway—also gave police hope of identifying and capturing the other two robbers.

From his hospital bed, George Prowse discussed the attempted robbery with a *Salt Lake Herald* reporter, saying that as soon as he saw the robbers were armed he went for his gun. The man who approached him, Prowse said, "immediately started to shoot. I was hit by the first ball. I thought he had killed me." After Prowse was hit, he returned fire: "If I had not been hit I would not have shot ... Anyway, I only winged him. He didn't give me half a chance."

Prowse underwent surgery at 7:00 p.m. as doctors attempted without success to locate and remove the bullet that had entered his thigh. Following surgery he "grew weaker and about 9 o'clock became unconscious" and died at 9:30 p.m. The post-mortem examination determined the cause of death to be "acute peritonitis" resulting from perforation of the intestines as the bullet traveled through his abdomen before lodging in his hipbone.

"It is doubtful if Salt Lake ever knew a sporting man more generally esteemed than was Colonel Prowse," eulogized the *Salt Lake Tribune,* noting that "He was a familiar figure on the streets during the afternoon. ... a very large man ... with a flowing grey moustache. ... During the summer his vest was invariably unbuttoned and a large fine diamond adorned the front of his colored shirt."

Although he may have been a "familiar figure" about town, not much was known about the murdered man. Prowse had bought the Sheep Ranch only the previous spring, but he had lived in Utah thirteen years—most of the time in Park City. It was believed he had been a railroad man in Arizona and New Mexico and a rancher in Colorado and Montana. He left only one survivor, a sickly twelve-year-old son who at the time of the shooting was en route to Florida to spend the winter in the care of a nurse. Friends told reporters his wife and another son had died in California years before.

Prowse's business establishment, the Sheep Ranch, was at 26 Commercial Street, a narrow thoroughfare one block long that ran between 100 and 200 South, parallel with Main and State streets. Although near the heart of the downtown business district and less than three blocks from the Mormon temple, Commercial Street was lined with saloons, gambling dens, and "sporting" houses.[3] Gambling was condemned by the Mormon church (as were other vices) and expressly prohibited by both state law and the state constitution. Nevertheless it created—along with drinking and "sporting"—a booming business day and night on Commercial Street. On even a relatively "slow night," such as Thursday, as many as 400 men and boys crowded the gambling establishments to try their luck.[4]

The police soon concluded the search for Lynch's companions in crime. Two days after the shooting, Detective George Sheets arrested a man he was certain had assisted Lynch with the hold-up. The man identified himself as Robert King.[5] Sheets said he had had his "eye on King" ever since the robbery and had been following him in the hope that he would lead him to the other robber.[6]

King was living at Walker House on West Temple Street, registered under the name of "Robert Martell." He was employed as a dealer at the Lone Star gambling house and said he had worked there from 1:00 to 5:00 p.m. the afternoon prior to the Sheep Ranch hold-up, a fact corroborated by the proprietor. He said he had gone to bed at the Walker House shortly before midnight the night of the shooting. King insisted that he was not involved and would have no trouble proving his innocence.

Before arresting King, Sheets had spoken with a store clerk, William Meyers, who identified the valise found near the Sheep Ranch as the one he had sold, along with three handkerchiefs, to a man the afternoon before the holdup. He had wrapped the merchandise in yellowish brown paper. After locking up King, Sheets searched his room at the Walker House where he found a piece of yellowish brown paper that fit the clerk's description. He also found burglary tools—steel drills, blasting powder, a powder blower, and a skeleton key. Sheets took the wrapping paper to Meyers who readily identified it. Later that evening Sheets escorted Meyers and the other eyewitness, the messenger boy Wittenberg, to the jail. Both identified King.

Despite the eyewitnesses found by Sheets and the incriminating wrapping paper, King continued to proclaim his innocence and sought to dispute the evidence against him: "That man Meyers is off base when he says I am the man who bought a valise from him. He's got me mixed up with someone else," King told newspaper reporters the day after his arrest.

The actual identity of the prisoner was unclear. He was registered at Walker House as Bob Martell, and yet he told police his name was King. To prove it he produced a membership card to the Elks Lodge of Los Angeles made out to Robert L. King. A few days after his arrest, a resident of Los Angeles who claimed to be a friend of

King came to Salt Lake City. King had been missing for some time, he explained, and hearing of the arrest he wanted to find out for himself King's condition. Upon seeing the prisoner, however, he told police this was definitely not the King he knew. Detective Sheets believed the prisoner's true name was the one under which he was registered at the boarding house—Bob Martell.[7] Regardless, the prisoner went to trial under the name of Robert King.[8]

After an inquest and preliminary hearing, King and Lynch were tried on October 30, 1900, in Third District Court, with Judge John Booth presiding. The prosecution was handled by Salt Lake County Attorney Graham F. Putnam assisted by Ray Van Cott; the defendants were represented by attorney Will F. Wanless.[9]

After two days for jury selection, the prosecution opened its case with several eyewitness accounts of the shooting; each identified Lynch as one of the three gunmen. Since Prowse's bullet had dropped Lynch to the floor, mask on face, gun at hand, it was easy for the prosecutor to link him to the robbery and shooting. Connecting King to the crime was more difficult. To establish that, the prosecution relied mainly on the testimony of the two eyewitnesses, Meyers and Wittenberg. The other potential witness, Sheep Ranch employee Frank Lyon, was not called to testify.[10]

When store clerk Meyers took the stand, he testified that on the afternoon prior to the shooting a man had entered Cressman's clothing store and purchased three handkerchiefs and a valise, which Meyers had wrapped for him. The prosecutor displayed the paper found in King's room, and Meyers identified it, pointing to some small tears he said had been made by the string used to secure the package. Meyers identified three handkerchiefs, including the one Lynch was wearing when he was arrested and two that were found in the Headquarters Saloon, as the merchandise he had sold on September 10.[11]

The prosecutor asked the clerk to identify who had bought the valise and handkerchiefs. "That man," said Meyers, pointing in King's direction. Since there were several people seated near King, a juror asked that "the man who was in the store stand up." "King, heard the [juror's] suggestion," wrote a *Herald* reporter, "and immediately started to rise from his chair. When about half straightened up he suddenly realized what his act implied and resumed his seat, looking very uncomfortable, while a hushed titter passed' round the courtroom."

In his cross-examination defense attorney Wanless sought to discredit the store clerk's powers of observation. Meyers had testified that King's hands were not the hardened hands of a laborer. When asked how he remembered such a minute detail, Meyers demonstrated how King "took a handful of change from his pocket with his left hand, holding it up with the thumb toward the clerk, so that he could see the hand quite distinctly." Wanless pressed him further: "Did you notice any other peculiarity about the hand except its smoothness and delicateness?" he asked. "No sir," was the clerk's reply. "Mr. King," Wanless said, "step up here and hold your hands up." King walked to the front of the courtroom and, facing the jury, raised his hands above his head. His left thumb had been cut off, leaving only a long scar.

After this cross-examination ended, the prosecutor called his second key witness, William Wittenberg, who told the court that he was in the nearby Vienna Cafe at the time of the shooting. He testified that he heard the shots, stepped into the alley at the rear of the cafe, and saw two masked men running from the direction of the Sheep Ranch. As they ran, he said, they removed the masks from their faces and disappeared into the back entrance of the Headquarters Saloon. Wittenberg then ran to the saloon's front door, walked in, and approached the two men who were now at the bar. One asked him to join him for a drink, the other left the saloon. Both seemed very nervous, he said. He identified King as one of the men.

During cross-examination Wanless asked Wittenberg how he knew the men were nervous. Wittenberg replied that he had noticed that King's hands were shaking but admitted he too had failed to see that the left thumb was missing.

When it was the defense's turn, Wanless sought to further damage the credibility of Wittenberg and Meyers. He began by challenging the conclusiveness of the paper found in King's room as evidence linking him to the crime. He called three witnesses. First, the owner of a Main Street clothing store testified that he used the same width and type of paper in his store. A clerk testified that he had sold a shirt to King and wrapped it in paper like that found in King's room. The manager of the Utah Paper Company, which sold wrapping paper to Salt Lake merchants, testified that it would be impossible to tell which store the paper came from since many stores used exactly the same kind.

To dispute Wittenberg's identification of King as the man he saw running through the alley and into the Headquarters Saloon, Wanless called on the proprietor and the desk clerk of the boarding house where King lived. Both testified they had never seen King wearing clothes that matched Wittenberg's description and that a search of King's room had revealed no clothes of any kind. The only things they had ever seen King wear, they said, were the clothes he had on right then.

In his closing argument Wanless tried to shift responsibility for the crime to the local police and city government for their tolerance of gambling, noting that it was in direct violation of Utah law. "The police and county attorney are sworn to uphold the laws," he declared; and "if they had done their duty there would have been no Prowse murder and no murder trial." Concluding, he told the jury that at most Lynch was guilty of manslaughter and King merited acquittal.

What is most striking about this defense is that the attorney did not attempt to establish an alibi for King. Newspapers reported at the time of King's arrest that he claimed to have an alibi that would prove his innocence. King said he had been working at the Lone Star gambling house during the time Meyers claimed to have sold him the valise and handkerchiefs. The proprietor of the Lone Star had corroborated this fact for the *Salt Lake Herald,* yet defense attorney Wanless did not seek to establish it in court. According to King, he had entered his room at the boarding house some two hours before the shooting and had passed the boarding house proprietor, Mr. Dudley, on the stairs. Someone would have noticed if he had left that night, King had argued. The defense neither presented this evidence nor put King on the stand to testify at all.[12]

On the eighth day of the trial, Judge Booth gave the jury formal instructions. It took only a few minutes for them to find Lynch guilty. Initially eleven jurors voted to convict King as charged, and one juror opted for a lesser charge. They deliberated for two hours. A second ballot was taken, and this time all twelve agreed to find both men guilty of murder in the first degree.[13]

When the verdict was read, King, according to press accounts, slumped in his chair and looked nervous and pale. Lynch sighed and "settled back into his usual indifferent attitude."

Leaving the courtroom, King and Lynch were asked by reporters for their reaction. Lynch had no comment, but King lashed out in what one account called "a volley of blasphemous abuse" against the jurors: "God-damn them, every one of them," King "hissed" between clenched teeth. "They're trying to job us, but I'll show them. The police, the sons of bitches, jobbed me, that's all."

Within a few days of the verdict, Wanless filed a motion for a new trial with Judge Booth based on a number of supposed procedural errors. On November 13 Booth denied the motion, saying he would make the same decisions again if a new trial were held.

Sentencing was held on November 15, scarcely two months after George Prowse had been killed. Before rendering the sentence Judge Booth asked each man in turn if he had anything to say. Lynch declined, but King responded by professing his innocence, claiming he was "bagged and brought in and placed in this position by Detective Sheets." Booth responded that "if it is a fact, Mr. King, that you are innocent, it is known only to you and to Lynch." Concluding, the judge said King and Lynch had "had a fair trial and were found guilty," and therefore "I have no discretion in the matter." Booth asked Lynch and King if they understood that the death penalty was the punishment affixed to this crime, and then informed them that under Utah law they had "the privilege of choosing whether you care to be hung or shot." Both chose the firing squad over the gallows, and the judge set their execution for January 11, 1901. Wanless told reporters he would appeal to the Utah State Supreme Court and hoped to place the matter before the court as soon as possible. King and Lynch were returned to jail where they were placed under the customary "death watch." While the pair waited for their case to be reviewed by the Utah Supreme Court, their initial execution date came and went uneventfully. A year later they were still waiting, but by then new developments in the case made it appear that at least Robert King might yet live to see many more Januarys.

Sometime during 1901 King secured the help of the government of Italy. He had written to the Italian ambassador in Washington, telling him that his real name was "Pedro Paguini"—a member of a distinguished Italian family—and that he was being held in Utah under sentence of death for a crime he had not committed. As an Italian subject, he solicited the help of his government in correcting this injustice. In September the ambassador instructed the Italian consul in Denver, Joseph Cuneo, to investigate the case. That fall Cuneo traveled to Utah, met with King and attorney Wanless, and provided funds for a private investigator to help uncover evidence that might lead to King's release.[14] This Italian connection solidified as King succeeded in enlisting the support of Charles Bonetti, a prominent Italian-American resident of Salt Lake. Bonetti rallied the support of the city's Italian community, which, according to one account, "became vehement in its protestations of innocence of its countryman ... [and] ready to offer any aid in its power."[15]

King also acquired the help of an unlikely ally—Salt Lake City police chief Thomas Hilton, who had been persuaded of King's innocence by a telegram he received in the summer of 1901 from the deputy warden of the Colorado penitentiary in Canon City. It told of John Mace, an inmate there, who said that King was mistaken for another Colorado inmate, John Strange. He was coming forward to reveal publicly what he knew, Mace said, because he had learned that King was about to be executed for a crime Strange had bragged about.[16]

During the next several months, Chief Hilton, Consul Cuneo, and defense attorney Wanless combined their efforts to verify the Colorado convict's story. On February 13 Mace signed an affidavit attesting to Strange's confession to him. On February 17 the affidavit was made public.

Mace told that he was in Ogden, Utah, the day after the Sheep Ranch hold-up. That evening he took a train east to Rawlins, Wyoming. On board he encountered Ed Davenport, whom he had met a week earlier in Ogden, and his partner John Strange. They told Mace that they were the two who were wanted for the Sheep Ranch hold-up. Strange told him "that he was the man who 'pumped' it into Prowse when he saw one of the 'lads' [Lynch] on the floor ... who was shot." Later, when Mace and Strange were serving time in the Colorado penitentiary, Strange told him that King had been convicted, which was the first Mace had known about it. Strange "laughed about it and said: 'Well King is innocent but they can do nothing with me ... now.'" Strange said, "'I am the man; I bought the valise ... handkerchiefs and so forth.'"[17]

This new evidence made a powerful impact. King took the news of Mace's affidavit as the vindication he had long sought. Interviewed by reporters, he said, "[I]t was the happiest news I ever received in my life. ... Had it come a little later, I would have been dead and in a dishonored grave. ... It is an awful thing to be condemned to die for a crime that you never committed."

Not everyone believed Mace's affidavit, however, or felt it proved King's innocence. District Attorney Dennis Eichnor said the affidavit "reads ... like a dime novel story and a mighty poor one at that." George Sheets, the detective who arrested King, said King was tried with the evidence "placed before as fair a jury as could be gotten anywhere, and they found him guilty." Surely a jury's judgment should mean more than the statement of a convict. Similarly Assistant County Attorney Frederick Loofbourow called the affidavit a convict's "trick," saying crooks "will go to great lengths to help one another out of trouble."[18]

Although these officials scoffed at the Mace affidavit, others, including Utah's governor, Heber M. Wells, took it seriously. Elected as the first chief executive when Utah achieved statehood in 1896, Wells was now in his second term. Called "a staunch friend of law and order" in one contemporary biography,[19] Wells, the son of Utah pioneer leader Daniel H. Wells, was one of the state's most respected citizens.

The morning after the affidavit became public, Governor Wells met with other top government officials to evaluate the case and discuss what should be done. Meeting with the governor were Secretary of State James T. Hammond, Attorney General M. D. Breeden, Salt Lake County Attorney Parley P. Christensen, District Attorney Eichnor, police chief Hilton, the deputy warden of the Colorado prison where Mace was held, and defense attorney Wanless. After deliberating, and hearing a fervent plea on King's behalf by the police chief, they concluded that further investigation was needed.[20]

The next day, February 19, 1902, attorney C. M. Garwood —hired by Consul Cuneo to assist in King's defense—arrived in Salt Lake City from Denver.[21] That afternoon Garwood visited Lynch in prison and Lynch agreed to sign an affidavit attesting to King's innocence. "He [King] is absolutely innocent and had nothing to do with the affair at all," Lynch stated; and "He has suffered for a crime he knew nothing about." Lynch also said that he and King had gone to trial together for financial reasons and that he had "told King that I did not see how he could be convicted and if he was I would some day tell all that happened and that would prove his innocence."[22]

Why Lynch waited eighteen months to tell the world of King's innocence remains an unanswered question. Police chief Hilton had met with Lynch a week earlier and tried unsuccessfully to persuade him to corroborate Mace's story.[23] Although now willing to testify of King's innocence, Lynch continued to be either unwilling or unable to name his accomplices. In speaking of his affidavit, Lynch said he was not "positive of the complicity" of Strange and Davenport, noting that he did not remember his accomplices "as distinctly as I once did." Lynch said his sole purpose in making a statement was to save the life of King, an innocent man. As for himself, Lynch said, "I am condemned to die and wish the thing were over." He realized "only too well that it is a matter of a very short time 'till it is over with me."[24]

The affidavits of Mace and Lynch attesting to King's innocence were published in the Salt Lake newspapers. Though from two convicts, the testimony cast doubt on King's guilt and caused one of the key prosecution witnesses, William Wittenberg, to recant his testimony. After seeing a photograph of John Strange, Wittenberg stated in an affidavit that he was "firmly convinced beyond a doubt in my own mind that the man whose photograph is attached [Strange] ... is the identical person whom I saw enter said ... saloon after shooting Colonel Prowse, and that the defendant Robert L. King is not the man."

Wittenberg explained why he was now positive that the man he had seen eighteen months earlier was Strange, after seeing only a photograph, when at the trial he had seemed equally certain of King's identity: "In my own conscience I then felt an uncertainty as to King being the man, but others said to me, 'We know he is the man and so do you.'" Furthermore, he said, "The influence being brought to bear on me was the principle [sic] reason I identified King."[25] Wittenberg told the *Salt Lake Herald* that "the more he thought of the part he took in the prosecution of King the more it has burned his conscience."[26]

Wittenberg had recently started working for Charles Bonetti—president of Salt Lake's Italian colony and an ardent advocate of King's innocence. It was Bonetti who informed Chief Hilton that Wittenberg wished to sign an affidavit changing his testimony, and it was Bonetti who notarized Wittenberg's affidavit.

With new evidence pointing to King's innocence, some thought a pardon might be appropriate. Attorney Wanless ruled it out. He said King not only would not ask for a pardon but that he would not accept one if offered. "A pardon always carries the impression that a man is guilty but has been punished enough," Wanless stated; "King will not leave the penitentiary until he has been fully exonerated."[27]

To either verify or disprove the charges made in Mace's affidavit, County Attorney Christensen and Sheriff Naylor traveled to Colorado on February 19. The pair hoped that questioning Mace, Strange, and others might provide the evidence necessary to extradite Strange to stand trial. Wanless was disappointed that Chief Hilton—the only law enforcement official who had sided with King—did not accompany them.

The county officials returned to Salt Lake a week later and reported that they had been unable to locate the two men who were in a position to corroborate Mace's statement—Ed Davenport and Mace's partner, Matthews, who had heard or participated in most of the pertinent conversations Mace said he had had with Strange. Both Davenport and Matthews had recently been paroled and could not be found.[28]

Naylor and Christensen did interview Mace and Strange. Strange denied involvement in the hold-up; at first he also denied knowing

Lynch until confronted with the fact that they had spent time together in Idaho's prison. The officials concluded, as Christensen told a reporter, that Strange "had something to do with the holdup" and that "Mace's affidavit was true in the main." Christensen believed that even if Strange had participated in the Sheep Ranch crime, that did not necessarily clear King. After all, there were three gunmen. "King is probably one of them," he said. Bolstering Wittenberg's claim that King and Strange shared a physical resemblance—contributing to confusion in identification—Sheriff Naylor said, "[T]hey look enough alike to be twin brothers." Three days after his return to Salt Lake, Naylor signed a complaint charging Strange with the murder of George Prowse.[29] Though willing to file charges, the sheriff believed "it would be a hard matter to convict him."[30]

While Chief Hilton, representatives of the government of Italy, and others sought to prove King's innocence, the courtroom battle continued. On March 17, 1902, the Utah Supreme Court considered the defense motion for a new trial, made two years earlier and based on alleged technical errors.[31] After arguments before the court, King fired attorney Will Wanless, saying he would now be represented solely by C. M. Garwood, the Denver attorney hired by the Italian government. Garwood had shown King a letter from Consul Cuneo telling him that as an Italian subject he "must do the bidding of Garwood."[32]

Wanless, who had defended King along with Lynch for nearly two years pro-bono, was bitter about losing him as a client just as money had become available to assist with the defense.[33] He vowed to continue to fight for Lynch's life. Making a veiled threat, he said he would now feel free to act in Lynch's behalf regardless of the effect his actions might have on King.[34]

On March 28, 1902, the Utah Supreme Court rejected the motion for a new trial and unanimously upheld the convictions of both King and Lynch, stating that "upon the whole record, no reversible error was found." In turning down the appeal, the justices ordered the district court to "execute the sentence in accordance with law."[35]

Although the court's decision was unfavorable, Will Wanless was not disheartened. He believed that the new evidence in support of King could also be used to benefit Lynch. Confident that a new trial would be ordered, the attorney insisted, "You may rest assured, Lynch will not be shot." The next day he, District Attorney Eichnor, and County Attorney Christensen met with Lynch at the state prison.[36] No one knows exactly what Lynch told these men, but the press reported that he "punctured the affidavit of John Mace" and convinced authorities that Strange had nothing to do with the Sheep Ranch hold-up.

His statements were made without any offer of immunity and in line with Wanless's new policy of "doing everything for his client regardless of the effect it may have on others," namely King.[37] Lynch did not recant his previous affidavit swearing to King's innocence; however, neither did he reveal the actual identity of his accomplices.

After consideration of Lynch's statements during a March 29 meeting, Salt Lake County dropped its charges against John Strange, "completely exonerating [him] from any part in the affair." The county authorities believed, lacking solid corroboration[38] of Mace's accusations from Lynch or anyone else, they simply did not have sufficient evidence to convict Strange.[39]

Although they agreed that the evidence was insufficient to implicate Strange, the defense argued that the same evidence was sufficient justification for a new trial for King and Lynch. On October 10 a hearing was held in Third District Court on the defense's second motion for a new trial. The motion was based on the Mace affidavit claiming Strange was guilty and King innocent, the Lynch affidavit stating King was innocent, and the Wittenberg affidavit in which the key eyewitness changed his account to say that it was Strange and not King he had seen fleeing from the Sheep Ranch.

Then the second eyewitness changed his story. Another piece of new evidence offered at the hearing was an affidavit signed by store clerk William Meyers. During the trial he had identified King as the man to whom he had sold the valise and handkerchiefs found at the crime scene. In his affidavit, signed June 30, Meyers said that after examining photographs of John Strange he was now "convinced in his own mind that it is probable that the person who really bought the goods from him" was Strange.[40]

The unexpected outcome of these developments occurred almost two months after the hearing, on December 23, 1902. That was when Judge Booth announced his decision to deny the motion for a new trial. Ironically he agreed with the defense that the new evidence would damage the state's case against the pair and, if presented at a new trial, might result in Lynch and King being acquitted. But Judge Booth had presided at their trial and remained personally convinced of their guilt. Acquittal, he said, "would be a miscarriage of justice."[41] He resentenced the men to be executed on February 20, 1903.

This second execution date passed with King and Lynch locked in their cells at the Utah State Prison. Their date with the firing squad was postponed pending the outcome of another appeal to the Utah Supreme Court. But before that appeal could be heard, the fate of both men would be profoundly affected by an incredible drama of daring and violence within the walls of the Utah State Prison in Sugar House.

Convicts at the prison[42] had just finished dinner around 6:00 p.m. on Friday, October 9, when three prisoners, Harry Waddell, Abe Majors, and Frank Conners, launched a plan to escape.[43] Armed with two revolvers and three "slung shots," the three men hid in the prison library adjacent to the dining room until guard Zebulon Jacobs came by. After beating him into semi-consciousness, the convicts overpowered another guard, David Wilckin, and took the keys to the cells along "murderer's row." Waddell walked past the cell of "Dutch Charlie" Botha, facing a death sentence[44] for killing his wife and her "paramour," and approached the cell occupied by James Lynch. "What the hell's up?" asked Lynch. "Get your clothes on," Waddell yelled. "There's a break, come along."

As Lynch walked out of his cell, Waddell handed him the keys and told him to let out another convicted murderer, Nick Haworth. Lynch opened Haworth's cell and then approached the cell of Robert King. Lynch told him "there was a break and he stood a good chance to escape." Remarkably, King refused, saying, "I do not care to go. ... I am innocent and will lose nothing by staying where I am." Another convicted murderer, Peter Mortensen, who was facing execution in less than six weeks for killing his wife, begged to be released but was refused.[45]

Lynch then joined Waddell, Majors, and Conners who had just finished dragging the guard Jacobs to the south cell house. "Well, what shall we do with him?" one of the prisoners asked. "Guess we had better finish him right here," the other replied. Seeing the badly bleeding guard, Lynch intervened. "Here boys, this won't do; there is no need. ... it will only aggravate this business." Waddell and Majors agreed to spare the old guard's life.

Seven prisoners ran for the outer wall of the prison grounds. One of them had secured a ladder. Lynch, first on the ladder, was shot in the arm by one of the guards as he reached the top of the wall. Though the impact almost knocked him over, he managed to slide down the outside of the wall and run to freedom. Haworth was right behind him. In a hail of gunfire, the remaining five convicts took turns climbing the nineteen-foot wall. Most made it but were unable to get past two guards who scurried to the outside and positioned themselves at the wall.

Only an hour after the prison break began, the siege was over. Three guards and five prisoners were injured. One prisoner was dead. Only two had succeeded in escaping the immediate area of the prison—James Lynch and Nick Haworth.

Guard Zebulon Jacobs's wounds were serious though not life threatening. He had two scalp wounds—so deep that his skull was exposed—each several inches long. Above one eye another cut had bled profusely, and on his right cheek was a gash. He told reporters that Lynch had saved his life.

Almost immediately after Lynch and Haworth dashed to freedom that Friday evening, a posse of twenty men started hunting for them. The next morning a fresh posse embarked, supplemented by bloodhounds. Many others volunteered to assist the manhunt. It did not take long to find the two. On Sunday, October 11, Haworth was captured in Holladay a few miles south of the prison. On Wednesday Lynch, haggard, weak, and going door to door begging for food, was identified and taken into custody in Woods Cross,[46] a small community a few miles north of Salt Lake City.

While Lynch was on the loose, his attorney, Will Wanless, went before the Utah Supreme Court as scheduled on Monday to argue for a new trial.[47] Prior to the hearing, Wanless joked with King's attorneys about the prison break. "Lynch is out hunting new evidence to be used in his new trial which the supreme court is going to grant him," Wanless quipped, which was met by "a hearty laugh from all who were near enough to hear."

While conceding that the new evidence presented to the Supreme Court dealt only with King's guilt and not Lynch's, Wanless argued that since both were originally tried together, if King were granted a new trial, so must Lynch.[48] This logic failed to persuade the court. On October 23 it granted King a new trial but upheld Lynch's conviction. The court expressed "doubt as to whether ... King would ever have been convicted without the testimony of Meyers and Wittenberg."[49] But no evidence had been presented that disputed or questioned Lynch's involvement in the shooting.

King and Lynch were brought before Judge Booth in Third District Court once again on November 18. District Attorney Eichnor moved to dismiss the charges against King due to insufficient evidence. Judge Booth granted the motion and all charges were dropped. Booth then sentenced Lynch to be executed on Friday, January 8, 1904.[50]

Robert King was jubilant. Imprisoned for over three years, he repeated his claim of innocence and said that he "knew it was only a question of time" before he would be released. He said he was going back to Italy for a few months to see his friends and family and to "tell them of my life here, and how I was in prison and was to die for a crime that I did not do." And then what? "I will ... come back to America. It is a good place and I want to live here."

Lynch, back in prison and facing execution for the third time, told reporters his attorney would ask the Board of Pardons to change his sentence to life imprisonment. If the board denied his request, Lynch said, "I suppose I will have to take my medicine like a man."

True to that pledge, his application for commutation came before the State Board of Pardons[51] on Saturday, December 19, 1903. Even though no new evidence had emerged bearing on Lynch's involvement, his attorney was able to show that nearly every member of the jury that had convicted him now wanted him spared the sentence they had imposed. Wanless presented the board with letters supporting commutation signed by ten of the twelve jurors. He also presented a petition signed by a number of the state's most prominent citizens, including the mayor of Salt Lake and other city and county officials.

It is both unusual and remarkable that prominent citizens would come to the defense of a drifter who was obviously guilty of participating in a hold-up and shooting that resulted in a man's death. Ironically support for Lynch can be traced to events surrounding his escape from prison when he intervened to save the life of prison guard Zebulon Jacobs. At age sixty-one Jacobs was one of the last surviving of Utah's early pioneers. Born in Nauvoo, Illinois, in 1842, Jacobs came to Utah in 1848 with his mother, Zina Diantha Huntington Young, a plural wife of Brigham Young.[52] Zina was, in her own right, one of Utah's most respected women. Well known throughout the territory, having been "set apart" by church leaders as a midwife, she personally helped bring hundreds of babies into the world. In 1880 she became president of the Deseret Hospital. In 1892 she became the third woman to head the Relief Society—the women's auxiliary of the Mormon church—a position she held until her death in 1901.[53] As a youth Zebulon had lived in the Lion House, built by his stepfather, Brigham Young.[54] And he was a veteran of the Black Hawk Indian War, a Mormon missionary to England, and had worked on the railroad.[55]

Jacobs himself now actively petitioned the Board of Pardons to prevent Lynch's execution.[56] In addition, the acting warden told the board that both before and after the prison break, Lynch had been a "model prisoner."[57] Despite this and pleas from Salt Lake City mayor Ezra Thompson and others, the board refused to commute Lynch's sentence. It now seemed certain that he would face a firing squad since the board was not scheduled to meet again until after his January 8 execution date.

Undaunted by the board's decision, Wanless continued to press for a life sentence. On December 30[58] he presented Governor Wells with another petition, signed by fourteen distinguished citizens and prominent attorneys, including future United States senator W. H. King and former U.S. senator Arthur Brown.[59] The petition focused on Lynch's role in preventing other prisoners from killing Jacobs during the prison break: "When offered an opportunity to escape,

Lynch paused long enough in the flight to render material assistance in saving the life of one of the officers at the prison." Continuing the petitioners reasoned: "Lynch must have known that delay endangered his chance of escape. We must regard this act, therefore, as both courageous and humane. If the principle of 'a life for a life' be urged, we answer that justice may well be satisfied with a life spared for a life saved. As Lynch saved innocent life, we urge that his own life be spared."

The petition worked. Soon after receiving it Governor Wells called a special meeting of the Board of Pardons for Saturday, January 2, 1904, to reconsider Lynch's application. Wells also instructed Lynch himself to appear before the board—the first time in state history that a condemned man was given the opportunity of appearing personally before the board to plead for mercy. This unusual circumstance, requiring the board members to actually face the person who would live or die by their decision, could only have placed added pressure on them to grant his plea for mercy.

Meeting in the chapel of the state prison,[60] the board listened to prisoners who told how Lynch convinced them to spare Jacobs. One of the prisoners quoted Lynch as insisting that no blood be shed or "you boys can count me out."

Questioned about the escape, Lynch said he didn't know anything about it until his cell door opened. He took full advantage of it, however, because "he saw nothing but death staring him in the face" if he remained. Lynch went on to point out that during his week of freedom he had not attacked or injured anyone.

At 1:15 p.m. the board unanimously voted to commute Lynch's sentence to life imprisonment. In their written decision, signed by Governor Wells and Secretary of State M. A. Breeden, they noted both the fact "that he saved the life of Guard Jacobs in the recent attempted jail delivery at the state Penitentiary, and the petitions numerously signed by citizens of Salt Lake City."[61] When told of the board's decision, Lynch was "so overcome by his feelings that he could make no reply. ... Then he sat down on his cot in the death cell and wept."[62]

In deciding to commute the sentence, the Board of Pardons may also have weighed the life spared by Lynch—Zebulon Jacobs—

against the life he had taken—George Prowse. Prowse was the owner of a gambling house who left no survivors or relatives in Utah. While a number of prominent men petitioned the board to spare Lynch's life, not one friend, relative, or acquaintance of Prowse had stepped forward to demand retribution. Weighing mercy with justice, they concluded that mercy was the right thing for Lynch.

For the next twelve years, Lynch remained incarcerated in the Utah State Prison. His reputation as a "model prisoner"[63] was enhanced. He won the confidence of prison officers and served for a number of years as a "trusty" in the prison office.[64] On December 18, 1915, he applied to the Board of Pardons for parole.[65] A month later, on January 22, 1916, the board considered his application along with six others. His was the only one granted.[66]

On the afternoon of Monday, January 24, 1916, less than sixteen years after the hold-up at the Sheep Ranch gambling house, Warden Arthur Pratt approached Lynch who was standing in the prison yard and told him he was free to leave the prison. Lynch stood as if frozen for a moment, and "then emotion took hold and he rejoiced like a child." After saying goodbye to former cell mates and guards, Lynch left prison and accepted a job in the copper mill at Garfield, west of Salt Lake City. Thus ended one of the most complicated and peculiar murder cases in Utah's history.

Notes

1. Accounts of the robbery were taken from the *Deseret News,* September 11 and 14, 1900; *Salt Lake Herald,* September 12 and 13, 1900; and *Salt Lake Tribune,* September 12 and 26, 1900.

2. Also known as Godfrey Prousse.

3. Later renamed Regent Street. Descriptions of Commercial Street are from the *Deseret News*, September 20, 1902, and *Salt Lake Tribune,* May 3, 1903.

4. *Deseret News,* September 20, 1902.

5. King was also known as Robert Martell, E. T. King, E. L. King, L. E. King, and Pedro Paguini.

6. Accounts of King's arrest are from the *Deseret News,* September 13, 1900; *Salt Lake Herald,* September 13, 1900; and *Salt Lake Tribune,* September 13 and 15, 1900.

7. *Salt Lake Tribune,* September 14, 1900; *Deseret News,* September 13, 1900.

8. Police chief Thomas Hilton disputed the prisoner's claim that he was Robert King of Los Angeles. The police had arranged for local members of the Elks Lodge to quiz the prisoner for "information every Elk should have known," which he was unable to provide. By November Chief Hilton thought the prisoner might be from Seattle and wanted for the murder of Robert L. King, and known variously as Robert LaDue, Robert Duvalle, William Loto, R. W. LeBlanche, and R. W. Martello, as a "forger, a burglar, and all around crook." *Deseret News,* November 26, 1900.

9. *Deseret News,* October 30, 1900.

10. It can be assumed that if Lyon had been able to positively identify King, he would have been called as another witness.

11. Accounts of the trial are primarily from the Trial Abstract, pages 8-49, Third District Court, Criminal Case 620, Utah State Archives, Salt Lake City, supplemented with newspaper reports from the *Deseret News,* November 7 and 8, 1900, and *Salt Lake Herald,* November 2 and 9, 1900.

12. Three years later in a newspaper interview, King was critical of the defense: "I was railroaded. ... I do not blame the court or the jury. ... [I]f I had witnesses to prove my innocence, why did I not put them on the stand? I wanted to have a separate trial; I wanted to put witnesses on the stand; witnesses who were well known and highly respected, who would have testified that I was with them on the night of the crime. But my attorney said no. 'We won't need them, you cannot be convicted,' he said. The first thing I knew it[,] I was 'guilty.'" *Deseret News*, October 23, 1903.

13. Accounts of the verdict and sentencing are from the *Deseret News,* November 9, 13, and 15, 1900; *Salt Lake Herald,* November 9 and 16, 1900; and *Salt Lake Tribune,* November 9 and 16, 1900.

14. *Deseret News,* February 17, 1902.

15. *Salt Lake Herald,* February 18, 1902.

16. *Deseret News,* February 17, 1902.

17. John Mace Affidavit, February 13, 1902, Third District Court, Criminal Case 620.

18. Accounts of the reactions to the Mace Affidavit are from the *Salt Lake Herald,* February 18, 1902, *Salt Lake Tribune,* February 18, 1902, and *Deseret News,* February 21, 1902.

19. *Drumm's Manual of Utah and Souvenir of the First State Legislature, 1896*, Special Collections, Marriott Library, University of Utah, Salt Lake City.

20. *Salt Lake Tribune,* February 19, 1902.

21. *Deseret News,* February 19, 1902.

22. James Lynch Affidavit, February 19, 1902, Third District Court, Criminal Case 620.

23. *Deseret News,* February 17, 1902.

24. *Salt Lake Herald,* February 20, 1902.

25. William Wittenberg Affidavit, February 20, 1902, Third District Court, Criminal Case 620.

26. *Salt Lake Herald,* February 21, 1902.

27. *Salt Lake Tribune,* February 21, 1902.

28. Reports of the county officials' visit to Colorado are from the *Deseret News,* February 27, 1902; *Salt Lake Herald,* February 28, 1902; and *Salt Lake Tribune,* February 28, 1902.

29. *Deseret News,* March 1, 1902.

30. Ibid., February 27, 1902.

31. Ibid., March 18, 1902.

32. *Salt Lake Herald,* March 18, 1902.

33. In an attempt to receive some payment for his work, Wanless wrote to Colorado's two U.S. senators and Italy's ambassador in Washington asking whether Cuneo and Garwood were acting on the ambassador's instructions in firing him. It is not known whether they responded or whether Wanless ever received any payment from the Italian government. *Deseret News,* March 19, 1902.

34. Wanless reacted sharply to his dismissal: "For a year and a half I have fought for King without any pay whatever. Now that the case is practically won and there is a little money in sight, Garwood and Cuneo step in." He said that Lynch was also "indignant," and added that it was now "exceedingly doubtful" that Lynch would say anything more that might benefit King (*Salt Lake Tribune,* March 18, 1902). In a parting shot Wanless remarked that he wondered what the Italian government would do "should they discover that he [King] is not an Italian, but an American-born Louisiana creole" (*Salt Lake Herald,* March 18, 1902).

35. Reports of the Supreme Court decision are from the *Deseret News,* March 28, 1902, and *Salt Lake Herald,* March 29, 1902.

36. Lynch and King were admitted to the state prison on May 1, 1901. Prior to that, they were incarcerated in the Salt Lake City jail.

37. *Salt Lake Tribune,* March 30, 1902.

38. They had limited corroboration of Mace's affidavit in that Wittenberg identified Strange from a picture. That Wittenberg said the same thing about King likely undermined his credibility.

39. *Salt Lake Tribune,* April 13, 1902, and *Deseret News,* April 12, 1902.

40. William Meyers Affidavit, June 30, 1902, Third District Court, Criminal Case 620.

41. *Deseret News,* December 23, 1902.

42. Originally constructed by the federal government in 1854, the territorial prison was expanded in 1888 and 1891 to house Mormon polygamists. The facility served as the Utah State Prison from statehood (1896) until 1948. See Richard D. Poll, ed., *Utah's History* (Logan: Utah State University Press, 1989), 286-87. The site is now occupied by Highland High School and Sugar House Park.

43. Accounts of the prison escape are from the *Salt Lake Tribune,* October 10, 1903; *Salt Lake Herald,* October 10 and 11, 1903; and *Deseret News,* October 15, 1903.

44. Botha's sentence was commuted to life imprisonment by the Board of Pardons on June 8, 1904.

45. Mortensen was executed, as scheduled, on November 20, 1903, a mere fourteen months after the murder.

46. *Deseret News,* October 15, 1903.

47. Ibid., October 12, 1903.

48. Ibid.

49. Ibid., October 23, 1903.

50. Accounts of the court's ruling and reaction to it are from the *Salt Lake Telegram,* November 18, 1903; *Salt Lake Herald,* November 19, 1903; and *Salt Lake Tribune,* November 19, 1903.

51. Under Utah's constitution, Governor Wells did not have the sole power to grant pardons or to commute sentences. This power was shared with the justices of the Supreme Court and the attorney general who, along with the governor, constituted the Board of Pardons.

52. *Salt Lake Herald,* September 23, 1914.

53. *Deseret News,* August 28, 1901. It is worth noting that among the speakers at Zina D. H. Young's funeral in 1901 was Emmeline B. Wells, a plural wife of Daniel Wells, the father of Governor Heber M. Wells. Mrs. Wells is quoted as saying, "I mourn for Sister Zina and I cannot help it. No woman was ever greater loved than Sister Zina." *Deseret News,* September 2, 1901.

54. Janet Peterson and LaRene Gaunt, *Elect Ladies* (Salt Lake City: Deseret Book, 1990), 52.

55. *Salt Lake Herald,* September 23, 1914.

56. *Deseret News,* December 21, 1903.

57. *Salt Lake Tribune,* December 20, 1903.

58. *Salt Lake Herald,* December 31, 1903, and *Deseret News,* December 31, 1903.

59. The petition was signed by M. P. Henderson, A. B. Irvine, Ashby Snow, M. M. Kaighn, William A. Lee, P. C. Evans, Fred T. McGurrin, Arthur Brown, W. H. King, A. R. Barnes, L. R. Rogers, H. J. Dinainy, M. P. Braffet, and A. A. Duncan.

60. *Salt Lake Herald*, January 3, 1904, and *Salt Lake Tribune*, January 3, 1904.

61. Board of Pardons Minutes, Series 332, Box 1, January 2, 1904, Utah State Archives.

62. *Salt Lake Herald*, January 3, 1904.

63. Ibid., March 19, 1911.

64. *Salt Lake Telegram,* January 23, 1916, and *Salt Lake Tribune,* January 23, 1916.

65. Lynch initially applied for commutation of his sentence on February 18, 1911. For some unknown reason, after it was considered by the board in executive session on March 18, Lynch withdrew the application "without prejudice." (See Board of Pardons Minutes, Utah State Archives Series 332, Box 2, pp. 143, 146.) Newspaper reports indicated that Lynch intended to ask for parole at a later time (*Deseret News,* March 20, 1911).

66. Board of Pardons Minutes, Series 332, Box 3, December 18, 1915, and January 22, 1916, pp. 134, 143.

6.

The Sensational Murder of James R. Hay and Trial of Peter Mortensen

Craig L. Foster

On the evening of Monday, December 16, 1901, in the quiet Salt Lake City suburb of Forest Dale, James R. Hay slipped out of his house and crossed the street to collect money from a friend and neighbor, Peter Mortensen, and then disappeared. By afternoon the next day, word was quickly spreading throughout the city that Hay had absconded with company money. By mid-morning Wednesday, however, Hay's murdered body was found in a shallow grave less than a mile from his home. Circumstantial evidence and Mortensen's strange behavior at the scene of exhumation led police to arrest him on the spot.

Thus began one of the most sensational trials in Utah history. Questions concerning the propriety of circumstantial evidence and of personal religious revelation loomed large during Mortensen's trial and attracted the attention of such noted writers as Sir Arthur Conan Doyle. In *The Edge of the Unknown* (1930), a work discussing the prevalence of spiritualism, Doyle described the Mortensen case as an example of psychic or spiritual phenomena. Thomas S. Duke in *Celebrated Criminal Cases of America* (1910) included it as one of the most talked about trials in the Rocky Mountain West.[1] On a local level the murder of a young, respected man by a friend and neighbor shocked the city. More tragically, it shattered the lives of those intimately associated with Hay and Mortensen.

James Robert Hay was born in 1869 in Maryborough, Victoria, Australia. Jimmy, as he was commonly known, was of Scottish stock, his parents having immigrated to Australia from their native home.[2] By the mid-1880s members of the Hay family had settled in Timaru, New Zealand, where they were baptized into the Latter-day Saint church. Following the death of Hay's father, the remaining family immigrated to Salt Lake City and resided in the Twentieth Ward. Jimmy obtained work as a clerk in ZCMI and through his ward activities met Aggie Sharp. In 1896 they were married in the Salt Lake temple.[3]

He clearly married above his social class. Aggie Sharp, born in 1876 to James Sharp and Lizzie Rogers, came from an extremely prominent family both in wealth and social status. She was a granddaughter of Bishop John Sharp of the Twentieth Ward who had been a personal friend and confidant of Brigham Young and a canny businessman himself who helped found ZCMI, Deseret National Bank, and several railroads. Aggie's father, James Sharp, was equally impressive. He had been closely associated with his father in railroading and banking and was, in 1901, president of Deseret National Bank and had an interest in several Utah railroads, including the Oregon Short Line. He was a former Speaker of the House in Utah's territorial legislature and a former mayor of Salt Lake City. In addition, he was a member of the LDS Board of Education and the University of Utah's Board of Regents.

Like his father-in-law, Hay was an enterprising, hardworking man seeking financial independence. In 1891 he left ZCMI and entered into a limited partnership with brothers George Ernest and William S. Romney to form the Pacific Lumber Company. By 1900 well-known financier David Eccles had joined the firm as a director and president. Hay was a director and secretary of the company.[4] At about that time, Hay, his wife Aggie, and their two young children moved into a home in Forest Dale in what was obviously a significant step in the young couple's upward climb toward social and financial comfort and respectability.[5] There Hay met Peter Mortensen.

Detective George A. Sheets worked on the case of James R. Hay's murder and that of George Prowse, detailed in the previous chapter in this anthology. Sheets became a patrolman in 1890 and a detective in 1893. *Utah State Historical Society, all rights reserved*

Some three years older than Hay, Mortensen was born in 1865 in Richfield, Sevier County, Utah, to hardscrabble Danish settlers. Their financial struggle continued into Peter's childhood as his father moved the family to several towns in search of carpentry work. Eventually the Mortensens settled in Ogden near a large English family by the name of Watkins.[6]

In 1891 Peter married his twenty-five-year-old neighbor, Ruth Elizabeth Watkins, in the Logan LDS temple. He followed his father into the carpentry business in Ogden. In 1897 he moved his young family to Forest Dale and took a job at the Pacific Lumber Company. By 1898 or 1899 he had decided to strike out on his own as an architect and contractor.[7] By 1901 he was a recognized builder in the greater Salt Lake City area. He was the father of five children and a teacher in the Forest Dale Ward's Sunday school. In that position he came into frequent and friendly contact with his neighbor, Jimmy, who was also actively involved in Sunday school.[8]

Although Mortensen was enjoying social stability, he was not having much success financially. Poor business practices had led him to overextend his credit. He continued to get building contracts, but when clients were slow to pay he, in turn, kept his former employer and supplier, Pacific Lumber Company, waiting for payments. In 1900 he was forced to take out a second mortgage on his home and to turn over the note to Ernest and Romney of Pacific Lumber. By December 1901 he owed the lumber company over $3,900. Both Hay and Romney pressured him to pay off his debt. Finally, on December 16, he arrived at the company office and informed both Hay and Romney that he could pay $3,800 of what he owed. Although he did not have the money with him—it was at his house—he nevertheless asked Hay to fill out a receipt and attach the mortgage note, which Hay did. As the men were preparing to leave the office, Romney specifically told Hay not to collect the money that evening as it would be risky to carry so much gold at night. He told him to get it from Mortensen in the morning. Hay and Mortensen rode home together on the Calder's Park tram, arriving a little after 8:00 p.m.

After a light supper Hay told his wife that he had to go over to "Brother Mortensen's for a few minutes to collect a large sum of money" because "Brother Mortensen tells me he must leave town early in the morning, to be gone for a couple of days ... and insists on paying it tonight."[9] Aggie proceeded to put their three children to bed and then went to bed herself at 10:20. At midnight she awoke to find that her husband had not returned. Worried, she sat up until 3:00 a.m. and then went across the street to ask the Mortensens if they had seen her husband. Peter said that her husband had left earlier with the money and appeared to be going into town to give it to Romney. He suggested that Hay might have missed the last tram back to Forest Dale and decided to stay downtown.[10]

By morning Aggie was frantic. Mortensen called on her to see if Hay had returned. When told that he had not, he took the tram into town and met with Romney. Mid-morning they contacted Jimmy's father-in-law, James Sharp, at his office in the Deseret National Bank to inform him that Hay had disappeared with $3,800. Sharp told the men to contact the police, and went to his daughter's house. Although he found Aggie in a state of panic, he took time to call on Ruth Mortensen across the street and was shown the mortgage note as evidence that Hay had received money from her husband. Sharp took the note and then escorted his daughter and her children to his own home in the city center.[11]

Later that afternoon Sharp, accompanied by several others, including Mortensen, Romney, and Detective George A. Sheets of the Salt Lake City Police Department, went to Forest Dale looking for evidence of Hay's disappearance. Several times during the day Mortensen mentioned that Hay had told him that it would be the perfect time to leave Salt Lake City and travel to New York. Mortensen and Romney checked the train depots to ascertain whether anyone had seen Hay the previous night.[12]

Mortensen described in detail how Hay had visited him at about 9:00 p.m. The two men had gone into Mortensen's sitting room where they sat on the settee and counted out the $3,800 in $20 gold pieces. Hay had then given Mortensen the receipt and took the money, after which Mortensen saw Hay out the door.

At the Mortensen house Sharp, who by then was very distraught, demanded to be shown exactly where Jimmy had last been seen. Mortensen pointed down the walk and said that it was about where Sharp was standing. Unsatisfied, Sharp insisted that he be shown the exact spot. Hesitantly Mortensen left the porch and walked to a spot about ten feet from the porch and twenty feet from the gate. Sharp exclaimed that the spot on which they were standing was where his son-in-law had been killed and that Mortensen was responsible. "How do you know he is dead?" Mortensen asked. Sharp responded, "The proof is that within twenty-four hours his body will be dug up in a field within a mile of this spot."[13]

By Wednesday morning there was still no trace of Jimmy Hay. Mortensen was about to catch a tram into town when he and Royal B. Young[14] were told by a young woman that "a body" (actually, what appeared to be a hastily dug grave) had been found. The two men rushed to the place where Frank Torgersen had been looking for a loose horse and stumbled upon a trail of blood and a mound of freshly turned earth. The shallow grave was close to the tracks of the Park City Branch of the Denver & Rio Grande Railway, between 500 and 700 East streets, about a half-mile from Peter Mortensen's home. There was a large quantity of blood on the tracks.

Torgersen asked Mortensen if he had a shovel, since his house was nearby. Mortensen replied that he did, specifically stating that the only shovel he had was a round nosed one. After retrieving the shovel, Mortensen and others watched while Torgersen began removing dirt, revealing marks that clearly showed that a square shovel had been used to dig the grave. Several of the small crowd also noted the footprints leading to and away from the grave. When they realized that the body was indeed Hay's, they contacted the police.[15] When the police arrived and exhumed the body, Mortensen paced back and forth nervously and acted as if he wanted to leave the gruesome scene. But when he headed toward home, a policeman stopped him about halfway there and placed him under arrest.

Family, friends, and neighbors initially reacted to the arrest with disbelief. Theodore Watkins, Peter's brother-in-law, stated, "If I believed Peter were guilty of this horrible crime I would not lift a finger to save him from the penalty, but I know he never did it, and I will spend every cent I possess, if necessary to prove his innocence."[16] Another brother-in-law, Richard C. Watkins, stated that he believed Peter was innocent and that he would investigate on his own. He added that had he believed Mortensen to be guilty, he would have taken his sister, Ruth Mortensen, to his home in Provo. Ruth, for her part, was on the verge of a nervous breakdown and had secluded herself from the public.

In the days following Mortensen's arrest, the police, aided by members of the Sharp family and neighbors like Royal Young, searched and re-searched the Mortensen property for evidence. Despite great activity, they found little. One significant discovery, though, was a recently washed square-nosed shovel hidden in the back of the Mortensen stable.

Hay had been killed by a shot to the back of the head from a .38-caliber pistol. The lengthy search of the Mortensen property and surrounding streets and fields conducted by the police failed to turn up the gun or Hay's missing hat.[17]

There was a flurry of activity on the part of Mortensen's lawyers. Barnard J. Stewart, a friend and neighbor, was retained to defend Mortensen. Bernard and his brother, Charles B. Stewart, acted to keep reporters away from Mortensen and tried to have him released from jail.[18] Despite their efforts to lessen publicity about the crime, the event and the circumstances surrounding it seemed to take on a life of their own. Every day, including Christmas, stories about the case and how Mortensen was reacting to the pressure appeared in the newspapers. One day the headlines read: "Mortensen is Breaking Down," while the next day's paper would carry the news that he was "feeling better." That, added to announcements of new witnesses and new doubts, created a circus-like atmosphere.[19]

About the time that James Hay was being laid to rest, Ruth Mortensen left with her children and brother Richard for Provo. She did not visit her husband in jail before she left. In fact, after his arrest she never again saw him. The newspapers reported that she was on the verge of hysteria. Although she had originally defended her husband and offered him a reasonable alibi, by December 23 she had changed her story and, at the insistence of her brother, told the police what she knew.

According to her, Hay had visited her husband on that fateful Monday night a little after 9:00 p.m. and, after about a half-hour, they had left the house together. In about twenty minutes her husband returned, breathless and red in the face. He told his sister-in-law, Henry's wife, who happened to be visiting, that if she wanted an escort back to her house, she had better hurry for he had "some work to do." He again left the house and was gone for about an hour.[20] When he returned, his wife realized something was wrong for he looked "simply ghastly" and appeared "so pale and ... had a wild look in his eyes." She asked him what was wrong, but he refused to answer and went to bed where he pretended to sleep. After a while Ruth again asked what had happened and he again refused to answer. Later, when Aggie Hay came to the house and called out for Peter, he did not respond until Ruth insisted. After he returned to bed, Ruth asked what he had done with Jimmy Hay. Peter became angry and said, "Don't you ever mention Hay's name to me again." When Ruth threatened to tell Aggie everything she knew, Peter said, "No you won't, even if you hear Hay is dead you must not say how long I was out last night."[21] Although Ruth's testimony to the police was damaging, it was never used in court because, as a matter of law, a spouse could not testify without a mate's prior consent.

While the evidence continued to mount against him, Peter strongly maintained his innocence. At one point he stated to the press, "There is no punishment too severe for the murderer of Hay."

The preliminary hearing began on January 21, 1902, in the Salt Lake City and County Building. Over an hour before the hearing commenced, the corridors were blocked with people waiting to enter the courtroom. During the next few days, the prosecution presented a number of witnesses, the defense none. By far the most intriguing and controversial event at the hearing was the testimony of James Sharp. After describing his confrontation with Mortensen and the subsequent discovery of the body, Sharp was asked by the defense how he had known that Hay was dead the afternoon before his body was discovered. Sharp replied, "God revealed it to me."[22] According to one reporter, the effect on Mortensen was devastating: "His head drooped, his eyes were half closed, and looked unseeingly into his lap; his chin quivered, the blood mounted to his neck, cheeks and forehead, coloring them a dull red. ... He glanced up appealingly as a stricken animal looks at the hunter about to take its life. Then his eyes fell again, but the look of helpless anguish lingered on his face."[23] Public reaction to Sharp's declaration was varied. The prosecuting attorney viewed it as "positive and splendid," while the defense emphasized that such testimony could "never be admitted in a court of law."[24]

The local clergy reacted to Sharp's declaration. The Reverend J. L. Albitron of the First Methodist Church, in a sermon following the testimony, accused Sharp of fanaticism and "declared that such a statement could not stand either before the law nor as the gospel."[25] Mormon leaders responded almost immediately in at least two publications. Probably the most critical reaction, penned by church president Joseph F. Smith and published in the *Juvenile Instructor,* an LDS magazine, read in part:

> Recently a man charged with murder of another man was examined before a committing magistrate in Salt Lake City. The father-in-law of the murdered man, during the examination ... laid the crime at the door of the accused. In the cross-examination the attorney for the defendant pressed the witness as to how he knew that the witness was guilty of the crime. The reply, as given in the press, was, because God had revealed it to him. ... No member of the Church of Jesus Christ of Latter-day Saints should, for one moment, regard such testimony as admissible in a court of law, and to make the case perfectly clear it may be further stated that such evidence would not be permissible even in a Church court, where rules of evidence, though not so technical, are founded largely upon the same principles that govern the rules of evidence in a court of law. Any attempt, therefore, to make it appear that such evidence is in keeping with the tenets of the "Mormon" faith is wholly unjustified.[26]

Another person who claimed inspiration in the case was Frank Torgersen, the young man who had discovered Hay's grave. After hearing of Sharp's claims to revelation, Torgersen admitted to a reporter that he had been inspired to search the field where the body was found:

> The moment I heard Jimmie Hay had disappeared something prompted me to go down to the field. I stood on the fence and took a casual view among the mass of burrs and tried to see beyond. I was not satisfied and started down the railroad track. ... Something seemed to urge me to go, something I could not understand and do not now.

> I stood on the cattle guard and just fought that feeling and went back where the folks were talking. The next morning when I wasn't thinking anything about the matter the fact that one of my horses was lying down attracted me to the spot and bumped me right on the grave, and then I didn't recognize what it was. It was the queerest experience of my life, fighting against that inclination to search the field.[27]

In spite of the controversy caused by Sharp's claims of revelation, the judge found enough other evidence to bind Mortensen over to trial for murder. Between the preliminary hearing and the actual trial, the police again searched the Mortensen house, by then occupied by his brother Henry, and the surrounding area for the missing murder weapon.

On May 5, 1902, the process of finding a jury began. District Attorney Dennis C. Eichnor had taken over for the prosecution, and Judge Charles W. Morse was appointed to preside over the trial.[28] Jury selection lasted almost three weeks, which was an enormous length of time at the turn of the twentieth century. The selection process proved to be as controversial as the case itself.

Each potential juror was asked about his personal belief in modern revelation, specifically if he believed that a person could receive personal revelation regarding the innocence or guilt of someone on trial for a crime such as murder. Potential jurors were also specifically asked about Sharp's statements.[29] Men who showed signs of believing the purported revelation or who refused to reveal their feelings on the subject were dismissed. Eventually over 1,000 men were summoned before twelve were selected.

Among those questioned and released by attorneys were Orson F. Whitney, assistant LDS church historian, and George F. Gibbs, secretary to the church's First Presidency. Both men knew Sharp and had been acquainted with Jimmy Hay.[30] When questioned about Sharp's statements, Whitney stated, "I believe Mr. Sharp believed he had a revelation." When asked if he believed that "God does reveal to man the guilt or innocence of a person charged with crime," Whitney replied, "I believe He can ... but I never knew of such a case." Pressed further about Sharp's purported revelation, Whitney finally admitted that he did not believe it.[31] Gibbs also "did not believe ... Sharp had received a revelation. He said, further, that such matters might be revealed by the Devil, and that God was blamed for many things He was not responsible for."[32] Seven of the twelve jurors eventually selected were members of the LDS church.[33]

From the outset District Attorney Eichnor and the prosecution team faced the difficult job of convincing the jury using only circumstantial evidence. Lacking both the murder weapon and an eyewitness to the crime, the prosecution aimed to weave a net of circumstantial evidence tight enough to convict.

Eichnor began the task with an opening statement wherein he described the events leading up to Hay's murder, including Mortensen's financial woes. He described Hay's disappearance and Sharp's accusations against Mortensen. At that point Eichnor reminded the jury, "This is not a question of religion or revelation. We will prove it [that Mortensen killed Hay] by both Mormons and non-Mormons."[34] Eichnor stated emphatically that Mortensen did not have sufficient funds to pay his debt to Pacific Lumber Company and detailed his receipts and disbursements, including $200 he had received on the day of the murder from John C. Sharp, for whom he was building a house. At that time Mortensen had told him that he had enough money to pay his debt to the lumber company. His accounts clearly showed otherwise.[35]

In building their case the prosecution called a total of forty-one witnesses.[36] Two of the most dramatic moments came when Hay's wife and father-in-law testified. Aggie Sharp Hay took the witness stand in "a courtroom packed to suffocation, yet as silent as a tomb." She described in quiet tones her husband's visit to Mortensen for the money and his subsequent disappearance. The defense made no attempt to cross-examine her.[37]

Her performance on the witness stand was in stark contrast to that of her father. James Sharp was described somewhat sensationally by one newspaper as "pouring forth the most bitter words, perhaps, that an accused man ever was compelled to listen to."[38] He described the search for his missing son-in-law and his retrieval of the unsigned receipt from the Mortensen home, which he showed to his son, Heber, and to George E. Romney. He then told of his confrontation with Mortensen and the eventual discovery of the body. At the end of his testimony, defense attorney Barnard Stewart cross-examined.

After several questions and answers, Stewart asked Sharp how he had known that Mortensen had killed Hay:

> After some hesitancy Mr. Sharp said, "I told you once."
> "Tell me again."
> "God revealed it to me."
> "How?"
> "By the utterance of my mouth. The words came from my mouth and I could not stop them. I will not deny the word of God, neither here nor in the presence of God hereafter."
> "Did God appear in person?"
> "Go and ask him."
> "Answer my question."
> "Ask God."
> [Judge Morse], "Answer the question Mr. Sharp."
> "He did not."
> "How did he appear?"
> "He appeared by the power of his spirit and told me. ..."
> "Is this, Mr. Sharp, the only manifestation you have had with reference to this case?"
> "No, sir."
> "When did you have any other?"
> "On Tuesday, at noon. I saw in a vision the trail of blood leading across the track to the grave. ..."[39]

Although Sharp's testimony was the most riveting of the trial, it was not the most damaging. Recognizing the controversial nature of Sharp's words, the prosecution sought to create a solid case that would not emphasize his accusations. With that in mind, they produced a parade of witnesses who provided bits of circumstantial evidence that, when combined, painted a dark picture, indeed, for the accused.

George A. Sheets, for example, testified that he had investigated the wall ledge in the basement where Mortensen had claimed to have kept the money in jars. He had found dust all along the ledge and no signs of jar prints. He also verified that Sharp had promised the body would be found within twenty-four hours. John Allen, the motorman for the Calder's Park tram, testified that he had seen Mortensen walking along the Rio Grande Railroad tracks carrying a shovel at 10:20 on the evening of December 16. Another witness, Charles

Watkins, stated that shortly after Mortensen's arrest he had asked him if he could show that he had paid Hay $3,800. Mortensen replied, "My books are in such shape that it will be necessary for you to say you loaned me $1,000 or $1,500," and suggested that Watkins alter his record books to make it look as though he had loaned Mortensen the money. Watkins refused to do so.[40]

The prosecution did not depend on testimony alone. Eichnor introduced material evidence such as the clothes Hay was wearing at the time of his murder and the gold watch found on his body. He also used courtroom demonstrations. For example, he brought Mortensen's settee into court and showed that two grown men could not sit comfortably on the settee at the same time. The square-nosed shovel found hidden in the back of Mortensen's stable was shown.[41]

Near the end of his presentation, Eichnor demonstrated to the court how much an ordinary quart fruit jar would hold in $20 gold pieces. Although Mortensen had claimed to have $3,800 in $20 gold pieces stored in three fruit jars, Eichnor easily placed $3,800 into one jar with about an inch and a half of space remaining. Mortensen was "visibly shocked," according to the newspaper. Three jars filled with gold coins, as Mortensen had claimed, would have amounted to about $13,000.[42]

After the prosecution rested, the defense called four witnesses to refute motorman John Allen's testimony, but they were unable to impeach it. No other witnesses were called, and no evidence was introduced to explain discrepancies in Mortensen's story. Most surprising to those in the courtroom was that Mortensen himself was not called to the witness stand. It appears that the defense strategy was simply to create enough doubt to produce a hung jury. After a total of fifty-five minutes, the defense rested.[43]

The prosecution then moved to allow members of the jury to visit Forest Dale and the scene of the crime. The defense agreed, and Royal Young was appointed to be their guide. Accompanied by four members of the police department, the jury visited the Mortensen home and cellar and then walked along the railroad tracks to the site of the grave.[44]

The next morning Judge Morse told defense attorney Barnard Stewart that during the visit to Forest Dale one juror had measured the distance between several points discussed during the trial. Morse expressed concern that Mortensen had not been present when the jury visited the site and offered the defense the opportunity to make another trip if desired. Surprisingly Stewart said that he had no objection to what had occurred during the trip. Eichnor suggested that the court record the jury's visit to Mortensen's house and cellar. Stewart again raised no objection.[45]

In summing up the case, Eichnor argued before a packed courtroom that Mortensen had had both the motive and the opportunity to kill Hay. In response, both Barnard and Charles Stewart addressed the jury and passionately pleaded for the life of their client. During his two-hour discourse, Barnard attacked Mortensen's brothers-in-law, Theodore and Richard Watkins, who had testified for the prosecution: "Where in this world can you find a brother-in-law who would be so willing to brand the children of his sister with the brand of infamy which would rest upon the children of a murderer? There are those conscientious brothers-in-law! Would you believe such men?" His words concerning the children brought tears to Mortensen's eyes as, for the first time during the trial, he broke down and wept.[46]

In a blistering attack that composed half of his speech, Barnard assailed the testimony of James Sharp as "an abuse of religion, a disgrace to the church, a mockery of God." He thundered:

> Do you believe a man who will come into the most sacred temple of justice on the most solemn of solemn occasions when a man's life is hanging in the balance and tell you, that the great God of the universe, the God whom you worship and the God that I worship came down here and revealed either in person or in spirit the guilt of this defendant. ...
>
> I do not believe it. In the words of one of the jurors, I believe that God that guides and controls this mighty universe has greater work than to communicate the guilt of this defendant to James Sharp.[47]

Skillfully adding another dimension to his rebuttal of Sharp's testimony, Stewart explained that Sharp had "been beside himself" and "lost in sorrow." Indeed, he had "laid awake at nights until his mind

[was] mystified." Sharp was no doubt an honorable man, the attorney said, who "had made statements under wrong impressions," for if his statements were not misguided but intended to influence the jury in order to convict Mortensen, then Sharp was "a man lost to honor." Stewart also reminded the jury that Sharp's statements "would be rejected in the councils of his own Church."[48]

For his part, Charles Stewart questioned the credibility of the circumstantial evidence and demanded, "Where is the gun? Where is the gun? Has anyone ever seen Peter Mortensen with a 38-caliber revolver? ... There is not a word of testimony here to show that Peter Mortensen ever had such a gun."[49]

In his closing statement Eichnor responded to questions concerning the gun and the circumstantial evidence. To achieve his goal of creating a net strong enough to convict, he listed what he termed fifty-five links of evidence. They began with Mortensen's failure to pay his debt and ended with his attempts to have his two brothers-in-law state that they had loaned him the money. Eichnor sarcastically berated Barnard Stewart for bringing out Sharp's claims of revelation: "Now then, about the subject of revelation. Who brought it out? Mr. Barnard Stewart, that brave man who pictured himself to you as a hero, this great knight, this great Napoleon of the bar, told you how brave he was to bring it out. Now why did he bring it out? May it not have been for the purpose of prejudicing those members of the jury, who, perchance, do not believe in the principle of revelation. It matters not whether I believe in it."[50] Eichnor explained that he had placed James Sharp on the witness stand in order to give his version of the search for Hay and the discovery of the victim's body.

Near the end of his closing statement, Eichnor dramatically declared: "Now gentlemen, if you find this defendant not guilty, when you go out of here and you meet Mrs. Hay, take her by the hand and say to her 'We had a reasonable doubt that Peter Mortensen murdered your husband.' Lay your hands upon the heads of those three little fatherless children and say, 'We had a reasonable doubt that Peter Mortensen murdered your father.' [G]o to the grave in the lonely field and place your hand upon that mound and say, 'We had a reasonable doubt that Peter Mortensen murdered you.' Do that if you can[,] gentlemen."[51]

In a little less than an hour and a half, the jury concluded its deliberations and delivered a verdict: guilty of murder in the first degree. Mortensen heard it without flinching or showing any sign of distress. His family was more demonstrative. Jesse, one of his brothers, glared angrily at the jury, while an uncle openly wept, and his father Morten wept as he privately thanked Judge Morse for his fairness in the trial.[52]

After the guilty verdict, one newspaper reported on evidence that had not been allowed in court: a .38-caliber shell found in a ditch beside Mortensen's house and his rubber galoshes, which police had taken to the grave site and found to fit what were suspected to be the footprints of the killer.[53]

Almost a year and a half passed before Mortensen was executed. During that time his lawyers attempted to overturn the verdict. Their first move was to seek a retrial, which was denied on October 5.[54] In November they attempted to have the verdict overturned based on fifty-two points in which, they asserted, the court had erred to the detriment of their client. The list of alleged errors included allowing Aggie Sharp Hay's and James Sharp's testimonies, as well as those of several other witnesses. The defense viewed them as hearsay and, therefore, incompetent, irrelevant, and immaterial to the case. They also objected to the introduction of the settee and the fruit jar demonstration. Perhaps the most significant and potentially damaging argument, supported by a signed affidavit from jury member Alma H. Rock, was that Mortensen was not allowed to accompany the jury and law officers to his home and to the murder site.[55] After a hearing that included testimonies or affidavits from Rock, Young, and others, it was judged that no improprieties had occurred.[56]

In a final attempt to save his life, Mortensen appeared before the State Board of Pardons, which consisted of Governor Heber M. Wells and members of the Utah Supreme Court. Mortensen asked the board to review the case and commute his sentence to life in prison. As part of the review process, District Attorney Eichnor and Judge Morse were asked for their opinions concerning Mortensen. Eichnor wrote that he had no new knowledge that would warrant commuting the sentence to life. Morse, on the other hand, stated that although there had been enough circumstantial evidence for the jury to find the defendant guilty beyond a reasonable doubt, he did not believe "that the death penalty ought ever to be inflicted upon a person whose conviction rests solely upon circumstantial evidence." Therefore, he recommended that commutation be granted.[57]

After its review, the Board of Pardons voted unanimously against commuting the sentence. Still hoping to live, Mortensen wrote Governor Wells on November 19, 1903, stating that he could adequately explain where he got the money he claimed to have given Hay. He asked to see the governor and explain the discrepancies in person. Later that day Wells did meet with Mortensen. After a lengthy interview, Wells refused to further consider Mortensen's plea for commutation.[58]

The next day, after a restless night and a small breakfast, Mortensen visited with his relatives for the last time.[59] He asked to be buried beside his mother in the Ogden City Cemetery and requested that no funeral be conducted over his body or any prayers said or flowers placed at the grave. After many tears, the family departed. Noticeable by their absence were Mortensen's wife and children. He had not seen them since his arrest. In fact, he had never seen his youngest child, Ruth, who was born after his arrest. Mortensen then met with the press, speaking passionately and emphatically at times and occasionally wiping away tears.[60] He maintained his innocence to the end: "To the world I want to say, and I swear by the heavens above, by the earth beneath, and by all that I hold near and dear on earth, that I am not guilty of that cowardly murder of my dearest friend. I ask, therefore, no man's pardon for aught that I may have done in life. I am confident that my life is an example to most people."[61]

At 10:27 a.m. he was led out to a chair against the east wall of the prison. He was shot by a firing squad at 10:31 a.m., and a wagon took his body away to be buried in Ogden. One final twist in the Mortensen saga was the refusal of the Ogden City Cemetery to accept his body for burial. Henry and David Mortensen were forced to have their brother's remains buried in the prison cemetery.[62]

After the execution and burial, family members were left to continue their lives. Morten Mortensen returned to California where he died in 1925. His body was returned to Utah and buried next to his wife's in Ogden. Henry, who had lived near, and worked with, his brother Peter, also moved to California. After the trial Peter's home was given to Barnard Stewart as payment for his legal services.[63]

Ruth Elizabeth Mortensen suffered greatly from emotional problems for years following the murder. Shortly after the arrest she and her children moved to Ogden to be close to her father and siblings. She depended upon her family to help make ends meet until her children were grown. By 1914 she and her children were using her maiden name Watkins as their surname.[64]

By 1925 she had moved to California. She married Alix Justesen and they settled in the Bay Area. She died on September 5, 1943, in relative anonymity. It appears that she went to great lengths to forget her earlier identity and protect herself from the scrutiny of people who might be aware of the Hay murder and her husband's sensational trial.[65]

James Sharp, on the other hand, remained prominent in the community until his death on May 7, 1904. Front page headlines announced that the former mayor of Salt Lake City had died from a sudden illness. After recounting his numerous business and political achievements, the news story stated:

> It is a matter of knowledge to the associates and friends of the deceased that he has not been in the best of health for some years, and that his condition was greatly aggravated in the tragic fate of James R. Hay, his son-in-law, who was so cruelly murdered. It will be remembered how he described in open court before judge, jury and accused that God had revealed to him the identity of the assassin. The statement was made in all soberness and created a tremendous sensation at the time and for months thereafter. The declaration made a pronounced impression upon all concerned and was very widely discussed. Through the long, legal battle that followed, Mr. Sharp maintained the correctness of that statement, though he maintained it unwillingly, it being drawn from him by the attorneys of the defense.
>
> The whole dreadful affair preyed heavily upon his mind and no one will know how much it had to do with hastening the closing chapter of his days upon earth. Certainly it broke down his health and brought sorrow and gloom to a life that had previously enjoyed much sunshine.[66]

Aggie Sharp Hay and her three young children eventually moved to Rexburg, Idaho, where her brother Heber and his wife had settled.[67] Apparently she felt forced to leave Salt Lake City because of the "stigma" of her husband's murder. She felt betrayed by the community's reaction to her father's claim of personal revelation.[68] However, according to a granddaughter, she suffered from "a serious thyroid disorder" that caused "terrible mood swings" and bouts of depression.[69] Some of her statements probably were the result of her illness. In April 1917 Aggie's thyroid problem reached a point where it was deemed necessary to operate, and she traveled to Salt Lake City for the surgery. Complications followed and she died on April 25. Her funeral was held in the Twentieth Ward chapel where she had been blessed by her grandfather, Bishop John Sharp, forty years before.

Eventually all three Hay children returned to the Salt Lake area. Ruth, who never married, worked for years in the Home Fire Insurance Company. Robert was so bitter and self-conscious about his father's murder that he changed his surname to Hays to avoid the impertinent inquiries that had faced him on his return from Idaho. James also returned to Salt Lake and became an accountant. While his two older siblings stopped attending church, but still recognized their affiliation as LDS, James never considered himself Mormon; however, both Robert and James married Mormon women and raised their children as Latter-day Saints.[70]

The children know very little about the murder of their grandfather in 1901. Jane Zobell recalled that she was about fifteen years old before she first heard of it. Her mother told her never to mention it to her father as the memories were too painful and the feelings too strong.[71]

As the *Salt Lake Tribune* adequately, although somewhat melodramatically, explained, "99 out of every 100 people in Salt Lake" believed that Peter Mortensen was guilty of murder:

> An immense and all-sufficing egotism was the keynote to his career. In the light of his subsequent career it is not difficult to believe that the motive for the murder of James R. Hay was not so much the financial gain as to avoid exposure for proposing a dishonorable scheme—an exposure which would have held him up to the scorn of those whom he

> sought to impress with the height of his virtue and the extent of his rectitude.
>
> Even when he could no longer doubt the feeling entertained toward him by the community, when his wife had deserted him, his brothers-in-law forsaken him, he kept up the sham. He never tired of parading his religion and holding himself up as a pattern of morality. The court, the jury, the witnesses, the Supreme Court, the Board of Pardons, the Governor, might be wrong, but he, Peter Mortensen, was always right.[72]

Thus, in the eyes of most people, a murderer had been caught and justice had been done. For most the story ended with the sound of gunshots from a firing squad; for others it went painfully on. For family members on both sides of this tragedy, the impact of the event was tinged with pathos and divided loved ones from each other. Although murder is always shocking, this particular homicide held an entire city and distant observers spell-bound in horror through a sensational trial that, for many, was the trial of the century.

Notes

1. Arthur Conan Doyle, *The Edge of the Unknown* (New York: G. P. Putnam's Sons, 1930), 197-98; Thomas S. Duke, *Celebrated Criminal Cases of America* (San Francisco: James H. Barry Co., 1910), 327-32. Interestingly the Hay-Mortensen case in Duke's work followed an entry concerning another celebrated Mormon criminal case, the Mountain Meadows Massacre and Philip Klingonsmith's damning testimony against John D. Lee. L. Kay Gillespie also discussed the case in *The Unforgiven: Utah's Executed Men* (Salt Lake City: Signature Books, 1991).

2. Information obtained from the International Genealogical Index, 1993 ed., Church of Jesus Christ of Latter-day Saints (hereafter LDS), Salt Lake City, Utah. The parents of James Hay were Robert Massey Hay and Ann McCrea.

3. Timaru Branch Records, 3, archives, LDS Historical Department. Jimmy's father was not baptized. The Ancestral File of the LDS church, 1993 edition, lists March 15, 1882, as his death date. However, the *Timaru Herald* lists a Robert Hay dying from consumption on January 31, 1872. This is a very early date, but it could explain why there are no baptismal records for him. James Hay and Aggie Sharp were married in the temple by John R. Winder. Witnesses were James Sharp and George

Romney. Marriage License #6003 for the County of Salt Lake, Utah, September 9, 1896.

4. According to the Articles of Incorporation for the Pacific Lumber Company, Utah State Archives, Salt Lake City, the original founders and officers were George Ernest Romney, William S. Romney, James R. Hay, and Joseph E. Jensen. In 1900 the company was re-incorporated with David Eccles as director and president, Ernest Romney as director and vice-president, James Hay as director and secretary, and Joseph E. Jensen and William S. Romney as directors. Eccles held 150 shares of stock valued at $15,000, Ernest Romney 147 shares valued at $14,700, and the other three men one share each valued at $100. Unfortunately the company suffered from economic problems and in 1911 had its charter of incorporation revoked for failure to pay taxes. George Ernest Romney (1868-1940), a close friend of Hay, was the son of Bishop George Romney and Jane Jamison and lived in the Twentieth Ward. Bishop Romney was involved in several business ventures with Eccles, including the Oregon and Mount Hood Lumber companies and Home Fire Insurance of which James Sharp was vice-president.

5. According to Andrew Jenson, *Encyclopedic History of the Church of Jesus Christ of Latter-day Saints* (Salt Lake City: Deseret News Publishing Co., 1941), 253-54, Forest Dale was a small community located on land that was originally part of Brigham Young's Forest Farm and later subdivided into individual home sites that attracted young families. In 1896 the Forest Dale Ward was created.

6. Monroe Ward Records, 3, LDS archives; U.S. Census of 1880 for the Territory of Utah, Sevier County, Monroe Precinct, 30; and Ogden Fourth Ward Records, LDS archives. According to the International Genealogical Index, 1993 ed., and the Ancestral File, Charles Frederick Watkins was born and raised in Somersetshire, England. He met his London-born wife Elizabeth Mary Loud in 1852. They eventually became the parents of eleven children, the last one born in Ogden where they settled after immigrating to America in the late 1870s.

7. Logan Temple Record, Book A:298, and Forest Dale Ward Record, LDS archives.

8. *Salt Lake Tribune*, December 19, 1901; *Jubilee History of Latter-day Saints Sunday Schools* (Salt Lake City: Deseret Sunday School Union, 1900), 310. Hay had previously served as second assistant superintendent of the Twentieth Ward Sunday school.

9. *Salt Lake Tribune*, December 19, 1901.

10. Ibid., January 23, 1902.

11. Ibid., January 24, 1901, and June 6, 1902. Sharp was accompanied by his son, Joseph Hyrum. The Sharp home at 411 East South Temple was the former residence of Abraham O. Smoot. After James Sharp's death the house was sold to Enos Wall who expanded it into a mansion; it presently houses the LDS Business College.

12. James Sharp appears to have been accompanied by at least one son, Heber Chase Sharp; a cousin, John C. Sharp (see n35); Officer Sheets; Peter Mortensen; George Ernest Romney; and a newspaper reporter, Edwin C. Penrose of the *Deseret News*. Romney recalled how he and Mortensen went to the train stations as reported in *Salt Lake Tribune*, January 23, 1902.

13. *Salt Lake Tribune*, January 24, 1902, and the *Salt Lake Herald*, January 24, 1902. Present at the time of Sharp's statement were Mortensen, Heber Sharp, George Romney, reporter Edwin Penrose, detective George Sheets, and at least one other police officer.

14. Royal Barney Sagers Young (1851-1929) was the adopted son of Brigham Young. He and at least two of his three wives resided in Forest Dale. He was president, secretary, and treasurer of Young Brothers Company which dealt in music, musical merchandise, bicycles, and sewing machines.

15. *Salt Lake Tribune*, December 19, 1901, and the *Deseret Evening News*, December 18, 1901.

16. *Ogden Standard*, December 20, 1901.

17. *Salt Lake Tribune*, December 21, 1901. The gun and the hat were never found. A pistol found two days after the discovery of Hay's body proved, after ballistics tests, to be the wrong weapon. Numerous man-hours were spent looking for the two items. In fact, a nearby pond was drained and thoroughly searched but produced no evidence.

18. According to *History of the Bench and Bar of Utah* (Salt Lake City, 1913), 202-204, Barnard (misspelled Bernard in places) Joseph Stewart, a graduate of the University of Utah and the University of Michigan Law School, was admitted to the Utah Bar in 1900. Charles B. Stewart, educated at the same institutions, became a member of the Utah Bar in 1893. An older brother, Samuel W. Stewart, was also an attorney and sometime law partner of Barnard and Charles and later a judge. See also *Biographical Record of Salt Lake City and Vicinity* (Chicago: National Historical Record Co., 1902), 619-20; Chad M. Orton, *More Faith Than Fear: The Los Angeles Stake Story* (Salt Lake City: Bookcraft, 1987), 57-59, 76; and, "C. B. Stewart, Ex-Utahn, Dies in L.A.," *Salt Lake Tribune*, May 21, 1945. Barnard (1873-1931) and Charles (1870-1945) were both born in Draper,

Utah, to prominent pioneer parents, Isaac M. and Elizabeth White Stewart. Both men married into prominent Mormon families. Barnard married Leonora Mousley Cannon, daughter of Angus M. Cannon, and Charles married Katherine Romney, daughter of Bishop George Romney and half-sister to Ernest Romney who later served as a witness for the prosecution. Barnard lived his entire life in the Salt Lake Valley; Charles later moved to Los Angeles.

19. *Deseret Evening News*, December 21, 1901, and the *Salt Lake Tribune*, December 23, 1901. As an example of the sensationalism produced by the press, a short article, "The Hoodoo House," in the *Salt Lake Tribune*, December 29, 1901, noted that James R. Hay had once lived in a house where two previous owners died tragically. Hay, the newspaper opined, may have succumbed to the curse of that house. The public also displayed a morbid fascination with the crime. According to the *Tribune*, December 24, 1901, crowds of curious people were destroying the Mortensen property. Hundreds had filed in and out of the Mortensen home and visited the burial site. The lawns and gardens had been trampled down by the numerous visitors, and some were bold enough to carry away tools and other personal household items as souvenirs. Elizabeth Jane Hay Zobell in a telephone interview on November 14, 1994, said her mother told her that the tops of the picket fence around the yard were torn off by curiosity seekers as souvenirs of the victim's house.

20. *Salt Lake Tribune*, December 24, 26, 1901; *Ogden Standard*, December 24, 26, 1901.

21. *Ogden Standard*, December 26, 1901. After Ruth Mortensen told the police all she knew, she evidently felt as if a great weight had been taken from her. Family members later reported that her nervousness left her and that she became more cheerful.

22. *Salt Lake Tribune*, January 24, 1902, and the *Salt Lake Herald*, January 23, 1902.

23. *Salt Lake Tribune*, January 24, 1902.

24. Ibid., January 25, 1902.

25. *Salt Lake Herald*, January 27, 1902.

26. *Juvenile Instructor* (February 15, 1902): 114, as quoted in Gillespie, *The Unforgiven*, 61. *The Deseret News* also carried two editorials, "That Startling Testimony" and "The Way of Revelation," on January 25 and 26, 1902, respectively.

27. *Deseret Evening News*, January 25, 1902.

28. According to the *Biographical Record of Salt Lake City and Vicinity*, 547-48, and the *Salt Lake Tribune*, April 9, 1904, Dennis Clay Eichnor

(1858-1904), a non-Mormon, was born in Pennsylvania to German-born parents. After law school he moved to Utah in 1888 where he was active in the Liberal Party and later the Republican Party and helped draft Utah's 1895 constitution. The *Salt Lake Tribune*, August 5, 1938, describes Judge Charles Wesley Morse as one of the West's most prominent Masons: 33rd degree in the Scottish Rite and a former grand master of the Utah lodge. A non-Mormon, he was born in Illinois and came to Utah in 1888. He served on the bench for sixteen years.

29. *Ogden Standard*, May 6, 1902. According to the *Salt Lake Tribune*, May 6, 1902, people were also asked to reveal their attitudes toward circumstantial evidence and capital punishment. See also the *Tribune*, May 7, 1902, and *Deseret Evening News*, May 2, 5, 6, 1902. One problem encountered during the jury selection process was the popularity of James Sharp. Because of his political and business activities, almost everyone had at least heard of him, and several prospective jurors stated that they would believe his story of personal revelation because of their respect for him.

30. *Ogden Standard*, May 29, 1902. Of the 1,105 men subpoenaed, 589 were examined by the court before the jury was finally selected. Orson F. Whitney, *Through Memory's Halls: The Life Story of Orson F. Whitney as Told by Himself* (Independence, MO: Zion's Printing & Publishing Co., 1930), 219, noted that James Sharp had once blessed a deathly ill child of Whitney's and promised that the child would live.

31. *Deseret Evening News*, May 8, 1902; the *Salt Lake Tribune*, May 8, 1902; and *Ogden Standard*, May 8, 1902. Whitney did not mention in his *Through Memory's Halls*, 240-41, that he had flatly rejected Sharp's claims of personal revelation. He quoted only part of his exchange with the defense attorney and then stated that the judge believed he had adequately answered the question and, to his relief, excused him from jury duty.

32. *Deseret Evening News*, May 8, 1902.

33. *Ogden Standard*, May 16, 28, 29, 1902; the *Deseret Evening News*, May 14, 1902; and *Salt Lake Tribune,* May 14, 1902, provided background data on the jurors. See also Andrew Jenson, *Latter-day Saint Biographical Encyclopedia* (Salt Lake City, 1936). **John R. Dailey** was a non-Mormon from Kansas who had recently settled in Salt Lake City and worked for the Rio Grande Western Railroad before turning to mining investments. Dailey had a slight acquaintance with Jimmy Hay; both were investors in the Copper Boy Mining Company. **Joseph Smith**, a merchant and a Mormon from Granger, was thirty-three at the time of the trial. **Samuel Bringhurst Jr.** (1850-1936) came from a prominent Mormon family and was a farmer in the Taylorsville area. **H. D. Shurtliff**,

age sixty-one, was a farmer from Mill Creek who declared himself to be non-Mormon and agnostic. He served as foreman. **James M. Barlow** (1857-1917), a Mormon, was a salesman and clerk at Eldredge & Co. in Salt Lake City. **Sterling Le Roy**, a forty-seven-year-old non-Mormon, worked for the railroad. **Henry Tribe** (1838-1909), another non-Mormon, was an English emigrant and manufacturer in Salt Lake City. **Michael Kopp**, a forty-nine-year-old candy manufacturer, apparently associated with the Salt Lake Candy Company, identified himself as an agnostic and refused to take the traditional oath that mentioned God. **William A. Bills** (1835-1915), at age sixty-seven the oldest member of the jury, was a farmer from South Jordan. A Mormon pioneer of 1848 and a former bishop of the South Jordan Ward, he was a polygamist with five wives. **John T. Alexander**, an English-born Mormon who came to Utah as a young child, was a forty-one-year-old sheepherder in Hunter. **Charles H. Ingham, Jr.**, thirty-six, was a sheep man and laborer from Salt Lake City and an active Mormon. **Alma Henry Rock** (1861-1943), born in Farmington, Davis County, to Mormon pioneer parents, had reportedly "drifted from his religious moorings." He was a farmer and merchant in West Jordan.

34. *Salt Lake Tribune*, May 30, 1902.

35. *Deseret Evening News*, May 29, 1902. Mortensen claimed to have received a total of $2,700 during December, including $2,100 from John C. Sharp, and to have paid Hay with that money. However, records showed that Mortensen had received only $1,546, including $1,000 from Sharp, and spent $1,485. John C. Sharp (1850-1915?), who played an important peripheral role in the case, was a cousin of James Sharp. According to Jenson, *Latter-Day Saint Biographical Encyclopedia*, 2:479-80, he was a bishop in Tooele for a number of years and a successful stock raiser in that area. In 1890 he moved to Salt Lake City where he was involved in banking and other businesses as well as LDS church activities.

36. Third District Court Minutes, 286-333, Utah State Archives, Salt Lake City.

37. *Salt Lake Tribune*, June 6, 1902.

38. *Ogden Standard*, June 6, 1902.

39. Ibid.; *Deseret Evening News*, June 5, 1902; *Salt Lake Tribune*, June 6, 1902. During the testimony it was shown that Mortensen had lied to Heber Sharp on Tuesday afternoon about the direction he had seen Hay take after he had left the front gate.

40. *Ogden Standard*, June 7, 1902; the *Salt Lake Tribune*, June 7, 1902.

41. *Salt Lake Tribune*, June 7, 1902; the *Deseret Evening News*, June 14, 1902.

42. *Deseret Evening News*, June 10, 1902.

43. Third District Court Minutes, 330. The defense called Royal B. Young, Martin Fesler, James C. Palmer, and Pearl Hill, but only three testified (*Salt Lake Tribune*, June 11, 1902).

44. *Ogden Standard*, June 11, 1902; the *Salt Lake Tribune*, June 11, 1902.

45. *Deseret Evening News*, June 11, 1902.

46. Ibid., June 13, 1902; *Ogden Standard*, June 13, 1902; the *Salt Lake Tribune*, June 13, 1902.

47. Ibid. The juror referred to was John B. Dailey.

48. Ibid. In conclusion Stewart explained that he had questioned James Sharp about his claims to revelation because he believed he would have been a coward if he had remained silent when the prosecution was trying to convict a man upon revelation and visions. He then accused the prosecution of trying to play on the emotions of the jury by having Aggie Sharp Hay and her father testify.

49. *Salt Lake Tribune*, June 14, 1902.

50. *Deseret Evening News*, June 14, 1902.

51. Ibid.

52. *Salt Lake Tribune*, June 15, 1902. The same article mentioned that a number of women had made comments like, "I think he is just as handsome as can be. A man as nice looking as that could never have done such a terrible thing."

53. *Ogden Standard*, June 17, 1902. The shell was not admitted because there was no definite proof that it was linked to the case. The rubber galoshes were not admitted because the defense attorneys argued successfully that Mortensen had been present at the exhumation so the footprints could very well have been made at that time. The newspaper claimed that Mortensen had talked in his sleep and made incriminating statements, an accusation that was never verified.

54. Salt Lake County, Third District Court, Criminal Case Files, September 1902, Utah State Archives.

55. Ibid, November 24, 1902.

56. Ibid., November 1902 to October 1903. It appears that all former jurors, except Michael Kopp who had died in May 1903, were contacted and questioned about this allegation.

57. Board of Pardons Case File, Utah State Archives.

58. *Deseret Evening News*, November 14, 16, 18, 19, 1903. See also Peter Mortensen to Honorable Heber M. Wells, Wells Correspondence, Utah State Archives.

59. Visitors included Morten Mortensen (father), Jessie Mortensen (brother), David Mortensen and his wife (brother and sister-in-law), a nephew (a son of Henry Mortensen), and attorneys Barnard and Charles Stewart. Henry and Elizabeth Mortensen (brother and sister-in-law) arrived too late to get into the prison. Most family members appear to have accepted Mortensen's fate, but brother David expressed intense anger and believed that Peter had not had a fair trail. A veteran of the Spanish-American War who served with Battery A of the Utah Artillery, he had decided to settle in Oakland after he was mustered out in San Francisco.

60. *Salt Lake Tribune*, November 21, 1903; the *Ogden Standard*, November 20, 1903; *Deseret Evening News*, November 20, 1903.

61. *Salt Lake Tribune*, November 21, 1903.

62. Ibid.; the *Deseret Evening News*, November 20, 21, 1903; *Ogden Standard*, November 20, 1903. Among the 93 people invited to witness the execution were John C. Sharp and Andrew Jenson. The same day that Mortensen was executed in Utah, the infamous bounty hunter and killer Tom Horn was executed in Wyoming.

63. *Ogden City Cemetery Records*, part 3 (Salt Lake City: Genealogical Society of Utah, 1940-42), 665. According to LDS Church Census records for the years 1914, 1920, 1925, 1930, and 1935, as well as records of the Berkeley, Oakland, and Hollywood wards, all in LDS archives, some members of the Mortensen family remained active Mormons while others did not.

64. LDS Church Census, 1914; *R. L. Polk & Co.'s Ogden City Directory* (1918), 444; ibid., (1919), 469-70; ibid.,(1920), 489-90; and U.S. Census, Ogden, Weber, Utah, sheets 11 and 17. Charles, Ernest, and Ruth were still living with their mother and working as a railroad switchman, railroad hostler, and department store saleswoman, respectively. Jesse was a construction carpenter.

65. Charles (Mortensen) Watkins was listed in the 1930 LDS Church Census as living in Sacramento, California. No trace of Ruth or her other children could be found, even after searching under variant names. It appears that Ruth and her children basically left the LDS church, although her death was noted in the Berkeley Ward records for 1943, 653, where it states that she was not known to ward members as she was not a member of record.

66. *Deseret Evening News*, May 7, 1904. Because James Sharp had been a regent for the University of Utah for almost thirty years, all classes were canceled the day of his funeral. It was held in the Assembly Hall on Temple Square. Seated on the stand were members of the LDS First Presidency, Twelve Apostles, and other church leaders. Among the numerous speakers were George F. Gibbs and Joseph F. Smith. Among the pallbearers were Governor Heber M. Wells and University of Utah president Joseph T. Kingsbury. *Deseret Evening News*, May 11, 1904.

67. Telephone interview with Marianne Sharp Long, December 17, 1994. By 1904 Heber Sharp had established a mercantile store in Rexburg, Idaho. In September 1902 he had married Vera Young Cannon, daughter of George Q. and Caroline Young Cannon, in the Salt Lake temple, James Sharp officiating. It appears that Aggie and her children moved to Idaho sometime in late 1906 or early 1907 and lived for a time with the Heber Sharp family.

68. Telephone interview with Elizabeth Jane Hay Zobell, a daughter of James Heber Hay, May 26, 1994.

69. Ibid., November 14, 1994.

70. Ibid.

71. Ibid. Zobell said she had never even discussed with her sister the murder of their grandfather.

72. *Salt Lake Tribune*, November 21, 1903. Regarding the exposure of a "dishonorable scheme," it should be noted that the *Ogden Standard*, June 17, 1902, mentioned that Mortensen had been overheard talking in his sleep. He is purported to have said, "Oh, Jimmie! If you had done as I wanted you to you would not be where you are and I would not be here!" He is also supposed to have repeated something about "divide up." This led a number of people to believe that Mortensen had led Hay down to the tracks on some pretense and then tried to convince him to claim that he had been paid and then robbed. For this, Mortensen would have given him half of what little money he had. Hay refused and was shot by Mortensen to keep him quiet.

7.

Ogden's "Horrible Tragedy"

The Lynching of George Segal

Larry R. Gerlach

As evidenced by the enormous popularity of Marlboro Country, the American West continues to excite the imaginations of modern Americans. To many people the term *American West* immediately calls forth a series of mental images associated with the heroic frontier—cowboys and Indians, farmers and trappers, wagon trains and mining camps. Less well appreciated is the ignoble dimension suggested by the term *back country*—a land of gamblers, prostitutes, thieves, killers, and a host of other social misfits trying to keep a step ahead of civilization. Because law and order was an essential yet fragile commodity in these nascent communities, it is not surprising that among the most vibrant images of the Old West are those associated with it—the posse heading off a band of desperadoes at the pass, the cavalry rescuing besieged pioneers, the sheriff confronting a gunslinger at high noon, a bad hombre dangling from a cottonwood tree. In the public mind, two-gun law enforcement and hempen justice appear as the dual symbols of the Code of the West. It is instructive that although a great deal is known about the quick-on-the-draw peace officer, relatively little is known about his back-country counterpart, the lyncher.

Like its corollary vigilantism, lynching is a uniquely American phenomenon. *Lynch law* originally referred to corporal punishment, the term deriving from the floggings administered by Judge Charles Lynch of Virginia to Tories during the American Revolution. As Americans spread across the Missouri in the nineteenth century, lynching became increasingly identified with citizens taking the law into their own hands in imitation of the famous English hangman, Jack Ketch. The popular tribunals caught on and, throughout the latter half of the nineteenth century and into the twentieth, lynching became an accepted, albeit abhorrent, method of administering capital punishment.[1] From 1882 to the present, at least 4,743 persons were lynched in the United States. The year 1952 was the first in more than three-quarters of a century in which none were recorded. From 1953 to 1964 there were ten. There have been no lynchings since 1965. Only four states—Massachusetts, New Hampshire, Rhode Island, and Vermont—have an entirely clean slate.[2]

Although it is generally known that Judge Lynch's extralegal brand of summary justice was practiced in Utah, the nature and extent of his bloodthirsty tenure has not yet received systematic investigation. A. J. Simmonds's recent studies of the hangings of Charlie Benson and Ah Sing are the only substantive published accounts of Utah mob justice.[3] Contemporary chronicles either ignored or gave incomplete tallies of victims,[4] while the modern state histories are virtually silent on the subject.[5] Indicative of the meager knowledge of extralegal hangings are conflicting and inaccurate reports that give the state total variously as from two to five.[6]

A review of early executions—legal as well as illegal—reveals that at least twelve lynchings have taken place in the state. Except for the hanging of Robert Marshall in Price on 18 June 1925, mob justice in Utah was confined to the territorial period. Research to date indicates that Judge Lynch claimed the lives of the following men prior to statehood:[7] three unidentified men at Wasatch Station during the winter of 1868-69; a black man identified only as "a damned nigger" in Uintah, 29 June 1869; Charles A. Benson in Logan, 18 February 1873; Ah Sing in Corinne, 13 April 1874; Thomas Forrest in St. George, 5 October 1880; William H. ("Sam Joe") Harvey in Salt Lake City, 25 August 1883; John Murphy in Park City, 26 August 1883; George Segal in Ogden, 20 April 1884; and Joseph Fisher in Eureka, 6 July 1886. In addition, there is the rumored hanging of

A street scene from one of Ogden's downtown entertainment districts about 1890, in this case the Saddle Rock Restaurant on 24th Street. Six years earlier a murder outside the Gem Restaurant on Fourth Street resulted in a lynching from the bell tower at city hall. The man who was lynched was a Japanese waiter and cook. *Photo from the* Ogden Standard Examiner, *Utah State Historical Society all rights reserved*

John Fletcher at Spring Hill Station on 24 August 1883 and the mob execution of William Thorrington on 14 June 1858 in Carson Valley, now part of Nevada but then part of Utah Territory.[8] Whatever the documented number, undoubtedly more illegal executions in Utah went unrecorded. And had it not been for the special vigilance of law enforcement officers, Lynch would have claimed additional victims from the approximately two dozen "near lynchings" reported in the press from the 1860s through the 1920s. (For the record, there were eleven judicial executions in territorial Utah beginning with the hanging of two Indians in 1854 to the death by firing squad of Patrick Coughlin in 1896.[9])

The Ogden entry in Judge Lynch's docket book, the little-known death of George Segal, is dated 20 April 1884.[10] The murder by popular tribunal in Utah's junction city began at approximately 11:30 p.m. on 19 April when Lizzie Gudgell was gunned down on Fourth Street in front of the Gem Restaurant. It ended shortly after 4:00 a.m. the next day when Segal was hanged from the south end of the fire bell tower located near the new Ogden City Hall. Although the circumstances and some of the proceedings of those fateful five hours are shrouded in uncertainty, the night of 19-20 April was indeed, as the *Ogden Daily Herald* put it, "the darkest in the annals of Ogden city."[11]

Frustratingly little is known about the two principals in the tragedy. Forty-eight-year-old Elizabeth Gudgell, who was apparently a widow, had come to Salt Lake City around 1880 and opened a dressmaking shop. In July 1883 she moved to Hailey, Idaho, but soon returned to Salt Lake City to receive treatment for a disease, erysipelas, which eventually destroyed the sight in one eye. About six months prior to her death, she moved to Ogden and assumed operation of the Gem Restaurant owned by Charles B. Irish. Her son, Frank B. Gudgell, and eldest daughter, the wife of produce merchant J. W. S. Smith, lived in Salt Lake; her youngest child, May, attended Sacred Heart Academy in Ogden.

Even less is known of Segal, a twenty-seven-year-old Japanese laborer. According to one report he was a "bad character" who had recently left Nevada "where he had a brother lynched for killing a man," and who himself "had been obliged to leave San Francisco because of some crime." But another report claimed that Segal had been in the United States since age ten, was "smart and intelligent, and as a rule honest and industrious," and was "liked by those who well knew him." All that is known for sure is that at the time of the lynching he was employed at the Chamberlain House earning $60 a month as a cook and waiter.[12]

Also unclear is the matter of motivation. The testimony of contemporaries, most of it hearsay, is fragmentary and confusing. This much is certain: three or four weeks before the murder, Segal had been discharged from the Gem Restaurant, reportedly because of "insolent conduct." Most people believed that he harbored a grudge against either Mrs. Gudgell, Mr. Irish, or both; but the nature of the hostility is uncertain. Some believed that Segal was simply irate over his dismissal. Others, noting that during the weeks following his discharge Segal had "frequently" returned to the Gem seeking to recover sundry personal articles as well as back wages of between $150 and $200, stressed that his anger stemmed from Mrs. Gudgell's alleged refusal to respond to his demands. Moreover, rumor had it that the "love-crazed" Segal had become enraged when Mrs. Gudgell rebuffed his amorous advances. To compound matters it was reported that Irish, who had allegedly purchased the Gem for Mrs. Gudgell, was Segal's rival for the woman's affections. Sad but true, the *Salt Lake Daily Herald* had the final word on the nature of the quarrel between Segal and Gudgell: "what passed between them will never be known."

Fortunately eyewitness testimony permits a more accurate reconstruction of the immediate events of the murder-lynching. The tragic train of events began about 10:30 the night of 19 April when an angry George Segal went to see his landlord, accountant William S. Lewis. Irate that Mrs. Gudgell persisted in denying back wages, Segal asked Lewis to help institute a lawsuit to recover the money. Lewis, later claiming that he detected "a wild and unnatural look" in Segal's eyes, tried to calm the man and suggested they discuss the matter further on Monday. Segal apparently would have none of it, for he stormed out of the house shouting: "God damn her! I will let her know whether she does not owe me."

He was armed with a .38-caliber pistol which he had been carrying for several weeks, supposedly because he feared an altercation with Irish. "The old man carries one for me, and I one for him," Segal declared. "There is likely to be a shooting match, some day, and I want to be ready for him." Segal apparently blamed Irish for his problems, for he told Lewis: "The old man will go off in a few days, and then I will be all right. I will have some of my money and go to work again." Segal had threatened Irish several times, and it may have been Irish whom he intended to encounter at the Gem. Segal saw him enter the restaurant around 10:30. But Irish stayed only a few minutes before going to the barbershop for a shave.

After leaving Lewis, Segal proceeded directly to the restaurant and the fateful confrontation with Mrs. Gudgell. According to the two principal witnesses, Gudgell and her friend, Fred Jackson, Segal searched behind counters and in the kitchen for some aprons and a carving knife he claimed to have left behind. When the proprietress began to berate him for spreading word about town that she owed him money, Segal became "excited, and began to talk very loud." Thereupon Mrs. Gudgell ordered him to leave. When he refused, she grabbed his arm as if to usher him out. At that point Segal drew his pistol, but when admonished by Gudgell and Jackson, he put the weapon back in his pocket.

It appeared that the crisis had passed. However, when Mrs. Gudgell, by then "somewhat excited" herself, announced her intention to hail the police, Segal became "desperate" and, according to the press, "no doubt insane."[13] As she opened the front door to summon the police, Segal fired a shot. At that she ran screaming into Fourth Street, pursued by Segal—pistol blazing. A second and then a third shot rang out. Mrs. Gudgell slumped to the ground. Segal, now clearly bereft of his senses, fired two more shots from close range.

In all, the assassin fired five shots. Four of the leaden insults found their mark. One lodged in the fleshy part of Mrs. Gudgell's right thigh, another shattered her left thigh bone, and another grazed her breast. The eventually fatal bullet entered her back just below the left shoulder and passed into the lung.

George Segal stood momentarily over his victim, smoking pistol in hand, and then fled into an alley next to the Corey Brothers' store. Fred Jackson gave brief pursuit but wound up ignominiously sprawled on the ground after tripping over a box in the dark alley. Police officers Thomas H. Ballantyne and James M. Brown heard the shots while making their rounds on Fifth Street. As they hurried toward the sound, they met Segal fleeing toward the Broom Hotel on the corner of Main and Fifth streets. The assailant immediately obeyed their order to halt and, with gun still in hand, confessed to the approaching policemen that he "had killed a woman" and was "willing to be hanged." The captive was promptly taken to the new city jail located on Main Street between Fifth and Sixth and was locked up under the custody of assistant jailer Moroni F. Brown who, appreciating the potential for further violence, hid the keys to the cell block.

The shooting immediately produced talk on the street. Officer Ballantyne heard the rumblings and threats when he arrived at the Gem Restaurant to begin his investigation. To avert any potential mob action, he returned to the jail, secured the keys to the cells from assistant jailer Brown, and delivered them to Mayor David H. Peery at his home on Fourth Street between Main and Spring. Ogden's chief magistrate took it upon himself to size up the public temper. But thinking that the men milling about the streets were simply coming from a dance, and finding only one citizen at the jail, he returned home convinced that there would be no violence unless Mrs. Gudgell died. Nonetheless he gave orders to transfer Segal to Salt Lake City on Sunday morning and posted two additional guards around the jail "lest some of the more daring spirits of the town should attempt to wreak the vengeance that was talked of."

It appeared at first that Ballantyne's fears were indeed unfounded. As the initial excitement passed, the milling crowd began to break up and people returned to their homes. But about 3:00 a.m. a group of twenty-five to thirty men (one estimate was thirty to forty) gathered to execute their retribution. It was no spontaneous gathering. That they were well organized and directed is evident from the course of events. With coats turned inside out and masks on their faces to prevent identification, and carrying chisels and sledgehammers, the men stealthily made their way to the jail.

At approximately 4:00 a.m. officers Ballantyne and Warren W. Elmer, on guard in front of the jail, spotted the men attempting to scale the fence around the city hall. Warning that this "was not the right thing to do," the officers pleaded with the masked mobsters to "let the law take its course." But four men brandished shotguns and ordered the policemen "to stand back." With the guards at bay, the other vigilantes scaled the fence, broke down the rear door of the city hall, and headed for the row of eight cells located on the first floor. En route they were met by jailer Brown who, finding himself staring down the barrel of a shotgun, felt "compelled to retire" to his office on the second floor. None of the mob bothered to ask for the keys. The cells were made of heavy boiler iron, but the sledgehammer-wielding avengers quickly smashed open Segal's 4'6"-by-8'7" cell, dragged the "trembling wretch" from his bunk, and hurried him down the corridor into the courtyard to the bell tower. Although Segal "made no resistance or noise," the look on his face revealed that he was "horribly excited by ... the avenging crowd who looked like fiends ... by the appearance of the candles they carried." A hangman's noose was looped around his neck and a gag placed in his mouth. Moments later Segal was suspended "between earth and sky." According to Brown, witnessing the hanging from the second-story jail window, Segal was given a couple of quick jerks and then hoisted up eight or ten times. Convinced that their victim was dead and that justice had been done, the lynchers disappeared as quickly as they had appeared. The tragic affair took less than ten minutes.[14]

Segal, "dead as a stone," remained hanging on the beam for about an hour. When notified of the lynching, Mayor Peery rushed to the jail. Shortly after 5:00 a.m. he summoned the coroner, Mark Hall, Sr., who pronounced the victim dead. The corpse was taken to the office of sexton Frank A. Gale where a coroner's jury comprised of P. G. Taylor, Samuel Hammond, and Mark Hall, Jr., rendered the final verdict: "The deceased had come to his death on Sunday morning, April 20, 1884, being hung with a rope from the bell tower near the city hall, Ogden City, by a masked mob of unknown men."[15] Shortly after the inquest Segal's remains were placed in a coffin and interred in the town cemetery.

While Segal was paying the ultimate price for his perfidy, Mrs. Gudgell was waging a losing battle for her life. After the shooting she was rushed to her apartment in Elizabeth Watkins's rooming house on Fifth Street between Main and Young. Doctor O. B. Adams was summoned from the Broom Hotel, but the patient's condition was such that he could do nothing "to materially help" until morning. The next day, Sunday, Adams called in Dr. John D. Carnahan, a surgeon, who removed the bullet from the victim's thigh. Attempts to extract the bullet from her lung were unsuccessful. Monday morning, 21 April, found her resting "comparatively comfortably," but her condition suddenly took "a more critical turn." Lizzie Gudgell died about 11:30 a.m.—almost exactly thirty-six hours after the shooting.

Her demise was not unexpected. The consensus all along had been that the wound, like most perforations of the lung, would be fatal. On 22 April her body was removed to the home of her daughter in Salt Lake City. The Reverend N. F. Putnam of Saint Mark's Cathedral officiated at the funeral held the following day. The double tragedy was finally over.[16]

Like every manifestation of lynch law, the hanging of George Segal is a story unique to itself. Yet in its salient features it exhibits characteristics common to other lynchings in Utah and elsewhere in the United States. As a case study of a peculiarly American brand of justice, the Segal lynching assumes a significance that transcends its particulars.

Almost without exception a lynching was a momentary sensation in a community, an event without lasting impact. The day George Segal was strung up, the bell tower, the jail, and the sexton's office were visited by "hundreds of people" drawn to the scenes of the tragedy by "a morbid curiosity." Extra copies of the *Ogden Daily Herald* hit the streets on 21 April as the murder-lynching became "the all absorbing topic in all circles" in the city. But by April 24 the *Salt Lake Herald* could, in truth, report that "the lynching excitement has about died out." There was no further public discussion of the matter as Ogdenites returned to business as usual. The sooner such ugly incidents were forgotten, the better. What could and should have been the basis of a community discussion of topics ranging from law and order to human dignity was put out of mind.

The identities of the lynchers, although often widely known in a given community, were infrequently disclosed. In only two of Utah's twelve known mob hangings—those of Robert Marshall and Joseph Fisher—were the names of the perpetrators made part of the public record. Witnesses of the Segal lynching ostensibly could not identify any of the vigilantes because of the masks and because, as the *Ogden Daily Herald* lamely noted, it was "a dark night." Another possible explanation for the anonymity was suggested by the *Salt Lake Chronicle*: "[P]ublic opinion is too strong in their favor."[17]

Without identification, it follows that lynchers were rarely held accountable for their acts. Of the henchmen in Utah, only the thirteen men who hanged Joseph Fisher in Eureka were indicted and brought to trial; six were convicted and sent to prison. In only two other instances, the Marshall and Segal cases, was a grand jury even impaneled; both times the investigation produced the same result —nothing.

In the Segal case Judge P. H. Emerson instructed a fifteen-member grand jury at the opening of the First District Court in Ogden on 5 May 1884 to pay "special attention" to the "late mock trial." His Honor urged them to be "specially diligent" in inquiring into what he flatly termed a "murder" in order that the "perpetrators of the foul deed" might be indicted for the crime and "brought to punishment." He noted that if "such atrocious outrages and violations of law" were permitted to pass unpunished, "no one can tell how soon and how often they will be repeated or who will be the next victims."[18] "Of course every lover of law and order," commented the *Deseret News,* "will endorse the sentiments of Judge Emerson, and will heartily congratulate the Grand Jury if they are successful in finding the offenders and bringing them to justice." Either the *Deseret News* was wrong in its prediction or there were no lovers of law and order in Ogden, for the grand jury obtained no information about the lynching. The law enforcement establishment thereupon pronounced the case closed. The Ogden City Council took no formal notice of the incident.

The failure to indict, let alone convict lynchers, suggests a community that for the most part either condoned the act or protected its perpetrators. The initial reaction was revulsion in the face of this travesty of justice. But as the *Ogden Daily Herald* noted, with the death of Mrs. Gudgell "public opinion has somewhat relented from the stern condemnation" initially directed towards the lynching. In the final analysis, as the *Salt Lake Tribune* observed, there was "divided opinion as to the justice or propriety" of the lynching. Although some citizens regretted it, others considered it "a moral lesson that will have a beneficial effect upon those who are disposed to be criminal or lawless."

Considerable blame for violence in American history is often laid at the doorstep of the press. There does seem to be a close correlation historically between the pointed and persistent denunciation of lawlessness by newspaper editors and the frequency of vigilantism. Although Utah's four largest newspapers spoke out against the Segal lynching, their stance was something less than crusading. The *Salt Lake Daily Herald* simply termed the "startling tragedy" the "Ogden Horror" and let it go at that. Labeling the "genuine lynching affair" a "Horrible Tragedy," the *Deseret Evening News* merely commented that "such lawlessness must be suppressed." The *Ogden Daily Herald* understandably was more fulsome in its commentary. Declaring that "the troubles of Saturday night and Sunday morning are the most tragic in the records of the Junction City," the paper went on "earnestly" to decry "the taking of retribution for crimes into the hands of others than the lawfully constituted authorities" and to express the hope that "this will be the last, as it was the first successful execution of Judge Lynch's law in this erstwhile peaceful and law-abiding community, in whose fair record such deeds are deplorable dark stains."

Although the major oracles of Utah's Fourth Estate agreed that the Segal hanging was "horrible" and "tragic" and denounced the affair in the course of reporting its occurrence, only the *Salt Lake Daily Tribune* formally and forcefully editorialized against lynch law. Noting that this was the third lynching in Utah that year, the *Tribune* deplored in no uncertain terms "the treading under foot of law and order": "It is a fearful thing for an angry mob to undertake the administration of justice. In the first place it is a total subversion of the very idea of social and legal authority ... and then, a mob is ungovernable, and may easily be turned into an engine of injustice and destruction so appalling that the very possibility might well make the stoutest heart quail from its consideration."[19]

But the effect of the *Tribune* editorial was diminished, if not negated, by its refusal to place the blame for the lynching where it properly belonged. Consistently—in Utah and elsewhere—opponents of lynching blamed not the lynchers but the legal system. The major portion of the *Tribune* editorial consisted of a condemnation of the state of criminal prosecution in America. Railing against the sluggishness of the courts, the appeal process, the legal loopholes exploited by defense lawyers, and the leniency of judges and parole officers, the *Tribune* concluded that "the machinery for the punishment of murders fails to do its proper work." As a result, the paper opined, "the mob spirit is formed and gains strength until few can be found to rigorously condemn an orderly lynching, which goes no further than slaying the murderer, after being sure of his identity." To remedy the situation the *Tribune* proposed a reversal of the cardinal tenet of jurisprudence: "after an indictment has been found against a person he should be required to prove his innocence." Whatever the defects in the legal system, such condemnation of judicial due process served to excuse the mob and, perhaps, by providing a convenient rationale, encourage similar future behavior.

The perpetrator of a particularly heinous crime, especially the murder of a police officer or a prominent community figure, was a good bet to wear a hemp necktie. National statistics demonstrate that the commission of a homicide was by far the single most frequent cause of lynchings, especially when allowances are made for the "racial transgressions" peculiar to the South. The next largest category is crimes against women.[20] Utah's experience with extralegal executions conforms to the national pattern. Of the ten lynchings where the alleged offense is known, all involved murder; three of the victims were police officers, the others popular or respected members of the community. George Segal's senseless, brutal riddling of Lizzie Gudgell's body made him a prime target. As the *Ogden Daily Herald* noted, the mob organized as "excitement over his cowardly, villainous assault of a defenseless woman spread through the streets." His crime was the sort calculated to arouse the basest passions in the community.

When one considers Segal's national origin along with the magnitude of his crime, his fate was sealed. The record of lynching in the United States is emphatic: a member of a racial minority was much more likely to be lynched than a Caucasian. Of the 4,743 persons known to have been lynched from 1882 to 1968, 3,445 were black. In 1884, the year of Segal's lynching, 51 of 211 were black.[21] Again the national pattern holds for Utah. Of nine instances where the race of the victim is known, five—more than 50 percent—were non-white: three blacks, one Chinese, and one Japanese.

There can be no doubt that racial prejudice played a role in the Segal lynching. Newspaper accounts repeatedly referred to "the Japanese," "Japan George," or, most frequently, "the Jap." The *Salt Lake Herald* proclaimed that the death of "the Jealous Jap" brought "a quietus" to his "infatuation for a white lady." The *Herald* explained that "as with the Asiatic in general, when the passions were excited by love, rivalry, jealousy, disappointment, and the like things, the murderous propensity prevailed, and he committed the diabolical deed."

Another factor was Segal's itinerant status. Of the twelve men lynched in Utah, only Charlie Benson was from a prominent family with social status. Had he not been a prodigal son, the black sheep of the family, it is difficult to imagine his getting short shift at the end of a long rope. The rest, like Segal, were drifters—usually laborers in the mines or on the railroad who had neither kith nor kin in the community. With few exceptions lynchings have been enabled by law enforcement looking the other way, during or after an event. In Utah the only instance of lynchers being indicted and convicted was when Constable Bert Either of Tintic turned state's evidence against those who hanged Joe Fisher.

The Segal lynching is a case in point. Although the mayor was concerned enough to order the prisoner's transfer to Salt Lake City the next morning, only two policemen plus a solitary night watchman were on guard duty at the jail. Moreover neither William W. Fyfe, the Ogden city marshal, nor Thomas Stevens, the Weber

County sheriff, rendered any assistance in safeguarding the public's prisoner. It simply was not true, as the *Tribune* claimed, that "every precaution that was deemed necessary was taken to prevent any uprising." More to the mark was the observance of the *Ogden Daily Herald:* "the keys might just as well have been left in the lock." Indeed, the previous year the Ogden constabulary had thwarted the popular execution of Robert A. Lee, who aroused community ire by "ravishing a woman," because they were "vigilant and determined to go through legal processes."[22] In short, the reign of Judge Lynch in Utah and elsewhere depended on a tacit collusion with respectable elements of society.

The lynching of George Segal—and the execution of other Utahns by vigilantes—was truly a dastardly deed perpetrated by people who should have known better. That such an event took place serves as a not-so-gentle reminder of human nature, that such things happen—here as well as elsewhere. We are less because of our uniquely American heritage of vigilantism. If there are solace and satisfaction to be derived from an examination of this violent dimension of our past, it is that we have hopefully learned from history. We profit from recalling historical tragedies only by pledging that they shall not happen again.

Notes

1. The three classic surveys of lynchings are James E. Cutler, *Lynch Law: An Investigation into the History of Lynching in the United States* (New York: Longmans, Green & Co., 1905); Walter White, *Rope & Faggot: A Biography of Judge Lynch* (New York: Alfred A. Knopf, 1929); and Arthur F. Raper, *The Tragedy of Lynching* (Chapel Hill: University of North Carolina Press, 1933). General studies of vigilantism include Richard Maxwell Brown, *Strain of Violence: Historical Studies of American Violence and Vigilantism* (New York: Oxford University Press, 1975); Robert Brent Toplin, *Unchallenged Violence: An American Ordeal* (Westport, CT: Greenwood Press, 1975); Thomas F. Parker, ed. *Violence in the United States*, 2 vols. (New York: Facts on File, 1974); and Hugh Davis Graham and Ted Robert Gurr, *Violence in America: Historical and Comparative Perspectives* (Washington, D.C.: Government Printing Office, 1969).

2. These figures are taken from "The Lynching Records at Tuskegee Institute," a typescript tabulation which is the most comprehensive yet made. Because there has not been a detailed state-by-state study of lynching, the figures, derived mainly from national newspapers, are clearly conservative. The usual number of lynchings given for Utah is eight, at least four fewer than actually documented.

3. A. J. Simmonds, "Chinaman's Chance," *Real West*, November 1972, 46-49, and "Cause of Death—Lynching," *The West*, January 1974, 26-27, 48. See also Simmonds's provocative connection between Mormon apostasy and the Benson lynching in *The Gentile Comes to Cache Valley* ... (Logan: Utah State University Press, 1976), 9-11. See also Lucille Randall, "The Hanging of Charley Benson," *Salt Lake Tribune*, September 7, 1975, a popular, derivative account; William M. McPhee, *The Trail of the Leprechaun: Early History of a Utah Mining Camp* (Hicksville, NY: Exposition Press, 1977), 57-59, offering a brief history of the Murphy lynching; Ted Deffendol, "The Lynching of Robert Marshall in Carbon County," an undergraduate essay at the College of Eastern Utah Library, Price, based on newspaper accounts; Steve Lacy, *The Lynching of Robert Marshall: The Last Lynching in the West* (n.p.: Castle Press, 1978), a brief and partly fictionalized account of the Marshall lynching that reprints important documents (to which it should be noted that Marshall was not the last person hanged in the West, as three white men were subsequently lynched in California); and my manuscripts: "Cops and Mobsters: The Lynching of Sam Joe Harvey" and "Forrest from a Tree: The Lynching of Tom Forrest."

4. Edward W. Tullidge, in his *Histories*, 2 vols. (Salt Lake City, 1889), makes no mention of lynchings; Robert W. Sloan, *Utah Gazetteer and Directory ... 1884* (Salt Lake City, 1884), 41-42, notes the mob executions of James Harvey, John Murphy, and "a Japanese" [Segal]; Andrew Jenson, *Church Chronology* ..., 2d ed. (Salt Lake City, 1914), 112-13, mentions the Harvey and Murphy incidents of 1883.

5. The standard school text by S. George Ellsworth, *Utah's Heritage* (Santa Barbara: Peregrine Smith, 1972), does not mention lynching, while Charles S. Peterson, *Utah: A Bicentennial History* (New York: W. W. Norton, 1977), 115, notes only the Marshall case. Of the contributors to Richard D. Poll, ed., *Utah's History* (Provo, UT: Brigham Young University Press, 1978), Richard O. Ulibarri in "Utah's Unassimilated Minorities," 634, alone mentions the topic—the Uintah hanging, the Marshall lynching, and the mob execution of "Sam J. Hairney in Salt

Lake City in 1885." The latter reference, apparently marred by typographical errors, is to William H. ("Sam Joe") Harvey in 1883.

6. The *Salt Lake Telegram,* June 18, 1925, listed Marshall, Charles Benson, and Harvey. The June 18 and 19 editions of the *Deseret News* and *Salt Lake Tribune,* respectively, listed four earlier lynchings—Marshall, Benson, Harvey, and Thomas Forrest—and erroneously mention "one Donovan" in Park City in 1888, due to confusion with the Murphy hanging. In the March 14, 1926, issue of the *Salt Lake Telegram,* Albert F. Phillips, in a supposedly comprehensive chronicle of capital crimes, mentioned that "two lynchings have occurred in Utah since the pioneers came in 1847, one in Logan and the other in Salt Lake City."

7. Information pertaining to eight of the lynchings can be found in public as well as private records. The lone account of the murder of a black man at Uintah is an entry in the diary of O. C. Smith, quoted in Robert G. Athearn, *Union Pacific Country* (New York: Rand McNally, 1971). The statement that three persons were hanged at Wasatch comes from George Hanson Beadle's *The Undeveloped West; or, Five Years in the Territories* (Philadelphia, 1873), 139, and *Western Wilds and the Men Who Redeem Them* (Cincinnati, 1878), 52. Beadle does not use the term "lynched," but one can assume as much because there was at the time no duly constituted judicial apparatus at the railroad camp. Beadle elsewhere (*Western Wilds,* 127) comments on the prevalence of lynching in such isolated communities.

8. *Deseret Evening News,* August 27, 1883, and *Salt Lake Herald,* August 28, 1883, report the Fletcher lynching. Bancroft, *Popular Tribunals,* 1:594-98, and *History of Utah, 1540-1886* (San Francisco, 1889), 592, report the Thorrington execution.

9. Although Coughlin's execution was on December 15, 1896, his sentence was imposed prior to statehood (January 4, 1896).

10. The Segal lynching is not widely known. Sloan, *Utah Gazetteer,* 42, notes that on April 22, 1884 (the date is wrong), "A Japanese shoots a woman in Ogden and is lynched." The WPA's *A History of Ogden,* 2 vols. (Ogden, 1940), 1:53, mentions that "in 1884 a mob hanged a Japanese near the city jail." The WPA account is derived from an interview with Gilbert A. Belnap in the *Ogden Standard Examiner,* February 3, 1924, in which he recalls the night he returned to Ogden from a church mission in Minnesota: "I walked up Twenty-fifth street and over near the jail, there was a man hanging from a pole, where he had been strung up a short time before. Calling the jailer's attention, he looked out and was as surprised as I was, for the mob had done its work so quietly and effec-

tively that none of the officers had been aroused. The victim was a Japanese who had killed a white woman in a fit of anger and unceremoniously a group of men took him, I am told, and lynched him within a few minutes after the crime was committed." Parts of the narration are erroneous. Neither John Q. Blaylock, "History of North Ogden: An Economic and Social Study" (M.A. thesis, University of Utah, 1922), Milton R. Hunter, *Beneath Ben Lomond's Peak: A History of Weber County, 1824-1900*, 2d ed. (Salt Lake City: Deseret News Press, 1945), nor any other historical study I have seen mentions the Segal lynching.

11. The most detailed reports of the murder-lynching are to be found in the April 21, 1884, issues of the *Deseret Evening News* and the *Ogden Daily Herald* and the April 22 editions of the *Salt Lake Daily Herald* and the *Salt Lake Daily Tribune*. Unless otherwise noted, all quotations in this essay are from these newspaper accounts.

12. Ibid. Some reports say that he was a cook, others that he was a waiter. The evidence and common practice at the time suggest that he worked in both capacities.

13. *Ogden Daily Herald*, April 21, 1884.

14. A report in the *Salt Lake Chronicle* stated that the police tried to hide Segal in the old city jail near the new Central School on the corner of Fifth and Young streets, but a passerby saw light in the building and alerted the mob which then hanged its victim from the belfry. As the *Ogden Daily Herald* said of the report: "It isn't true." Information concerning the size, construction, and location of the cells is in Hunter, *Beneath Ben Lomond's Peak*, 480.

15. *Ogden Daily Herald*, April 21, 1884.

16. *Salt Lake Tribune*, April 23, 1884.

17. Quoted in the *Ogden Daily Herald*, April 22, 1884.

18. *Deseret Evening News*, May 6, 1884.

19. April 22, 1884.

20. "Lynching Records at Tuskegee."

21. Ibid.

22. *Ogden Junction*, March 12, 1873.

8.

Justice Denied

The Lynching of Robert Marshall (A Memorial Delivered on the Anniversary of the Event)

Larry R. Gerlach

On June 18, 1925, Robert "Bob" Marshall, an itinerant coal miner of African-American descent, was murdered by a lynch mob in Carbon County, Utah. Afterward newspapers throughout the state and across the nation carried stories about an occurrence that was, tragically, not uncommon. From 1882 to 1964, the year of the last recorded lynching in the United States, at least 4,743 people were executed by mob henchmen; 3,446 (73 percent) of the victims were black. The majority of lynchings (3,224 or 68 percent) occurred prior to World War I; they decreased as the twentieth century progressed and were confined primarily to the Deep South.[1]

Robert Marshall was not the first to be lynched in Utah. Between 1869 and 1886, at least eleven men, two of whom were black and two Asian, received this kind of short shrift at the end of a long rope; Corinne, Eureka, Logan, Ogden, Park City, St. George, and Salt Lake City witnessed such violence.[2] It was thought that with the passing of the frontier and the onset of statehood—i.e., social stability, institutionalized law enforcement, regularized judicial procedures, and a watchful press—lynchings would be a thing of the past. Alas, some forty years after Sam Joe Harvey was strung up and dragged lifeless through the streets of Salt Lake City, another itinerant black man would receive the same treatment: Robert Marshall was the last black man to be lynched in the West.[3]

On the evening of Monday, June 15, 1925, at approximately 7:30 p.m., James Milton Burns, town marshal of Castle Gate and night watchman for the Utah Fuel Company, was shot and fatally wounded while making his rounds. It was a brutal murder, likely the result of a personal grudge. He was shot five times, beaten about the head with a revolver, and kicked in the face. There were no eyewitnesses. But two or three young boys playing near the scene saw Marshall flee into the surrounding hills immediately after the shooting. A search party organized by Carbon County sheriff Ray Deming and eventually numbering upwards of 150 men combed the hills in pursuit. After Burns died on June 16, community anger over the heinous murder of a popular lawman increased to a fever pitch during a 2.5-day manhunt, including a brief exchange of gunfire with Marshall.[4]

Sometime during the night of June 17, the exhausted fugitive returned to the cabin he shared with fellow black miner George Gray, a mere half-mile from the murder scene. The next morning while Marshall slept, Gray went to Utah Fuel headquarters in Castle Gate and advised authorities of Marshall's whereabouts. It was approximately 9:30 a.m. when a nine-man posse led by Deputy Sheriff Henry East descended upon the cabin and captured Marshall without any resistance. A three-car procession transported him to Price about ten miles away. En route the party met up with Sheriff Deming who told them of reports that a lynch mob was forming in town. Deming then sped away in the opposite direction. Upon reaching town the caravan stopped in front of the county courthouse amid an angry crowd. Instead of taking Marshall directly to jail, East went into the courthouse, leaving the prisoner unattended. The crowd commandeered the vehicle and headed out as a parade of "at least 100 cars."[5]

As extralegal executions, lynchings typically were out-of-sight occurrences, but in this instance Carbon County residents knew in advance of the "necktie party." Several hundred—some estimates say upwards of 1,000 men, women, and children—gathered at approxi-

This view of Robert Marshall's 1925 lynching was displayed in store windows and sold as postcards in Price, Utah, in the aftermath of its occurrence there. *Utah State Historical Society, all rights reserved*

mately 10:20 a.m. around a tall cottonwood tree on the Critchlow farm some 2.5 miles east of Price, near Wellington. The crowd was described by a reporter on the scene as consisting not of "disorderly, violent, undesirables" but of "your neighbors, your friends, the tradespeople with whom you are wont to barter ... public employees, [and] folks prominent in church and social circles." They watched as a noose was placed around Marshall's neck and he was hoisted into the air and hanged.[6] Ten minutes later three deputies belatedly arrived and cut him down; when the lynchers detected evidence of life, Marshall was hanged a second time and died from a broken neck.

Although the newspapers reported that "no attempt at concealment was made by any member of the lynching party [and] in fact, participation in the affair seemed to be a matter of boasting," Deming and his deputies professed not to know the identity of those responsible.[7] But an investigation conducted by District Attorney Fred W. Keller and County Attorney Oliver K. Clay resulted in warrants being issued on June 20 for the arrest of five ringleaders, four of whom were charged with "pulling the rope"; the next day warrants were issued for the arrest of six accomplices.[8] All eleven men, six of whom were employees of Utah Fuel Company, were charged with murder in the first degree. They waived a preliminary hearing and were bound over for trial. But instead of proceeding to trial, Keller and Clay, against their better judgment, bowed to the insistence of Utah governor George Dern and State Attorney General Harvey Cluff and agreed to summon a grand jury—whereupon the eleven men, whose time in jail had resembled more a celebration than an incarceration, were released on bail on June 30, itself an unusual act in a first-degree murder case.[9] The grand jury opened on July 28. The identity of the lynchers was common knowledge, but none of the 125 witnesses summoned would testify against any of the suspects. On August 18 the grand jury concluded that there was insufficient evidence to indict, and the Carbon County Eleven were released.

The basic facts of the Marshall lynching are well known, as they are part of the public record. Less well known and therefore difficult to explain succinctly are the actions taken—and not taken—by those directly and indirectly involved, from the murder of J. Milton Burns through the conclusion of the grand jury proceedings. Explanations run the gamut from ethnic tensions and labor unrest to social vigilantism in the guise of the Ku Klux Klan, from irresponsible hooliganism and mob psychology to racism. These complicated and complex issues need not concern us here; what does concern us is the meaning of the Marshall lynching.

The summer of 1925 claimed numerous victims, to wit:

1. Robert Marshall, victim of premeditated, cruel, and unusual murder, and his wife Pearl of Van Buren, Arkansas, for her loss; similarly J. Milton Burns, the victim of a brutal, senseless murder, and his wife Olivia and six children for their loss.

2. Impartial and honest law enforcement. Lynchings rarely occurred when police showed the determination to protect a prisoner. In this case police officers who were sworn to uphold the law were derelict in turning Marshall over to a mob and then by failing to intercede to stop the proceeding, by refusing to cooperate with the district and county attorneys, and by lying to the grand jury. If any one person is not protected when in the custody of the police, then no one is.

3. The judicial process and the sanctity of the law. Not only did the vigilantes take matters into their own hands and thereby deny Bob Marshall his fundamental rights of due process and trial by jury, but public officials and judicial officers from the statehouse in Salt Lake City to the courthouse in Carbon County conspired to undermine the legal system and prevent the accused from coming to trial. Newspapers in Price and elsewhere in the state expressed a common rationalization: the lynching, while unfortunate, merely expedited the administration of justice to a guilty party. The hallmark of a civilized society is rule by law, not justice. That Marshall may have been guilty—an assumption never proved—is irrelevant. The crime against J. Milton Burns was compounded by the crime against Robert Marshall, and both were overshadowed by the subsequent lawlessness within the law. As the Bible states: "[T]he law is good, if a man use it lawfully; ... the law is not made for a righteous man, but for the lawless and disobedient ... for murderers [and] manslayers."[10] The worst injustice was use of government means to perpetuate a wrong. What happened—the murders of Burns and Marshall—was tragic. What did not happen was the more tragic: the impediment to the

investigation and the fact that the lynchers were not brought to trial. At the conclusion of the grand jury, Fred Keller declared: "I am ashamed at the disgraceful mockery of law and order which has resulted in the affair right from the beginning, and the manner in which the state has been held up to ridicule."[11]

4. The moral fiber of a community. Hundreds of people witnessed the deed, but none were mindful enough of their civic responsibility to tell the truth under oath! The lynching was a miscarriage of justice not only because Bob Marshall was illegally executed but because so many good people behaved so badly by either directly abetting the subversion of law or by indirectly raising no voice in protest, thereby helping erect a wall of silence. Their commitment to protecting fellow community members transcended their commitment to protecting inalienable constitutional and legal rights. Most residents either condoned the lynching or acquiesced in it.[12] A thin line separates civility from savagery, and whenever normally decent, law-abiding people decline the obligations of citizenship and of conscience, commit injustice in the name of justice, and engage in lawless disorder in the pursuit of law and order, the line is crossed.

5. The integrity of the press. The two newspapers in Price, as well as papers in some other Utah communities, failed to denounce these acts. Upon the arrest of the alleged lynchers, the *Sun* [Price] proclaimed, "If these eleven men are in any danger of severe punishment this community is not awake to such a condition. And there is fast growing a feeling that it is about time that the matter was closed up." At the conclusion of the grand jury, the same paper ran a front-page editorial headlined: "All is well that ends well." The editor explained, "The general sentiment of the folks of Carbon county is that even [if these were] the actual perpetrators of the lynching there was little to be gained by carrying the matter to a point where they would be severely dealt with."[13] Instead of condemning the lynchers, exposing the manipulation of the system, and acting as the voice of community conscience, the press excused the lawlessness, the perversion of justice, and the community cover-up and thus was a party to the judicial travesty.

6. History. Therein lies the final victim. Those responsible for culling official government files in Salt Lake City and destroying legal

records in the Carbon County Courthouse are guilty of obstructing historical justice. We can never know the full story of the Marshall lynching or, more precisely, the role of state and local officials and private citizens in ensuring that justice would not be served.

There are those who would say that events of long ago, like the Marshall lynching, should be consigned to the dustbins of history as they have no relevance to our lives today. That was then, and this is now. But history is cumulative, for good and for ill. Mr. Jefferson's Declaration of Independence lives today, as do Lincoln's quest to preserve the Union and the achievements of the immigrants and pioneers who settled America. So, too, we today live with the legacy of slavery, of Japanese internment camps, and lynchings such as Robert Marshall's. Freedom comes from knowing the past, learning from the past, and using the lessons of the past to elevate the human condition.

What do we learn from the Marshall lynching? We learn that the circumstances of the affair and its aftermath are complex, but that the root cause is simple—racism. Bob Marshall was hanged primarily because he was an itinerant black man. The language used by those who were a party to this violence underscores that it was an act of racial aggression. And subsequent justice was denied for the same reason: the victim was black and without standing in the community.

We gather here today because Robert Marshall was lynched near Price and is buried in the city cemetery. However, we gather not to commemorate the lynching but rather to address its importance, and that is less about what happened in Price and Carbon County than about what was happening in Utah, the Intermountain West, and America itself. The Marshall incident was symptomatic of an ill—the racism that afflicted, and still afflicts, America. The lynching affords the occasion for us to meet in a ceremony of historical recognition and racial reconciliation.

Reconciliation cannot truly occur unless past injustices are fully acknowledged. The lynching is representative of past injustices; and acknowledging the miscarriage of justice and the subversion of the judicial process is an essential part of the healing process. Sometimes in trying to save face, we lose face; in trying to forget, we are unable to forget. We remember past unpleasantness because that is one way of making amends to past victims. It is a means whereby we as individuals and as communities can cleanse our historical souls. Admission is the first step toward reconciliation.

A second necessary requirement for reconciliation is the sincere extension of understanding and respect to others. Because Marshall died without family in Utah, some of the estimated 100–150 blacks in Carbon County at the time pooled their resources to pay his funeral expenses, but had no money for a marker. Today a broader group of friends, not of Bob Marshall but of tolerance, gather to dedicate a headstone—a tangible act of atonement that symbolically links the recognition of past tragedy with present-day efforts to promote racial harmony and hopes for a future marked by brotherhood and sisterhood. We cannot turn back the hands of time and do what should have been done in 1925. But we can, in our time, recognize the injustice that was done to Mr. Marshall and accord him the most basic of human dignities by marking his grave with a proper headstone. It is the least we can do. The best we can do is to strive to affect racial reconciliation and understanding.

As the African-American scholar Cornel West reminds us with the title of his 1993 book, *Race Matters*, race does matter, now as then. The cultural polarization that fueled the Marshall murder persists to a disturbing degree today. In recent months we have learned about racial incidents at a junior high in Davis County, Utah, at the Martinsville High School in Indiana, and at the University of Indiana; if racism continues to manifest itself in schools, supposed bastions of education and enlightenment, then we assuredly face nothing less than a national crisis. Thus President Bill Clinton's "Initiative on Race" is welcome; a national dialogue on the issues of race for the purpose of creating a more just and more united America is an admirable objective.[14] Personally I am not optimistic about its success. Local dialogue is more likely to be effective in promoting social understanding. We cannot mobilize nationally to combat racism unless individual communities, and communities within communities, act to recognize and confront the issues as we are doing here today.

But community dialogue will not be successful unless we as individuals make a personal commitment to keep the faith. Summarizing the history of the Marshall lynching, dedicating a headstone, and offering spiritual pronouncements will not get the job done. Others may not, indeed many do not, share our sense of historical justice, embrace our belief in the importance of racial healing today, or endorse our vision of tomorrow. We cannot help that. But we can learn from today's events and resolve to have conversations with our individual consciences, with our family and friends, and within our communities. Do not look to others to resolve the problem. Instead, embrace the challenge of the poet Robert Frost: "I bid you to the one man revolution—the only one that is coming."

So it is that we gather at the site of a historical tragedy, the Marshall lynching, on the date of another historical tragedy, the assassination of Dr. Martin Luther King, to address the racism that caused each tragic event. In front of the Lincoln Memorial in Washington, D.C., on August 28, 1963, Dr. King told us that he had a dream; he later told us we would not have to go far and that it would not take long to reach the goal. Today his dream remains vision, not a reality, and it is clear that we still have far to go and will not soon reach our goals.

In an essay entitled "Where Do We Go From Here?" published in April 1972, Dr. King said, "We must first recognize honestly where we are now." I would add that we cannot understand where we are unless we first recognize honestly where we have been. We cannot realistically envision the future without understanding the past. History is not a compendium of dates and names. It is a tool. We learn from history, we gain solace from it, we derive inspiration from and find meaning in it. We cannot undo the past, but we can recognize what has happened and why. To ignore past misdeeds is to seem to condone them, if only by silence; to acknowledge past misdeeds is to educate, and to educate is to prepare the way for a better tomorrow. Historical tragedies must not be forgotten but should be kept alive in our individual and collective memories. They are tangible reminders of what can never be allowed to happen again. Take with you, as an appropriate conclusion to our discussion of the Marshall lynching, the insightful, inspiring words from Maya Angelou's poem, "On the Pulse of Morning":

History, despite its wrenching pain,
Cannot be unlived, but if faced
With courage, need not be lived again.

Notes

1. Lynching records are admittedly incomplete, and thus statistics underestimate the number of actual victims. The finest compilation of source material is Norton H. Moses's *Lynching and Vigilantism in the United States: An Annotated Bibliography* (Westport, CT: Greenwood Press, 1997). For other sources, see my piece, "Ogden's 'Horrible Tragedy': The Lynching of George Segal," immediately preceding this article in the current anthology, as well as Ralph Ginzburg, ed., *100 Years of Lynchings* (New York: Lancer Books, 1962); Robert L. Zangrando, *The NAACP Crusade against Lynching, 1909-1950* (Philadelphia: Temple University Press, 1980); and Stewart E. Tolnay and E. M. Beck, *A Festival of Violence: An Analysis of Southern Lynchings, 1882-1930* (Urbana: University of Illinois Press, 1995).

2. For a summary of eleven known lynchings in Utah (and one in what is now Nevada), see my article, "Ogden's 'Horrible Tragedy,'" ibid. The commonly used tallies, all unquestionably low, for 1882-1903 are: Montana 85, Colorado 64, Wyoming 37, New Mexico 34, Arizona 28, Idaho 19, and Nevada 5. The usual number that is given for Utah is 7.

3. For the Harvey lynching, see my chapter, "Vengeance vs. the Law: The Lynching of Sam Joe Harvey in Salt Lake City," in Jessie L. Embry and Howard A. Christy, eds., *Community Development in the American West: Past and Present Nineteenth and Twentieth Century Frontiers*, Charles Redd Monographs in Western History, No. 15 (Provo, UT: Brigham Young University, 1985), 201-37. For other detailed studies, see my source notations in "Ogden's 'Horrible Tragedy,'" in this anthology, as well as Allan Kent Powell, "A History of Labor Union Activity in the Eastern Utah Coal Fields, 1900-1934" (Ph.D. dissertation, University of Utah, 1976), 280-87.

4. The account of the Marshall lynching and its aftermath is based upon the author's research for a monograph on the subject. The basic sources include reports of events contained in the two Price newspapers, the *Sun* and the *News-Advocate,* and in other newspapers published in the state, as well as regional and national dailies and the leading African-American papers; official government records; archival materials in local and national depositories; and oral interviews.

5. *The Sun,* June 19, 1925.

6. Ibid.

7. Ibid.

8. The five initial arrest warrants were issued for Charlie Atwood, barber; Joseph Golding, proprietor of Golding Brothers Vulcanizing

Works; George O'Neill, barber; Morgan King, Price city electrician; and Henry East, deputy sheriff of Castle Gate and special agent for the Utah Fuel Company. The subsequent six arrest warrants were for E. E. Jones, superintendent of Utah Fuel Company at Castle Gate; Warren Peacock, Price city marshal; Joseph Parmley, chief clerk of the Utah Fuel Company; John Daskalakis, night watchman for Utah Fuel; L. T. Davis, store manager for Utah Fuel; and Joseph Caldwell, Utah Fuel employee.

9. The *Salt Lake Telegram*, June 30, 1925, reported, "The prisoners have been the idols of the Carbon County citizens since they have been incarcerated in the county jail; according to sheriff's officers, citizens in sympathy with the alleged lynchers made pilgrimages from various sections of the county and brought foodstuffs, delicacies and candy to the prisoners during the past ten days."

10. 1 Timothy 1:8-9.

11. Quoted in the *Salt Lake Tribune* and the *Ogden Standard-Examiner*, August 19, 1925.

12. A photograph of Marshall hanging from the tree limb was displayed in some store windows and sold as postcards.

13. *The Sun*, June 26 and September 11, 1925.

14. On June 14, 1997, U.S. president Bill Clinton announced a program, "One America in the 21st Century: The President's Initiative On Race," to encourage discussions on racial issues as a means for reconciliation. He also appointed a seven-member advisory board chaired by the distinguished African-American historian John Hope Franklin to assist in promoting the initiative and its objectives.

9.

Red Lights in Zion

Salt Lake City's Stockade, 1908-11

John S. McCormick

The history of prostitution in the United States is not a frivolous subject, though it is often treated that way. In recent years a number of historians have given it the serious treatment it deserves. They have focused particularly on the midwestern and western United States, writing, for example, about late nineteenth- and early twentieth-century Saint Louis, Kansas, Helena, Nevada's Comstock, San Diego, and San Francisco.[1]

Thus far historians have had little to say about Utah. Yet the situation here was little different from the rest of the country. In Salt Lake City, as elsewhere, laws prohibiting prostitution were on the books. But in general, local officials saw them as politically expedient concessions to middle-class morality. Prostitution, it was felt, could not be eliminated. It could only be controlled. The best way to do that was to confine it to particular parts of town known as "red-light districts" where it could be watched and regulated. As Arthur Pratt, Salt Lake City police chief in 1895, said, "I think the best plan is to put them [prostitutes] in one locality as much as possible and keep them under surveillance. The evil cannot be suppressed, but it must be restrained and kept under strict police control. It is a more difficult problem to handle when the women are scattered out than when they are kept together."[2]

Red-light districts varied from place to place, ranging from a discreet house or two in or near small towns to block after bawdy block of Manhattan's "Tenderloin," Chicago's "Levee," Baltimore's "Block," San Francisco's "Barbary Coast," New Orleans's "Storyville," and San Diego's "Stingaree." In Salt Lake City an area near the central business district was well established within a generation of settlement. In the early twentieth century, Salt Lake, following the example of other cities, adopted a "compound" or "stockade" policy. Under the direction of the mayor and city council, the interior of a block on the city's west side near the railroad tracks was walled off, "cribs" and "parlor houses" were built within the enclosure, and prostitutes were allowed to work essentially unhindered within the confines of the block. They were arrested only when they plied their trade elsewhere. Though little known,[3] the history of the stockade is not only fascinating in itself but is a rich source of information about prostitution in general and is valuable in providing insight into the larger history of Salt Lake City, as a lens through which to view a range of issues.

The origin of Salt Lake's first red-light district is unknown. It is not clear whether it evolved gradually or whether city officials at some point unofficially established it. What is clear is that by the early 1870s it was located at what is now Regent Street, or what was originally, rather appropriately, named Commercial Street. The *Salt Lake Tribune* in 1903 referred to the area as a "resort of gamblers and fast women."[4] According to the *Deseret News* half a dozen years later, the occupants of Commercial Street were "the demi-monde, the male parasite, the dope fiend, the gambler, and the beggar."[5]

John Held's description is one of the most interesting. A native of Salt Lake who became a nationally known illustrator in the 1920s, Held said his information came from considerable first-hand experience:

> Within the street were saloons, cafes and parlor houses, with cribs that were rented nightly to the itinerate "Ladies of the Calling." Soliciting was taboo, so these ladies sat at the top of the stairs and called their invitation to "come on up, kid." The parlor houses allowed no such publicity. There was no outward display to gain entrants to a parlor house. One pushed an electric bell and was admitted by a uniformed maid or an attendant. The luxury of these houses always included a "Professor"

Dora B. Topham, a.k.a. "Belle London," was the madam of Ogden's "Electric Avenue." In 1908 she was asked by Salt Lake City mayor John Bransford and Councilman Martin Mulvey to build and operate a compound in Salt Lake called "the stockade," the intent being to contain prostitution within a single city block. The experiment lasted three years. *Utah State Historical Society, all rights reserved*

> at the piano. There was none of the brashness of the mechanical piano; those were heard in the saloons and shooting galleries of the street. The names of two of the madams are engraved on my memory, just as they were cut on the copper plates that Dad had made for printing the ladies' personal cards. In Dad's engraving shop an order for cards from the madams was always welcome. They demanded the finest and most expensive engraving, and the cards were of the finest stock, pure rag vellum. ... One of the madams called herself Miss Ada Wilson. Hers was a lavish house on Commercial Street. Another gave her name as Miss Helen Blazes. Her establishment catered to the big money, and in it only wine was served. In other houses, beer was the popular refreshment, at one dollar a bottle, served to the guests in small whiskey glasses.[6]

Of several dozen buildings on Commercial Street that were once houses of prostitution, three remained standing in 1982 at 165, 167, and 169. As elsewhere in the United States, leading citizens commonly owned the land and buildings in such districts.[7] In 1893, for example, Gustave S. Holmes constructed the buildings at 165 and 167 Regent Street. A well-known businessman, he owned the fashionable Knutsford Hotel which stood where the Broadway Center is now on Third South and State streets, and served as a director of the National Bank of the Republic, had extensive mining interests, and in 1909 was reportedly the fifth or sixth largest taxpayer in Salt Lake County.[8] "Female boarders," as the common euphemism went, occupied the upper floors of each building. In 1909, according to the *Deseret News,* the prostitutes at 167 Regent Street were "French women."[9] Legitimate businesses were located on the first floor of both buildings. A cigar factory, one of about a dozen in the city at the time, was originally in one building, and a printing establishment was in the other. The liquor business was always closely associated with prostitution, and in 1900 a saloon replaced the printers.[10]

The third building has a similar history. It was built in 1899 for Stephen Hays, a Salt Lake merchant, real estate speculator, and, like Holmes, a director of the National Bank of the Republic.[11] It was designed by prominent Utah architect Walter E. Ware, who also had to his credit the city's First Presbyterian Church, First Church of Christ Scientist, Saint Mark's Hospital, and the Westminster College gymnasium.[12] For several years, Martin E. Mulvey, a member of the city council from 1906 until 1912, operated a saloon on the building's first floor.[13] Upstairs was the so-called parlor house where prostitutes received their customers in a common parlor or sitting room. Though long vacant, its original design and layout remain unchanged in the 1980s: a large center room surrounded by 8- by-10-foot rooms, or "cribs," just large enough for a bed, washstand, and one or two chairs.

As in other American cities at the time, an unofficial licensing system existed in Salt Lake. The police would typically arrest the prostitutes and escort them to police court where they routinely paid a fine for being an "inmate" or a "keeper" of a "disorderly house." In many places the money derived in this way became an important revenue source so that the aim of anti-prostitution ordinances and periodic arrests was often not so much to suppress vice as to produce income for the city. In Wichita, Kansas, for example, the city treasurer reported at the end of August 1873 that the income from fining prostitutes was so large that general business taxes were unnecessary.[14]

The way the system operated in Salt Lake City varied from time to time. In 1886 police regularly arrested several dozen prostitutes, fined them a maximum of $50 each, gave them physical examinations, and released them. Between arrests, according to the *Salt Lake Herald,* the women were "allowed to go along without fear of molestation, as long as they did not ply their trade so openly and brazenly as to offend the public eye."[15] By 1908 the police kept track of names and addresses of madams and their houses. The madams, in turn, gave up-to-date lists of their "girls" to police. Every month each woman was expected to pay a "fine" of $10. The *Deseret News* examined the book with the list of prostitutes and found that during the summer of 1908 an average of 148 women paid fines each month. The nearly $1,500 collected monthly was part of the city's general fund.[16] In the mid-1910s city policy was to license brothels as "rooming houses" and require that prostitutes work only in them.

Around the turn of the century, various individuals and groups advocated that the city relocate the red-light district farther away from the business area. In 1903 the *Deseret News* reported, "It is now proposed to purge Commercial Street and move it to a less public district where their presence will not be a constant blot, defacing the business center and forcing itself upon public attention." In the view of the *News,* "The project is commendable. ... Whether it is practicable remains to be seen."[17] In another story the *News* quoted Nephi W. Clayton, a prominent businessman and Mormon church leader, as favoring the continuation of a restricted district but relocating it on the far west side of the city.[18] The *Tribune,* on the other hand, preferred to "open up a new street into the interior of some of the downtown blocks."[19] The general feeling was that prostitution could not be entirely eliminated, but that it had a harmful effect on downtown business. It offended and drove away potential customers and led to higher rents since space for legitimate business was scarce. In addition, it was pointed out, prostitution had begun to spread beyond the bounds of Commercial Street. Several brothels were operating on Main Street itself, another was located on Brigham Street, and the notorious Helen Blazes was reported to have opened a parlor house near the corner of Seventh South and Main streets. Formal involvement of Salt Lake City officials came in 1907 when police chief Thomas D. Pitt recommended in his annual report that a change be made. In his view the red-light district needed to be moved and a "stockade" established: "This question [of prostitution] is certainly a question hard to dispose of, and, being a necessary evil, there is only one way in which it can be successfully handled, which is as follows: Let the city set aside a piece of ground of sufficient size to accommodate several hundred of these prostitutes. Enclose same carefully with high fences; build cottages or houses to accommodate these inmates; charge them rent; license them and place them under control of the Police Department as to their safety and confinement, and to the Board of Health as to their cleanliness and sanitary conditions."[20] Mayor John Bransford and the Salt Lake City Council accepted Pitt's recommendation and in the spring of 1908 began to plan the stockade.

A prominent businessman, deeply involved in real estate and mining activities, Bransford was a member of the American Party, as were nine of the fifteen members of the council.[21] This explicitly anti-Mormon political party was founded in 1904 to oppose what it saw as the church's continued domination of political affairs in Utah.

In many ways a reincarnation of the Liberal Party which existed in Utah from 1870 to 1893, it was never successful state-wide, but it grew rapidly in Salt Lake City and between 1906 and 1912 dominated city government.[22] However, the stockade policy received support from council members of all parties, the clearest indication of which occurred when Chief Pitt changed his mind and refused to help implement the policy. Mayor Bransford fired him, and the city council supported the mayor by a vote of twelve to two.[23]

The council made no public announcement of their intention until December 1908 when the project was nearly completed and about to open. Bransford then held a press conference and frankly explained his own attitude toward prostitution and the way the stockade had come about. "With reference to the new district," he said, "the houses of which are in the process of construction, I wish to say that I am thoroughly in favor of it and that it was at my suggestion that the work was begun." Prostitution would always exist, he asserted. It could only be minimized under official supervision. Accordingly, he said, "I propose to take these women from the business section of the city and put them in a district which will be one of the best, if not the very best, regulated districts in the country."[24]

Having explained his approach to the problem, Bransford went on to outline the stockade's history. In the spring of 1908, he said, he and Councilman Martin E. Mulvey, with the approval of the rest of the council, met with Mrs. Dora B. Topham, perhaps Utah's most notorious madam. Better known as "Belle London," she operated much of the sex-for-hire business on Ogden's "Electric Avenue."[25] Bransford and Mulvey asked her to form a corporation, purchase land on Salt Lake's west side in the center of Block 64, Plat A, which was between 500 and 600 West and 100 and 200 South, and set up and operate a stockade. According to Bransford, "I told her that if she did as I wished, and followed out the directions, ... I would see to it that the women of the downtown district were removed to the new location."[26] London agreed. Later she explained: "I know, and you know, that prostitution has existed since the earliest ages, and if you are honest with yourselves, you will admit that it will continue to exist, no matter what may be said or done from the pulpit or through the exertions of women's clubs." She believed that she could "segregate the evil, that I could control it, and that I could decrease disease by an intelligent management, and while profiting financially myself, do some good."[27]

In the summer of 1908, Belle London formed the Citizen's Investment Company. During the next two months, it purchased land in the interior of Block 64 and commissioned architect Lewis D. Martin, a member of the city council, to draw up plans. Construction began in September 1908 and work was completed three months later.

On the evening of December 18, ten days after Mayor Bransford's press conference, city police told all prostitutes on Commercial Street and nearby Victoria Alley that they had until 4:00 a.m. the next morning to vacate the area. According to Councilman Mulvey, "The women of the town will not be told that they must reside within the shelter, but they will be given to understand that if they do not, things will be made unpleasant for them, while they will be given to understand that they will be allowed to live undisturbed within the stockade."[28] In other words, the women had three choices: they could leave town, they could go to jail, or they could go to the stockade. Evidently most of the women, perhaps one hundred in all, went to the stockade.

Salt Lake City newspapers, in particular the *Deseret News* and *Intermountain Republican,* provide important information about the stockade, as do the 1911 Sanborn Fire Insurance Maps. It consisted of about one hundred small brick and frame dwellings called "cribs," built in rows, or on "line." Hence the phrase, "Going down the line." Belle London rented these cribs to prostitutes for from $1 to $4 a day. The cribs were about 10 feet square, with a door and a window in front. Soliciting was usually carried out from the windows. According to the *News,* "... only two feet above the sidewalk, sits the painted denizen of the underworld calling to the passers between puffs on her cigarette."[29] A curtain or wooden partition divided the inside of the crib. In the front half were a chair or two and a combination bureau and washstand. In the rear half was a white enameled iron bed. There were also half a dozen larger buildings at the stockade. A "landlady" operated each of these "parlor houses," renting it from London for $175 a month. The half a dozen or so women in each house split their earnings with their landlady. In addition, a large structure at the end of one row of cribs served as a storehouse for beer and liquor, always an important part of the business. A brick wall partially enclosed the entire compound. Outside the stockade on 100 South, London built a two-story brick building as her office and residence. Its architect was Councilman Mulvey. There were three entrances to the stockade, one on 200 South and two on 100 South, with a guard at each one. Their job was to keep children out and to warn stockade occupants of periodic police raids that were conducted largely as a matter of form. To give warning, an elaborate alarm system was installed. The effectiveness of the system and the extent of cooperation between police and prostitutes are shown by the fact that in March 1910, 453 warrants were issued for the arrest of women in the stockade. Not one was served. The reason, the police officers in charge explained, was that each night when they went to the stockade to serve the warrants, they found it dark and deserted.[30]

Why was the stockade located at that particular place on the west side? No one wanted to be near it, Mayor Bransford explained, but it had to be somewhere. Those in charge of the project looked for an area where it would have as little negative effect as possible. According to Councilman Mulvey: "The location of the new district is the best which could possibly have been secured. There are railroad tracks on two sides of the district, and when the Western Pacific tracks are completed, the tracks will surround the district on three sides. The block is the dividing line between two school districts, and no children will be compelled to pass the place on their way to and from school. From the outside, nothing can be seen of the movements within, and the offensive sights which have greeted passers-by in the neighborhood of Commercial Street will be absent."[31]

There was a second reason why city officials chose this location for the stockade, Mulvey said: "We found that most of the better class of residents were leaving the area anyway, because of the influx of Italians and Greeks who live in that neighborhood."[32] The conclusion was that the "foreign element" had so destroyed the area that establishing prostitution there would not harm it any further and could even be rationalized as catering to the "immoral foreigners."

Mayor Bransford and Councilman Mulvey failed to mention one other fact that played a role in the selection of the site: Bransford owned property across the street. On it he built a large two-story building. Its upper floors served as a rooming house for prostitutes while the ground floor housed a variety of small Greek businesses, including originally a saloon, a barbershop, and a coffeehouse.[33]

During the nearly three years the stockade operated, reaction to it was mixed. On December 13, 1908, a few days before it opened, a group of fifty west side residents submitted a petition to the City Council endorsing the stockade policy. It would keep prostitution from spreading, they said, would not interfere with business nor "contaminate" residents of the area, and it would "add to the safety and respectability of that portion of the City known as W. Second South."[34] At the same time, other residents formed a West Side Citizens League and submitted contrary petitions to the council. They held mass meetings at which they protested the location and demanded prosecution of those responsible.[35] The league remained in existence for the life of the stockade. Of Salt Lake's five daily newspapers, the *Tribune* and the *Telegram* supported the stockade, while the *News,* the *Herald,* and the *Intermountain Republican* opposed it. In December 1908 and again in May 1910, the *News* ran a series of sensational articles purporting to expose conditions in the stockade. Mayor Bransford and a majority of the council continued to support the enterprise; but Bransford's own American Party opposed it, as did both the Republican and Democratic parties. Salt Lake City police chief Samuel Barlow supported the idea. County sheriff John C. Sharpe did not, and conducted occasional raids with dubious authority. Women in the stockade, and London herself, were periodically arrested, but charges were usually dismissed. Only a handful of women were ever convicted. When they were, they were given the usual choice of paying a fine, going to jail, or leaving town. The Salt Lake Ministerial Association periodically spoke out against the stockade, on one occasion characterizing it as "a system of brutality, debauchery ... that Rome never out did."[36] Mormon church leaders, in contrast, made no public statements about it.

On September 28, 1911, London made an unexpected announcement: "The stockade will be closed on Thursday and the same will not be opened again. So soon as I can arrange my business I shall advertize the property for sale."[37] Reaction was mixed. The *Telegram* published an editorial expressing regret at the stockade's closing. Prostitution was inevitable, the paper said, and closing the stockade would make regulation more difficult.[38] Chief Barlow agreed, saying that control of prostitution would become "infinitely more difficult."[39] The *News* and *Herald* were skeptical that London really intended to close the stockade permanently. As the *Herald* saw it, her intent was "merely to embarrass the good citizens of the community by turning a flood of scarlet women into the streets, thus creating a condition more horrible, if possible, than the stockade itself."[40] That accomplished, the paper predicted, the stockade would soon reopen. The *News* agreed, pointing out that "this turning loose of 300 prostitutes in Salt Lake where they will infiltrate the business district, flaunt themselves on the streets, and offend the public morals" would occur during the weekend of the Mormon church's general conference when the city would be filled with out-of-town visitors.[41]

According to the *Telegram* the decision to close the stockade was made at a meeting of London, Bransford, and Mulvey. London denied that, saying that the decision had been entirely her own. She had reached it, she said, because "there is a strong public sentiment in favor of such a course."[42] Bransford agreed, without being specific, that "opposition from various sources" led to the stockade's closing.[43]

The precise circumstances surrounding this development remain unclear. The important point, however, is that its demise brought no substantial changes. It did not mean the end of prostitution in Salt Lake City nor the end of segregated vice districts. Prostitution continued to exist, and everyone knew it; though, as before, the subject was excluded from polite conversation. According to newspaper reports, no more than a dozen women accepted the offer of the Women's League to "leave their lives of sin" and come to the Women's Rescue Station where jobs as maids and domestic servants would be found for them. The rest of the former occupants of the stockade either returned to Commercial Street or remained near west 200 South. Laws prohibiting prostitution remained on the books but were only selectively enforced. The continued goal of public officials was not the elimination of the vice but its regulation by de facto licensing and attempted confinement to certain areas. Commercial Street remained a red-light district until the late 1930s, as did the west end of 200 South until the late 1970s. Prostitution continued to be an integral part of the life of Salt Lake City.

Notes

1. John C. Burnham, "The Social Evil Ordinance: A Social Experiment in Nineteenth-Century St. Louis," *Missouri Historical Society Bulletin* 27 (April 1971): 203-17; Carol Leonard and Isidor Wallimann, "Prostitution and Changing Morality in the Frontier Cattle Towns of Kansas," *Kansas History* 2 (Spring 1979): 34-53; Elliott West, "Scarlet West: The Oldest Profession in the Trans-Mississippi West," *Montana, the Magazine of Western History* 31 (April 1981): 16-27; Paula Petrik, "Capitalists with Rooms: Prostitution in Helena, Montana, 1865-1900," *Montana, the Magazine of Western History* 31 (April 1981): 28-41; Marion Goldman, "Sexual Commerce on the Comstock Lode," *Nevada Historical Society Quarterly* 21 (Summer 1978): 98-129; Elizabeth C. MacPhail, "When the Red Lights Went Out in San Diego," *Journal of San Diego History* 20 (Spring 1974): 1-28; Neil Larry Shumsky, "Vice Responds to Reform: San Francisco, 1910-1914," *Journal of Urban History* 7 (November 1980): 31-47. Other valuable studies include David J. Pivar, "Cleansing the Nation: The War on Prostitution, 1917-1921," *Prologue* 12 (Spring 1980): 29-40; Pivar, *Purity Crusade* (Westport, CT: Greenwood Press, 1976); Mark Connelly, *The Response to Prostitution in the Progressive Era* (Chapel Hill: University of North Carolina Press, 1980); Robert E. Riegel, "Changing American Attitudes Toward Prostitution, 1800-1920," *Journal of the History of Ideas* 29 (July-September 1968): 437-52; and John C. Burnham, "The Progressive Era Revolution in American Attitudes Towards Sex," *Journal of American History* 59 (March 1973): 885-908.

2. *Salt Lake Tribune,* January 4, 1895, 8. For similar statements, see the comment of Frank B. Stephens, a member of the Salt Lake Police and Fire Commission, in the *Tribune,* February 8, 1896, 5; an editorial in the *Tribune,* February 9, 1896; and a note in *Truth* 1 (September 6, 1902): 6.

3. Reuben J. Snow's master's thesis, "The American Party in Utah: A Study of Political Struggles during the Early Years of Statehood" (University of Utah, 1964), deals with the stockade in its discussion of the American Party. There was no other study of any aspect of Utah prostitution at the time this article was written. Readers may now also want to

consult Jeffrey D. Nichols, "Prostitution and Polygamy: The Contest over Morality in Salt Lake City, 1847-1918," Ph.D. dissertation, University of Utah, 1998.

4. March 31, 1903, 11.

5. June 24, 1909, 2.

6. *The Most of John Held, Jr.* (Brattleboro, VT: Stephen Greene Press, 1972), 99-100.

7. See, for example, Goldman, "Sexual Commerce on the Comstock Lode," 106-108.

8. For biographical information on Holmes, see his obituary in the *Deseret News,* July 3, 1935, 3, and *Sketches of the Inter-Mountain States* (Salt Lake City: Salt Lake Tribune Publishing Co., 1909), 226-27.

9. June 24, 1909, 22.

10. *Insurance Maps, Salt Lake City, Utah* (New York: Sanborn-Perris Map Co., 1898), 2:103; *Salt Lake City Directory, 1894-95* (Salt Lake City: R. L. Polk and Co., Publishers, 1894-95), 824; *Salt Lake City Directory, 1898,* 844, 846, 893, 643; *Salt Lake City Directory, 1899,* 505; *Salt Lake City Directory, 1900,* 440, 512; *Salt Lake City Directory, 1901,* 926.

11. For biographical information on Hays, see his obituary in the *Deseret News,* January 29, 1927, 1, sec. 2, and the *Salt Lake Tribune,* January 30, 1927, 22, sec. 3.

12. For information on Ware, see the Architects File, Preservation Office, Utah State Historical Society, Salt Lake City.

13. *Salt Lake City Directory, 1900,* 517; *Salt Lake City Directory, 1901,* 926; For biographical information on Mulvey, see his obituary, *Salt Lake Tribune,* April 22, 1951.

14. Leonard and Wallimann, "Prostitution and Changing Morality in the Frontier Cattle Towns of Kansas," 44-45.

15. June 2, 1886, 4.

16. *Deseret News,* September 23, 1908, 1.

17. April 3, 1903, 4.

18. Ibid., 1.

19. March 31, 1903, 11.

20. *Message of the Mayor, with the Annual Report of the Officers of Salt Lake City, Utah, for the year 1907* (Salt Lake City, 1907), 371-75.

21. For a short biography of Bransford, see *Sketches of the Inter-Mountain States,* 97.

22. The only study of the American Party is Snow, "The American Party in Utah."

23. Salt Lake City, "Minutes of the Meeting of the City Council," December 7, 1908, 831; December 14, 1908, 856-58.

24. *Salt Lake Herald,* December 8, 1908, 1.

25. Little is known about London. For some fragments, see Lyle J. Barnes, "Ogden's Notorious 'Two-Bit Street,' 1870-1954" (Master's thesis, Utah State University, 1969), 19-20.

26. *Salt Lake Herald,* December 8, 1908, 1.

27. *Salt Lake Tribune,* September 28, 1911, 2.

28. *Salt Lake Herald,* December 10, 1908, 12.

29. May 18, 1909, 1.

30. *Salt Lake Times,* July 23, 1910, 1.

31. *Salt Lake Herald,* December 18, 1908, 2.

32. Ibid.

33. *Salt Lake City Directory, 1911,* 108, 153, 774, 987.

34. *Salt Lake Herald,* December 13, 1908, 7.

35. See, for example, Salt Lake City, "Minutes of the Meeting of the City Council," June 21, 1909, 448.

36. *Intermountain Republican,* December 15, 1908, 7.

37. *Salt Lake Tribune,* September 28, 1911, 1.

38. September 29, 1911, 4.

39. *Salt Lake Telegram,* September 28, 1911, 10.

40. September 29, 1911, 1.

41. September 28, 1911, 1.

42. *Salt Lake Tribune,* September 28, 1911, 1.

43. Ibid., 1.

10.

Cigarette Prohibition in Utah, 1921-23

John S. H. Smith

The early twentieth century was marked by profound and significant changes in the nature of American life. None had more significance than the will exerted by elements within the Progressive movement to eliminate "social evils."

The most colorful manifestation of this effort was the prohibition of alcohol. Similar but less well known was the companion legislation between 1896 and 1921 to ban public consumption of tobacco products.[1] During this time no fewer than fourteen states prohibited the sale of cigarettes entirely, the last of these laws remaining as late as 1927.[2]

Cigarette prohibition never attained the notoriety of liquor laws, partly because its advocates were ultimately unsuccessful in promoting it as a national policy and partly because the difficulties of enforcing anti-cigarette statutes usually brought about their repeal within one or two legislative sessions. But the temporary successes of the No-Tobacco League, the Clean Life Army of the Anti-Cigarette International League, the indefatigable Women's Christian Temperance Union, and allied bodies are not easily dismissed. These "evil weed" warriors were usually the same who opposed "demon rum," and only their overriding concern with liquor prevented them from pressing the anti-cigarette campaign with full vigor. By the time the liquor victory had been won, a new age had begun—one in which the defense of hard-won Prohibition diverted these activists from successfully promoting anti-tobacco laws. However, the will was there. Thundered Billy Sunday in his most exuberant mood: "Prohibition is won; now for tobacco."[3]

That challenge was taken up with particular enthusiasm in Utah where the cigarette suffered not only from its reputation as a habit of creatures of low morals and bringer of disease but also because it constituted a specific violation of the Word of Wisdom, the health code of the Church of Jesus Christ of Latter-day Saints (LDS).

The earliest tobacco legislation placed on Utah law books concerned itself with forbidding the sale of cigarettes and related products to minors. This 1896 law was never enforced with any degree of effectiveness, which later led organized opposition to the anti-cigarette legislation to question the viability of a much tougher law banning sale to and use by adults.

LDS church leaders, concerned with the moral and physical well being of their young people, periodically attacked both this laxity and the habit itself in semi-annual conference sermons and through articles in church publications. But their rhetorical attitudes were not acted upon with any vigor until the post-World War I period. In 1919 at a special meeting of the Social Advisory Committee of the LDS church, a suggestion was offered and adopted "that we use every effort, in kindness, to do away with cigarette smoking."[4] The committee, chaired at this point by Elder Stephen L. Richards, responded enthusiastically and would expend considerable energy over the next two years planning and executing an anti-tobacco campaign.

Meanwhile, outside the LDS church, a Utah chapter of the Indiana-based No-Tobacco League of America had been established a few months earlier with Fred L. W. Bennett as president.[5] This organization proceeded to publish its own local organ, the *No-Tobacco News,* to promote the idea of control and prohibition in Utah on a non-sectarian basis.[6]

Although to the community at large it appeared that little had happened other than observable propaganda from pulpit and prohibition groups, it would seem that, in fact, a great deal of well coordinated activity was underway. In March 1920 an LDS church

Edgar L. Newhouse, an executive with the American Smelting and Refining Company, was arrested in Salt Lake City in 1923 for smoking. The legislature's total ban on tobacco products had been enacted two years earlier, but such arrests proved to be the death knell for the statute. In this photograph (date unknown), notice the stogie in Newhouse's mouth. *Utah State Historical Society, all rights reserved*

publication editorialized, "We believe that the abolition of the entire tobacco business would be beneficial to the higher interests of the human race."[7] This was followed quickly by an announcement at the June church conference that the theme and slogan of the Mutual Improvement Associations, the church's youth groups, for the 1920-21 year would be: "We stand for the non-use and non-sale of tobacco."[8]

The Social Advisory Committee re-emphasized the church's interest through a newsletter sent out in July 1920. The publication contained specific recommendations for "coercive and persuasive" measures to be carried out by church committees on the local stake level in order to produce awareness of "the cigarette evil" and the possibilities of prohibitory legislation.[9]

Further indications that this committee may have been acting as a spearhead for promoting legislation is suggested by a letter dated November 19 from the general secretary of the Young Men's group to the Social Advisory Committee: "Dear Brethren: At the meeting of the General Board of the YMMIA held last Wednesday evening, the matter of following up our Slogan on the Tobacco Evil was considered, and it was recommended that your committee take measures to ascertain, how the members of the next Legislature stand on the three propositions, Prohibition of the Cigarette Smoking, Prohibition of Smoking in Public Places, and Prohibition of Advertising Tobacco in the State. This is to be done through the respective Stake Social Committees."[10]

The result was that on November 30, the newly renamed Conjoint Correlation and Social Advisory Committee's Tobacco Sub-Committee made several recommendations, including that "Stake Presidents [be asked] to interview legislators, their attitude [to be] obtained on an anti-cigarette law, a law forbidding smoking in certain public places, and a non-advertising of tobacco law insofar as state control is concerned." They also recommended that "a committee be appointed to formulate the bills covered by these points." It was decided by the committee that a suitable letter should be framed with the assistance of Elder Richards and sent to the chairmen of stake Social Committees "asking them to secure this information as tactfully as possible, and that in addition, the assistance and advice of the

Council of the Twelve be sought." It was also moved and passed that proper legal counsel be procured to draft suitable bills.[11]

Events began to move quickly following this meeting. On December 10 the Conjoint Committee could send out a letter notifying stakes that the week of January 17 to 23, 1921, was the time when "the Church will concentrate its energies in an anti-tobacco campaign." The letter concluded, "Stake and Ward Social Committees should marshall their forces and carefully plan for this effort. This should not be interpreted to mean undue publicity. The effectiveness of any strategy, particularly a campaign, often depends upon the extent to which it is a surprise."[12]

Surprise it was. Although the number of articles about tobacco in church publications had risen considerably and although national publications were examining the possibility of tobacco prohibition,[13] there appears to have been no airing of the subject as a political issue during the election campaign period of late 1920. As the *Salt Lake Tribune* noted later in a bitter editorial, it was not "a campaign issue in any sense, not withstanding what private pledges were, more or less secretly, extracted from candidates over the state."[14]

But the importance of the campaign was clearly reflected in the New Year's message from LDS church president Heber J. Grant which concentrated on the tobacco menace and the responsibility of Latter-day Saints to eschew this evil.[15] This lead was quickly reinforced. The same issue of the church's *Improvement Era* that published the New Year's message carried a lengthy article by University of Utah professor Frederick J. Pack proving tobacco harmful to human efficiency.[16] Other church magazines carried similar articles and instructions for special programs to be carried out by church organizations during the week beginning January 17. *The Relief Society Magazine* specifically noted that the church would be concentrating all its efforts on an anti-tobacco campaign during that week.[17] This included the Sunday schools of the church, with a program for January 23 that was to conclude with everyone standing to join the pledge, "We stand for the non-use and non-sale of tobacco."[18]

The coordinated details of the campaign were outlined in the church's *Young Woman's Journal*. It reported that the Young Men's organization would concentrate on scientific arguments for tobacco prohibition and subsequent law enforcement. The Young Women's organization was to concentrate on absorbing the "ideals of womanliness," with a suggested program that reduced the issues to handy slogans: "It makes men selfish in their disregard of woman's sense of refinement"; "Smoking fathers are likely to have smoking children"; and "It impairs physical strength and intellectual power." Other church organizations had similar programs in store.[19]

The *Deseret News* launched its drive for tobacco prohibition on January 15 with a lengthy article attributed to the Social Advisory Committee.[20] Two days later an item datelined Washington, D.C., alerted the city to the fact that Utah senator Reed Smoot had introduced a bill to prohibit cigarette use in government buildings.[21] The combination of Smoot's bill and the notable church activity on the subject prompted the Advertising Club of Salt Lake City to draw an obvious conclusion; it quickly issued a statement deploring any action to prohibit cigarettes or other tobacco products.[22] On the same day, the *News* editorialized in favor of cigarette prohibition, stating that the public was ready for such action. The following day it added a novel argument to the campaign by claiming that the cost of the habit could be more profitably used to feed the starving millions in the Near East and China.[23]

On January 19 the point of the campaign was revealed when Senate Bill 12 was introduced into Utah's upper house by Senator Edward Southwick.[24] As the public began to register its reaction, the support and opposition to the bill fell into two clearly defined groups. The proponents were the hierarchy and most of the membership of the LDS church and evangelical Christian groups.[25] The opponents consisted mainly of the gentile (non-Mormon) business community and a few concerned Latter-day Saints, joined by the *Salt Lake Tribune*, the *Salt Lake Telegram*, and the weekly *Citizen*. However, they suffered from lack of prior warning and a reluctance to believe that such "freak" legislation, as they called it, could stand any chance in the legislature. The *Tribune*, especially, felt that inevitable amendments would render the bill harmless.

One clergyman spoke out against the bill. The Reverend Elmer I. Goshen of the First Congregational Church called for common sense in the matter, stating that smoking was surely a personal matter and the enforcement of an anti-cigarette law would bring all the laws of the state into contempt.[26] Perhaps the most pertinent observation about the bill came from the *Citizen:* "A cigarette does not mean life, but to some it may mean liberty, and the pursuit of happiness."[27]

But to arguments that doctrines of "the dominant Church" were being introduced into legislation to the detriment of personal freedom, proponents like Senator Southwick had a ready answer. He rebutted that it was the duty of the minority to abide by majority legislation. He added that smokers, by nature of the vice, infringed on the rights of non-smokers.[28]

The bill's progress through the legislative process was unchecked by the rapidly growing opposition. Groups like the Printers' Union and the Veterans of Foreign Wars voiced their concern, but the bill encountered no serious obstacles. Amendments to provide for licensing and more effective enforcement of the old law concerning sale to minors were defeated in both the Senate and House. Petitions initiated by local tobacco sellers were overshadowed by the greater number of petitions submitted by the anti-cigarette forces.[29] There can be no doubt that some petitions carried more weight than others as, for example, that submitted by the board of the Deseret Sunday School Union representing 127,000 Sunday school supporters in the state of Utah.[30]

The prohibition forces generated a great deal of publicity. One advertisement, paid for by the young people's Mutual Improvement Associations of Salt Lake County, called anyone who smoked "defective—a physical, mental and moral defective. The cigarette smoker is not a degenerate because he smokes cigarettes. Quite often he is a cigarette smoker because he is a degenerate."[31]

Further fuel for the debate was contributed by the Women's Christian Temperance Union which charged the Red Cross with having corrupted the morals of young soldiers by shipping cigarettes to France during World War I. The program of the Red Cross was defended in a special resolution passed by Legion of Foreign Wars Post No. 2 of Salt Lake City.[32]

The controversy had no effect on the nature of Senate Bill 12. Having been favorably reported out of committee, it survived a few mild attempts at a licensing amendment and was finally passed by the

Senate 14 to 3, with one member absent. Clearly the selection of the Senate for the introduction of the bill had been prudent.[33]

The House presented more of a challenge to the bill in that a substantial number of its members were willing to accept some kind of tobacco licensing system. During a special order of business on February 24, an amendment to this effect deadlocked on a vote of 23 for and 23 against, one absent. When the bill itself was immediately put forward for a vote, the results were 33 to 13,[34] the moderates having switched to full support of the Southwick bill.

The closing debate was both bitter and revealing. Representative O. F. McShane of Beaver County, sponsor of the defeated licensing amendment, referred to LDS support and predicted the resurrection of the anti-Mormon American party.[35] Also of interest was a statement by Representative M. S. Winder of Salt Lake County, one of those who had switched his vote: "I regard as the most regrettable feature of this affair the lobbying done by a certain group of men who are members of my Church, whose methods I consider despicable in the extreme. However, since I have pledged myself to my constituency to vote for anti-tobacco legislation, I am compelled to vote aye on this question."[36]

The law was signed by Governor Charles R. Mabey on March 8 and took effect on June 7, 1921, accompanied by some approving words from the *Deseret News* but otherwise without fanfare. The *Citizen* voiced the attitude of many who wondered what was next when it asked sarcastically: "Shall we allow our people to go on being stimulated by demon caffeine, when a mere law can dash the cup of inebriety from their lips?"[37]

In July and August a few perfunctory arrests were made but, as predicted, the law was largely ignored. The various law enforcement agencies disclaimed responsibility. The city police suggested that state law should really be enforced by county sheriffs, and the county sheriffs excused themselves on the grounds of the pressure of other work. It was a transparent evasion of legal responsibilities but a good indication of how the police regarded the legislation. The new law created only minor problems for the attorney general who found himself deliberating whether Dr. R. Shiffman's Asthmador Cigarettes came under the ban (they did) and whether cartons of legal pipe tobacco displayed in shop windows contravened that section of the law that concerned advertising (they did not).[38]

For the next year and a half, the law was in essence simply ignored and seemingly forgotten apart from occasional sharp remarks in the *Deseret News*.[39] The indifference toward the anti-cigarette law was decried by President Grant who demanded that in the upcoming elections of 1922, the Latter-day Saints should vote for no candidate who would not declare his support for it. He added that the law should be "enforced, not repealed."[40] Following the elections that is exactly what happened. The new Salt Lake County sheriff, Benjamin R. Harries, a man openly backed by the prohibitionist-dominated Social Welfare League, began to enforce the law in earnest.[41]

Simultaneous with Sheriff Harries's announced intention to enforce the law, a move was put under way to repeal or amend it. The movement drew largely on the business community that lamented the loss of revenue and the adverse effect on tourism. The bill to amend was introduced by Senator Henry N. Standish of Salt Lake County on February 14, 1923, and referred to the Public Affairs Committee. After a brief closed-door session, the Standish bill, which was a simple licensing system, was returned with an adverse report. This prompted the *Salt Lake Telegram* to cry foul—claiming that the same influence which had promoted the Southwick law was still at work, as confirmed by other information in their possession, as well.[42]

All these charges paled into insignificance when four prominent Utah businessmen were arrested for smoking an after-dinner cigar in the Vienna Cafe in Salt Lake City. Ernest Bamberger, National Republican committeeman and former senatorial candidate; Edgar L. Newhouse, a director of the American Smelting and Refining Company; A. N. McKay, manager of the *Salt Lake Tribune*; and John C. Lynch, manager of the Salt Lake Ice Company, were marched down Main Street to the county jail to be booked.[43] Immediately the Utah law became subject to editorial comment throughout the nation, which was particularly annoying to the local business community then in the midst of a municipal promotion campaign. Newspapers as far afield as Boston and San Francisco had the opportunity to wax indignant over this infringement of personal liberty.[44]

Sheriff Harries's deputies did not stop with the arrest of those four businessmen. In the following days they scoured the lobbies of the Hotel Utah and the state capitol with considerable success. Utah restaurants blossomed with signs reading, "Look out for Mike and John," meaning deputy sheriffs Michael Mauss and John Harris, quickly two of the best known men in Salt Lake City.[45] Mauss, one deduces, tackled his job with the same enthusiasm he exhibited when he led a four-man, pro-prohibition team that submitted a petition to the House in 1921.[46]

Now the anti-prohibition forces had fodder for their own lobbying efforts. The obvious ridicule to which Utah was being subjected and the affronts to personal dignity involved in the arrests gave them better ammunition than before. The *Tribune* daily recounted how Utah had become the laughing stock of out-of-state newspaper opinion.[47] Suddenly on March 2, a *Deseret News* editorial signaled the partial capitulation of the prohibition group. After arguing defensively that the law would have worked if it had been vigorously enforced from the first, the editorial allowed that the substitute bill met with most of the requirements for protecting youth. It noted with approval that the advertising clause was even stronger and forbade the advertising of any tobacco, not just cigarettes. This extra safeguard, it was felt, would effectively protect against "alluring" advertisements for pipe and chewing tobacco.[48]

With the sudden notoriety showered on the state, the change in public temper must have been clear to all interested parties. The fact that the *News* commented favorably on substitute Senate Bill 184 on the day following its introduction was significant, especially since it was introduced by the same committee that had turned down Senator Standish's licensing bill. On March 3 the new bill was unanimously approved by the Senate and passed to the House where it received the prompt treatment of something everyone was eager to be done with. On its final reading it passed 34 to 20, one absent.[49] That same day, March 8, the bill received Governor Mabey's signature.

It can be argued that the demise of tobacco prohibition was the result of exactly the sort of public debate that the sponsors had sought to avoid at the time the law was being promoted in 1921. In combining private pressure with a massive and well-timed public campaign, the prohibitionist force had been able to persuade the 1921 legislature as to where its duty lay.[50] The opposition, caught by surprise, did not take the issue seriously enough to mount an effective counter-campaign. However, 1923 found the situation reversed, with a well-organized group centered around the *Tribune* and the *Telegram* and bolstered by the Chamber of Commerce and many businessmen. This, coupled with the publicity generated by the arrest of prominent citizens like Ernest Bamberger, created a movement and a cause capable of repeal.[51] Intensive and critical public examination of the issue at this stage did what the proponents had rightly feared would be the result if the opposition had been allowed ample warning in 1921.

Despite the support the Mormon church received from other churches, the cigarette prohibition movement in Utah was largely an LDS effort. In a sermon at general conference in April 1921, Elder Richard R. Lyman could say: "Mutual Improvement workers and others, in and out of the Church, have waged a rather intense campaign against the use of the cigarette in the state of Utah, and wherever else the Church of Jesus Christ of Latter-day Saints has members. ... I am proud to have helped to secure the following result: The State of Utah has passed a law prohibiting the sale or giving away of cigarettes or cigarette paper. This work has not been a matter of hysteria. With us it is not a mania. We have proceeded deliberately. We feel as if with mathematical certainty we have done something for the lasting benefit of the young people of our communities. ... If we have been too intense in this campaign, may we be forgiven."[52]

The whole affair could be dismissed as part of the season of excess in America in the 1920s, but much more than the right to legislate on moral questions was involved in the Utah case. In a more or less open exercise of its authority and influence, the Mormon church regenerated some old antagonisms in Utah politics.[53] It was no secret that the church wanted cigarettes outlawed. Throughout the campaign it stressed that society had an obligation, for example, to protect minors from the vice, and non-smokers from the tyranny of smokers in enclosed public places. Where the movement erred was in promoting an unrealistic law that went far beyond those goals.

From the standpoint of today's medical knowledge, there was considerable merit in the attack on tobacco. Had the LDS church confined itself to educational efforts, aimed at both members and non-members, its moral concern likely would have been well received. In an open society prohibition is a problematic violation of individual freedom. Unless carefully and specifically defined in terms of the actual—not idealistically presumed—prevailing moral and social climate, it has a built-in guarantee of failure—human nature.

Notes

1. While the reformers were against tobacco in general, it was the cigarette that bore the brunt of the attack. One interesting reason is suggested by Richard B. Tennant, *The American Cigarette Industry,* Yale Studies in Economics, vol. 1 (New Haven, 1950), 134: "The first users of cigarettes in this country were the immigrant populations of the large cities, and this alone was enough to make the xenophobic hinterland suspicious." Another reason was that pipes and cigars were somehow considered more manly and less harmful. The most probable reason for the cigarette's prohibition lay in the fact that it was an inexpensive habit and usable by women and young people.

2. Ibid., 134.

3. Robert K. Heiman, *Tobacco and Americans* (New York, 1960), 250.

4. Social Advisory Committee Minutes, June 2, 1919, archives, Historical Department, The Church of Jesus Christ of Latter-day Saints, Salt Lake City; hereafter cited as LDS archives.

5. *Improvement Era* 22 (May 1919): 645. Bennett had shown his interest in this subject in an article, "Selling Tobacco, Tea, and Coffee," *Improvement Era* 20 (July 1917): 797-99, in which he related how he as a recent convert to Mormonism found it inexplicable that Mormon merchants could sell these products in good conscience. He called for the women of the church to boycott such stores.

6. This magazine appears to have been published at least twice and was remarked upon approvingly by the church's *Improvement Era* 23 (December 1920): 181. Earlier, in volume 22 (September 1919), p. 1,016, the *Era* had quoted the following from the national *No-Tobacco Journal*: "How would you like to have women and girls not only smoking the poison-

ous, stinking stuff, but chewing, slubbering and spitting the stuff around while they are baking the pies and the cookies?"

7. *Improvement Era* 23 (March 1920): 451.

8. Ibid. 23 (August 1920): 875-81. In his address on the subject of tobacco, Elder Melvin J. Ballard noted the precedent of liquor legislation and urged a similar battle on behalf of tobacco.

9. Social Advisory Committee, Newsletter No. 3, July 12, 1920, LDS archives.

10. Social Advisory Committee Minutes, November 19, 1920.

11. Conjoint Correlation and Social Advisory Committee Minutes, November 30, 1920, LDS archives.

12. Ibid., December 10, 1920.

13. See, for example, L. Ames Brown, "Is a Tobacco Crusade Coming?" *Atlantic Monthly* (October 1920), 446-55.

14. *Salt Lake Tribune,* February 17, 1921, 6.

15. Printed in the *Improvement Era* 24 (January 1921): 259-62, with a similar message carried by *Liahona: The Elders' Journal* 18 (January 18, 1921): 275.

16. Frederick J. Pack, "How the Impending Tobacco Crusade Can Be Avoided," *Improvement Era* 24 (January 1921): 218-28. Dr. Pack was a leading church authority on the subject, with a number of publications to his credit. His *Tobacco and Human Efficiency* (Salt Lake City, 1917) was to be used as a standard text during the coming church education campaign. The thrust of his argument, indeed the general tenor of prohibitionist rhetoric, was that there existed a close identity between moral and physical fitness. Although smoking was damned as a hazard to health, most commentators seemed more concerned with its effect on spiritual and material growth. An article by Elder Richard R. Lyman, "The Cigarette Menace," *Improvement Era* 23 (December 1920): 144-45, handily lists nearly all the moralistic catch phrases of prohibitionist literature. "Boys who smoke cigarettes are like wormy apples. They drop off long before harvest time." "I consider cigarette smoking the greatest menace devastating humanity today because it is doing more than any other vice to deteriorate the race." "I consider any young man at school, in college, or in any professional school is seriously, indeed almost fatally handicapped by the habit of smoking." "One-half the truth has never been told about the evils of cigarette smoking. It blunts the whole moral nature and has an appalling effect upon the physical system as well. I have seen bright boys turned into dunces and straightforward, honest boys made into cowards by cigarette smoking." "The tobacco habit leads to vice, and is frequently

the forerunner of crime. This is because tobacco is a drug, and dulls the moral sense." These moralistic quotations will come as no surprise to those familiar with the dying years of the Progressive movement.

17. *Relief Society Magazine* 8 (January 1921): 43.

18. *Juvenile Instructor* 56 (January 21, 1921): 18.

19. *Young Woman's Journal* 32 (January 1921): 28-29. Before listing the planned activities, the magazine made a statement of authority: "This campaign has been inaugurated by the Correlation and Social Advisory Committee, with the approval of the First Presidency and General Authorities, and the General Boards of the Church."

20. *Deseret News*, January 15, 1921, 6.

21. Ibid., January 17, 1921, 7.

22. *Salt Lake Tribune*, January 18, 1921, 10.

23. *Deseret News*, January 19, 1921, 9.

24. The final version of the bill was substantially that proposed in State of Utah, *Laws of the State of Utah ... 1921* (Salt Lake City, 1921), chap. 145: "An act making it unlawful to sell cigarettes and cigarette papers, to advertise cigarettes and cigarette papers, to permit minors to smoke in certain places of business for any person to smoke in certain enclosed public places."

25. *Deseret News*, February 8, 1921, 7. The Salt Lake Ministerial Association formally endorsed the Southwick anti-cigarette bill and pledged full support.

26. *Salt Lake Tribune*, January 29, 1921, 22.

27. "Cigarettes as Symbol of Liberty," *Citizen*, January 29, 1921, 9.

28. *Deseret News*, February 3, 1921, 6. But in response to this self-righteousness, the *Citizen* of February 5, 1921, 9, carried a pointed satirical essay on a personal habit of Senator Southwick which they felt infringed on the sensitivities of others. "The solon who would suppress the offensive cigarette masticates the maddening chicle." Senator Southwick, it appeared, had not had the grace to remove his chewing gum during his tirade against the cigarette in the Senate chamber.

29. *Salt Lake Tribune*, February 5, 1921, 22.

30. State of Utah, Legislature, Senate, *Senate Journal,* 14th Sess., 1921, p. 275. Following the introduction of the Southwick bill, the Senate and House received petitions favoring the bill almost daily. Even a casual glance through either the House or Senate journals will register the fact that the bulk of these were from wards, stakes, and other Mormon church groups.

31. *Deseret News*, February 9, 1921, 10.

32. The Red Cross cigarette program was generally supposed to have been masterminded by the American Tobacco Company. See *Deseret News*, February 16, 1921, 2, and "Too Much Fire in the Smoke of the Tobacco Battle," *Citizen*, February 19, 1921, 4. The program called for citizens to raise funds to send cigarettes abroad. Spokesmen for the LDS church had spoken against this practice at the time. See The Church of Jesus Christ of Latter-day Saints, *Eighty-eighth Semi-annual Conference of the Church of Jesus Christ of Latter-day Saints* (Salt Lake City, 1917), 59.

33. *Senate Journal*, 14th Sess., 1921, pp. 199 and 275.

34. State of Utah, Legislature, House, *House Journal,* 14th Sess., 1921, pp. 378-80.

35. *Salt Lake Tribune*, February 25, 1921, 1.

36. *Ibid*., 12.

37. "Why Not a Special Session to Eradicate Sin?" *Citizen*, March 19, 1921, 3.

38. State of Utah, Attorney General, *Biennial Report of the Attorney General ... for the Period Ending November 30, 1922* (Salt Lake City, 1922), bound as no. 3 in State of Utah, *Public Documents, 1921-1922*, vol. 1.

39. *Deseret News*, November 18, 1921, 4. "Utah's anti-cigarette law, carefully prepared and triumphantly passed though it was, has had about as lax enforcement as any statute that was ever placed upon the books. ... the law has practically remained a dead letter ... dealers have violated it with scarcely a pretense of secrecy."

40. *Improvement Era* 25 (September 1922): 955.

41. "The Plunge into the Blue" *Citizen*, January 6, 1923, 3. Sheriff Harries's election was the subject of a court case in which sixty-eight plaintiffs charged that his election was with the connivance of the Ministerial Association and the LDS church.

42. *Salt Lake Telegram*, February 20, 1923, 1.

43. *Salt Lake Tribune*, February 21, 1923, 22.

44. "Utah's 'No Smoking' Signs," *Literary Digest*, March 24, 1923, 14-15.

45. *Salt Lake Tribune*, February 22, 1923, 20.

46. *House Journal,* 14th Sess., 1921, p. 223.

47. *Salt Lake Tribune*, February 25, 1923, 2.

48. *Deseret News*, March 2, 1923, 4.

49. *House Journal,* 15th Sess., 1923, p. 542.

50. *Improvement Era* 24 (April 1921): 575, printed a list of who had voted for and against the bill.

51. *Salt Lake Tribune*, February 25, 1923, 1. A mass meeting held in Salt Lake's Orpheum Theatre was a huge success. Every seat was taken and crowds waited outside. A delegation of 250 people was welcomed from Ogden.

52. *Ninety-first Annual Conference of the Church of Jesus Christ of Latter-day Saints* (Salt Lake City, 1921), 143-44.

53. *Citizen*, February 19, 1921, 7. A cleric threatened to create a new party to fight along religious lines. See also the *Tribune,* February 24, 1923, 1, where Rabbi Adolph Steiner of Temple B'nai Israel attacks "blue" laws as having replaced the fagot and the rack once used by those who joined church and state.

11.

Bootlegging in Zion

Making and Selling the "Good Stuff"

Helen Papanikolas

"The greatest blessing since Christ," the *Deseret News* called Prohibition on the evening before Utah went dry. "A splendid measure," Governor Simon Bamberger said before the law took effect on August 1, 1917. The *Salt Lake Tribune* assured its readers that "No Prohibition bill ever became law with a better chance of being enforced." But instead Prohibition introduced the speakeasy, the silver hip flask, and the padded suitcase. The era of the bootlegger was about to begin in Utah as it had in other dry states.[1]

While the legislature was still debating the fine points of implementing the statewide ban, opportunists were busily hoarding liquor in anticipation of its advent. An enterprising Marysvale, Utah, druggist accumulated 600 gallons, supposedly to be dispensed by physicians in Piute County which was already dry under a local option law. In Salt Lake City, legally wet until August 1, the *Tribune* reported that residents were "keeping ear and eye open to the call of the 'tangle foot' vendor and many a quart, gallon and barrel has been snugly stowed away for future reference."[2]

Until midnight of July 31, liquor dealers sold their inventories at any cost. People flocked to buy whatever alcohol was available, ignoring provisions in the law for stringent fines, jail, or both for possession of it. Throughout the state throngs celebrated the end of an era by toasting with liquor. The *News* called the revelry a night of debauchery. The *Kaysville Weekly Reflex* complained that if people were as careful in saving food for the war effort as they had been in the past few days "in conserving the supply of booze there would be a very large surplus this fall." In Richfield "they celebrated the death of John Barleycorn with lots of wetting and washing down." The *Tooele Transcript* decried "a night of disorder that was much to be regretted by all the sober citizens of Utah." The *Tribune* said, "Old Man Booze ... died game ... like the spirit of the west ... with his boots on ... [and with] wine, women and song." At midnight in Park City "a wild scene was enacted on Main Street, and empty barrels and empty ice cream freezers and everything else that would roll down the paved street were set to motion ... [with] drunken yells and loud hurrahs by the midnight revelers."[3]

By January 16, 1920, the 18th Amendment imposing nationwide Prohibition had been ratified by the states; to enforce it Congress passed the Volstead Act. The evangelist Billy Sunday said: "[T]he reign of tears is over. The slums will soon be a memory. We will turn our prisons into factories and our jails into storehouses and corncribs. ... Hell will be forever for rent."[4]

The naive belief that Prohibition would solve the country's social problems was unaffected by the weariness of the population over wartime shortages and sacrifices, the trauma of the worldwide influenza epidemic that killed more than a half-million Americans, and, most important, the cynicism accompanying the carnage of "the war to end all wars." In the revolt against old virtues, forbidden liquor became the symbol of a new sybaritism. For many, Prohibition was an assault on Constitutional liberties.

While ministers, politicians, editors, and the Women's Christian Temperance Union enjoyed a putative victory, speakeasies immediately proliferated in basements and walkups on shabby streets. A knock on a door was answered by the opening of a peephole through which suspicious eyes looked out waiting for the password. "Joe sent me" and the words *flivver, rumble seat, booze, flapper, jazz,* and *bootleg* (an

A downtown scene in Price, Utah, during Prohibition. Federal agents "especially feared going into Carbon County where scoffing at Prohibition was an amusement." In all, "agents uncovered 448 distilleries and 702 stills in Utah [1923-32] ... over 47,000 gallons of spirits, malt liquor, wine, and cider; and 332,000 gallons of mash." *Photo by G. L. Beam, Utah State Historical Society; all rights reserved*

old word for liquor smuggled in a tall boot) became indelible accretions to the American vocabulary.

Joining Americans in these illegal activities were recent immigrants from the Balkans, Mediterranean, and Asia who were free from the American-Puritan attitude toward alcohol. In moderation it was traditionally part of the ceremonial and communal festivities of their cultures. Especially among the Mediterranean people, drunkenness was censured. But the immigrants derided Prohibition as peculiar; their wine and *saké* were staples that accompanied meals. A popular Greek phonograph record of the era asked in perplexity, "Why is America dry?"[5]

The foreign language newspapers subsidized by the LDS church —such as the German *Beobachter* and Danish *Bikuben*—could only mirror its stance in favor of Prohibition, but the Japanese *Utah Nippo* predicted the impossibility of monitoring the law and deplored the evils that followed, in particular blindness that afflicted people who had turned to drinking wood alcohol. The Greek-language *To Fos* ("The Light") said: "By a large majority doctors consider alcoholic beverages useful for therapy, most priests as well as [other] knowledgeable people, want the abolition of this law that rather than saving a few drunkards from degeneracy and catastrophe, has sent a multitude to Hades by means of liquor sold for evil and unscrupulous gain." *To Fos* asserted that morphine and cocaine addiction had increased tenfold since Prohibition. "Statistics show the Volstead Act is harmful not beneficial," it said. In ethnic communities bootleggers were not outcasts unless they combined liquor pursuits with prostitution.[6] In contrast, the predominately Mormon communities of Sanpete County gave Prohibition "whole-hearted approval, but the law would be violated in Sanpete just as it was in areas with no tradition of abstention. Although possibly exaggerating, one former resident recalled that, 'Bootleggers almost had to wear badges so they wouldn't sell to each other.'"[7]

Yet in Utah, immigrants and the American-born never embroiled themselves in bootlegging to the extent of those in large cities where young thugs were taking their first steps toward becoming leading gangsters. Utah was only slightly touched by gangsterism, but residents, including mothers and children, became lawbreakers; bootlegging flourished, and shootings were regular events. Drinkers had not resigned themselves to becoming abstinent, even if it meant drinking flavoring extracts that contained as much as 85 percent alcohol (for lemon) and which, in spontaneous accommodation to their need, were being bottled in pints, quarts, and gallons.

Former governor J. Bracken Lee recalled Prohibition's debut: "Whiskey immediately began coming in from Rock Springs, Wyoming." Rolla West, a mayor of Price, Utah, during the Prohibition era, wrote: "One of the biggest and most astute politicians of the early 1920s discovered that White Mule, Panther wettings, moonshine, embalming fluid, Bootleg or even Bourbon whiskey, by throwing in a little burnt sugar and tobacco juice [for flavor and color], was available in Private distilleries in Wyoming."[8]

The making and selling of liquor had suddenly passed from commercial distilleries to the underground. Immigrants who used the grape residue from wine-making for their households' liqueurs, Americans who sporadically made a small amount of whiskey for their own consumption, and an eager number of novices who learned the easy rudiments of production set up stills in towns, cities, and isolated areas of the state. The Utah legislature was as busily engaged for the next sixteen years in formulating a complex system of rules to govern patent medicines and flavoring extracts (a favorite of young people and housewives), denatured wood alcohol, cider, vinegar, mincemeat, and communion wine ("to follow the commands of the Divine Master"), and the associated fines, imprisonment, and confiscation of liquor apparatus and other property, including automobiles used for its transportation.[9]

Although the phenomenal new liquor business was surreptitious, bootleggers became instantly known. Usually they carried on a legitimate business as camouflage. Others worked part time at it, especially after the stock market crash of 1929 and the economic depression that followed. They came from the professions, from business, and from labor: unsuccessful doctors and attorneys, successful druggists, sheepmen who left their wives to run camp stills during lambing and shearing, railroad workers, miners, shop owners, and particularly those who operated shoeshine stands.

Many American-born druggists actively engaged in bootlegging since medicinal liquor had always been dispensed by them. In their back rooms—as well as in poolhalls, candy stores, and hotels where "traveling men," the old-time drummers, congregated—liquor was readily available.

Shoeshine shop owners became middlemen through another long-established American custom. Until World War II doctors, attorneys, and businessmen were in the habit of having their shoes shined during their work day in the business district. According to one shop owner, while the polish was being applied his customers "asked us all the time where to get some whiskey."[10] In Utah, as in the nation, Greek immigrants had almost exclusively taken over shoeshine parlors, once the province of blacks and the Irish, and often owned chains of them. As boys of nine and older, they had been brought to the United States by *somatoempori* ("flesh merchants") and indentured in return for their highly inflated ship's passage.[11] In Salt Lake City and elsewhere in Utah, they served as conduits between their countrymen's bubbling stills and respected, insatiable citizens. As the shoeshine parlors became increasingly popular fronts, the once modestly dressed, obsequious shoe shiners began wearing monogrammed silk shirts and being chauffeured in Cadillacs. Several extended their activities into Canada. As the best man at a wedding in the mid-1920s, one of them brought cases of Canadian whiskey as a gift for the large reception; marriage celebrations in Greek immigrant days were communal.[12]

If illegal whiskey flavored the wedding festivities of immigrants, it also spiced the dancing parties of the American-born. Reports in the *Provo Herald* complained of "immoral dancing" and intoxication at Utah County locations throughout the early 1920s. L. R. Hebertson who managed the Geneva resort "admitted that drinking had been rampant at the resort the entire season. 'There hasn't been a dance at Geneva this summer,' he said, 'when Salt Lake bootleggers didn't come down, loaded with liquor, which was sold to the dancers and others.'" In Vivian Park, another resort in the Provo area, manager J. F. Carter told the *Herald* that "there had been 'drunkenness and improper dancing at the resort all summer.'"[13]

Middlemen did well, but those who sold their liquor directly did even better. In cellars, basements, and empty buildings, they set up stills with exhaust pipes leading to chimneys to disperse the potentially betraying fumes. Beyond, on farms and in half-hidden gulleys and washes where scrub oak and tall sagebrush screened chimneys on shacks, lucrative distillation progressed. Small canyons and mountain draws were ideal: Burch Creek in Weber County, the Mount Olympus area of Salt Lake County, Barney's Canyon north of West Jordan, the junction of Red Creek and the Strawberry River, Johnson's Pass in Tooele County, Twelve Mile Canyon in Sanpete County, the mouth of Provo Canyon, Crandall Canyon north of Castle Gate in Carbon County, and Nine Mile Canyon between Price and Duchesne. To allay suspicion, bootleggers in Nine Mile Canyon kept a few old ewes grazing outside the shacks, supplied by authentic sheepmen who left old and injured animals behind when they trailed their flocks into high country for summer grazing.

Fermenting grapes for wine and barley and hops for beer required no special equipment, but setting up a still depended on a coppersmith's craftsmanship to solder sheets of metal into round or box-shaped containers ranging from a few feet in circumference for individual needs to those of massive dimensions for wholesale business. The "feds," federal liquor agents, sought out coppersmiths as diligently as bootleggers did and used ruses to entrap them.[14] Fortunately most stills were made of copper. When a lead-coil still was discovered in Sanpete County, the information "presumably did more to discourage tippling ... than any number of sermons."[15]

Making whiskey was simple once the still was ready; recipes for mash became common property. Producers drove to farms and grain elevators to buy great amounts of rye, wheat, and corn "for fodder"; to stores for hundred-pound sacks of sugar "for putting up fruit"; and to wholesalers for pounds of yeast "to bake bread." To distill 100 gallons of whiskey a day, a plant in an empty four-story warehouse on 100 South and 400 West in Salt Lake City used a ton of sugar, sixty-five pounds of yeast, and a sack of rye every four days.[16] The industry utilized great quantities of raisins, molasses, and a lesser amount of fresh fruit. Tobacco juice or iodine gave the required amber color and "bite" to the whiskey.

Sugar whiskey made without fusel oil that had to be filtered over charcoal was of the highest quality. Grapes were often added to the grain and sugar for taste. The mash was then left to ferment in a crock for seventy-two hours, strained through cloth, and distilled. The first distillation was whiskey. The bootlegger periodically lighted matches to the distillation: the higher the alcohol content, the bluer the flame. When the flame turned yellow, more water than alcohol was being distilled.

"Raw" whiskey, also called "white lightning," was unaged and sold straight from the still.[17] Much cheaper than aged whiskey that was handled by trusted bootleggers who supplied men in business and the professions, it satisfied transients, cowboys, sheepherders, and the poor.

Capturing distillers was a monumental problem.[18] Following usual political practice, the state legislature had passed a Prohibition bill that entailed an enormous expenditure of time by a vast force of personnel but had not provided commensurate funds to pay officers. Governor Bamberger asked health officials and other state officers to take on Prohibition duties with their regular work, and he deputized others. Governor Charles R. Mabey continued the policy of giving commissions to people who traveled about the state and were interested in uncovering liquor violations.[19] Not enough honest agents were employed, however, to cope with stills sprouting up everywhere and the ceaseless demand of the public: "People went crazy over whiskey. Looking for it, getting it, hiding it."[20]

After the Utah bill became law, the liquor agents' first duty was to stop alcohol from being imported into the state, especially from Wyoming which was still legally wet. According to Rolla West: "Any unattached man who had enough money to make a down payment on a fast car and enough money to pay for his 'load' to the Wyoming supplier could get directions [from him] where he could sell his 'load' at a handsome profit. Full time or part time. Part time being preferr[ed] since a regular job was a good front."

When agents found the two-lane dirt roads that smugglers used between Utah and Wyoming, some shipments were thwarted and local alcohol production increased. In Carbon County "'Kentucky' moonshine whiskey makers who had never been as far east as Grand

Junction, Colo., arrived on the scene on very short notice. Back rooms and basements strategically situated became quietly active and hush-hush. ... [You could get it] anywhere in town."[21]

To transport alcohol, bootleggers used cars, stages, trains, horses, and, in one instance, an airplane. One man recalled: "I drove the old Bingham Stage Line starting in 1919. We'd regularly pick up two unmarked suitcases in Salt Lake—no name or tag on them—and deposit them outside Johnny Jimson's place in Bingham. This way no one could accuse us of knowing the suitcases were filled with Wyoming whiskey."[22]

An ingenious bootlegger in Wales, Sanpete County, loaded whiskey into the pack saddle of his trained horse and then turned the animal loose to make its way home over twenty miles of mountain road. The man returned home by car on the highway. Although the officers "knew he was bootlegging," when they stopped his car and searched it, they never found any liquor in it.[23]

Agents checked boxcars regularly. Because few officers were available to examine every freight train, they relied on rumors and informers. In Ogden agents discovered two boxcars filled with $100,000 of "fine liquor" and stood guard while curious onlookers came to the rail yards and milled about.[24]

Railroaders themselves made deliveries. Engineers, conductors, and brakemen traveled throughout Utah and into surrounding states and were able to buy their own whiskey, but railroad officials and men working in roundhouses and depots in division points had stationary jobs and depended on others for liquor. Two gallons in pint bottles could be fitted into a padded suitcase. Railroaders had few qualms about carrying their heavy luggage into YMCAs which had been built mainly to house railroad workers on their overnight runs.

A long-retired Union Pacific brakeman recalled that as an eighteen-year-old he was introduced to the Milford mayor by a conductor. In return for a room above the mayor's drugstore, freedom to read any magazine on the rack, and all the malted milks he wanted, he was recruited to bring Delmuse Whiskey at $20 a gallon from Caliente, Nevada: "It was a good deal. I had the experience. The year before I spent two months in Monterey, California, in an army program for young men to get a taste of army life. The sergeant was confined to the base. He was an alcoholic and he'd whipped all the Monterey police force. His nerves were a jangle and he had to rely on vanilla and lemon extract. Twice a week I went into Monterey for supplies and the sergeant gave me some money and a note to take to this guy in a certain poolhall. I'd go to the toilet and the guy would follow me. I'd give him the note and money and he'd give me the booze."[25]

Using the rails to transport alcohol was easiest and least subject to detection, but automobiles were still the most common means. When horses carried product through impassable draws and canyons, several trips had to be made to highways where cars awaited their arrival. In a dugout a half-mile off the Lincoln Highway in Tooele County, agents found a 200-gallon still, forty gallons of whiskey, and 1,500 gallons of mash. The bootleggers brought the liquor on horseback to the highway with a cedar tree dragging behind to erase their tracks.[26]

Whiskey runners spent a large portion of their time eluding and trying to outwit agents. In Salt Lake City a wholesaler rode streetcars to empty houses throughout the city to tend his stills. To cover his trail he stopped off at various corners and transferred to later streetcars. For alleviating the sag at the back of automobiles that gave officials the clue that contraband was being transported, bootleggers placed blocks under the rear springs. With loads of liquor in their cars, they drove slowly toward semaphore lights to prevent sloshing in the bottles that might arouse suspicion. Recalling this precaution, the owner of the Grand Central grocery chain, Maurice Warshaw, told a television audience about creeping toward an intersection light while looking apprehensively into the rearview mirror at a sheriff's car following him.[27]

Bootleggers quickly learned it was useless to hide bottles in toilet tanks or pour liquor down the sink, for agents became adept at removing the gooseneck pipe underneath and finding the incriminating residue. However, bootleggers were equally adept at devising new subterfuges to avoid detection.

An imaginative Sanpete County resident "kept his stocks in bed—with his wife ready to jump in and feign sickness should the law appear with a search warrant." Another Sanpete merchant transported his booze "in a specially designed rumble seat." In Summit County, when the newly elected Coalville sheriff set up road-blocks to stop Wyoming whiskey from coming in, Park City connoisseurs had to drink less desirable brew until the town mortician, J. E. "Jimmy" Flynn, drove a hearse to Kemmerer, Wyoming, with other town notables following, ostensibly to the site of a mine disaster. After filling the coffin with whiskey, the funeral cortege drove through the roadblock, reverently waved on, and into Park City.[28]

Heine Hernon, who since 1901 had owned a Park City saloon, converted it to a soda fountain the day after Prohibition went into effect ("There were seventeen saloons in Park City before that day and seventeen soda fountains the day after," residents said). But Hernon then installed a partition, suspended by weights, under a second-story window of his saloon. When raided, he rolled barrels of Wyoming whiskey against the partition, which lifted from the pressure, and the kegs came to rest in the attic of the adjacent one-story building. More common was the approach of the Metropol Hotel in Price that constructed removable baseboards behind which whiskey bottles could be safely hidden. In the Granger-Hunter area of Salt Lake County, farmers successfully hid bottles and small kegs in designated sections of irrigation ditches for nighttime retrieval by middlemen.

Copper tubing leading to storage containers was conclusive proof of illegal activities. After a diligent hunt in a combination restaurant and soft-drink parlor near 100 West 200 South in Salt Lake City, agents found a copper tube between the woodwork running from the first floor to the basement and back to a supply tank on the second floor.[29]

No one, of course, could explain away the presence of working stills; bootleggers frantically tried to dismantle them when agents swept through neighborhoods on raids. During the 1922 Carbon County coal strike, National Guard troops, while systematically searching mine company houses, saw a young South Slav girl running down the road, her long blond hair streaming. Sensing she was holding contraband, they ran after her. The girl threw a coil of copper tubing into a clump of bushes, climbed a tree outside Menotti's grocery store, and remained there until a wagon passed below. She jumped into it, hid, and escaped to her house. She then had her hair cut like a boy's and dyed black, and until the National Guard left the county she dressed in overalls.[30]

The potential profit to be made from illegal drinks was so tempting that individuals often took foolish risks. Frank Lyons built a 40-gallon still in his Provo home, less than two blocks from the courthouse; it was raided in 1921. A number of larger stills was discovered by agents in downtown Provo, the largest, destroyed by officials in 1928, "was capable of producing over 200 gallons of whiskey every 24 hours," with most of the product sold to Provoans in anticipation of the Christmas holiday season.[31]

The elements often helped federal agents. Counting on surprising the immigrant neighborhoods in Magna, agents began a raid after snowfall. Hearing the commotion and the cries, "They're coming!" a mill worker emptied several barrels of wine into the gutter in front of his house. The agents followed the red rivulets to his doorstep and arrested him.[32] To absorb fumes, a bootlegger in Price dug a trench and buried two parallel pipes that led from his basement still to an underground septic tank. While agents prowled the neighborhood after snow had fallen, they noticed two lines where the snow had melted, dug, and uncovered the pipes.[33]

Stills exploded frequently and neighborhood fires were a constant menace. Firemen repeatedly detected stored whiskey while extinguishing flames. A disastrous 1932 fire in Highland Boy destroyed the school, houses, and businesses a third of a mile on either side of Carr Fork, leaving 300 people homeless.[34] Above the roar of the fire, stills blew up, one after the other.

Agents were also aided by hunters and boys. During every pheasant, duck, and deer season, hunters came upon hidden stills and informed police. Playing football on 400 South between 1000 and 1100 East in Salt Lake City, boys discovered a 10-gallon keg of whiskey buried in a hillside to age. They carried the prize a distance and then called police. One of the largest distilleries in the West was found by boys playing near an old westside warehouse, supposedly used to store furs and hides. When the boys saw two men enter the building, they notified the police. Nine 500-gallon vats and twelve 55-gallon barrels filled with mash were found. Inadvertently a small boy betrayed his bootlegging grandfather when several agents appeared at a farmhouse in American Fork and asked him if his grandfather made whiskey. The boy answered that he did and led them to the barn, then watched in horror as they demolished the still and barrels with axes.[35]

Liquor agents were almost always Protestants or Mormons and reflected the anti-immigrant prejudice of the era that culminated in the 1924-25 Ku Klux Klan campaigns.[36] As immigrants from the Mediterranean and the Balkans began marrying American women, hostility against them grew. In retribution liquor agents often tried to fake bootlegging charges. A young Greek in Magna who eloped with a Mormon woman to Farmington and returned to find crosses burning in front of his cafe and her parents' house was continually on the alert for approaching agents. By banging on the wall, the other side of which was a Greek coffeehouse, he gave the signal to his countrymen to rush over to prevent agents from planting a bottle of whiskey and then arresting him.[37]

Ignorant of, or indifferent to, immigrant cultures, agents were often harsher than necessary. They trivialized the need of wine for communion, for the common cup from which a bride and groom must drink, and for toasting the health of a newly baptized infant. In Helper the sheriff entered a below-the-sidewalk restaurant to arrest the owner for a liquor violation. The proprietor was eating and lifted his palm in a staying motion. He had come from the island of Crete, from a pocket of land where a large population of Turks lived, and had acquired their Moslem tenet of not rising from the table until a meal was completed. Fuming, the sheriff waited, taking this religious custom as a sign of contempt.[38]

The Price newspaper resented the attention focused on illegal operations in Carbon County. It accused federal Prohibition director Mathonihah Thomas of not having "the nerve to tackle the booze problem in Salt Lake City" where "all a man has to do to get booze most anywhere ... is pay the price.... The trouble is that if the Democratic office holder undertook to clean up Salt Lake he would run into too many of his friends." Accusations that law enforcement protected some violators became common during Prohibition. The city marshal of Milford in 1928 was reported by federal official George A. Goates to be protecting his sister, "the chief offender" in his jurisdiction. State legislator Lorenzo Argyle complained to Governor Bamberger that law officers in Spanish Fork were turning a blind eye toward "Bootlegging, Drinking and Carousing."[39]

Caught with alcohol in one's possession was not the only hazard in Prohibition days. Lacking reputably made liquor, drinkers consumed canned heat and wood alcohol that could cause blindness. Some learned how to neutralize the methane in denatured alcohol bought at service stations. Lead salts from car radiators—used by unscrupulous still operators as cheapjack condensers instead of copper tubing—could poison drinkers. Another danger was posed by caves and other poorly ventilated hideouts that nearly asphyxiated bootleggers and agents alike.[40] Proper storage presented problems that sometimes required sophisticated knowledge. J. Bracken Lee recalled: "Someone gave me a gallon of moonshine and I went to the druggist and asked him if he had any empty wooden casks. He gave me a small, empty formaldehyde barrel and told me to wash it out several times with boiling water. Later that day two friends came by and I offered them a drink. I saw them the next day downtown. Their mouths were blistered. I found out you can't ever get formaldehyde out of wood."[41]

Bootleggers could be as clean and as honest or as unclean and dishonest as they wanted to be. Agents raiding a grocery store in Salt Lake City seized forty-four gallons of wine made in a dirty 50-gallon barrel: "The mash was a conglomeration that respectable pigs would have scorned—being composed of decomposed grapes, apples and other refuse from the store."[42] Drinkers, therefore, deemed it important to know their suppliers, and they searched until they found "decent liquor that wouldn't make a person sick." The two most frequently mentioned as "men you could trust" and who "made good stuff" were John Diamanti of Helper and Jimmy McG— of Salt Lake City who made whiskey in his 1st Avenue house and sold most of it in the Moxum Hotel; the guests were mainly permanent residents, stockmen, and traveling salesmen.

People needed suppliers, and bootleggers needed attorneys to extricate them from the law. It was a period of halcyon days for many lawyers who otherwise would have made a modest or substandard living. Word-of-mouth elevated several attorneys, among them Samuel A. King and R. Verne McCullough, the latter also well known as a businessman. More so than American bootleggers, immigrants required effective attorneys. Judges used their discretion in handing down sentences and were especially severe toward the foreign-born who flouted the nation's laws. Meanwhile local juries so often refused to convict their fellow citizens of possession that the Utah attorney general's office complained.[43]

Women, too, often faced trial for bootlegging. Among nine Carbon County residents caught in a raid was a Helper woman of "old" American stock who owned a "brewery of magnificent proportions." Her operation included a complete bottling plant. Women who owned boardinghouses were under constant scrutiny. The French owner of the Allies Hotel in Price was arrested twice in one week. In Bingham a woman was charged with making whiskey in the old Boston Con Hotel, and in Salt Lake City a mother of nine children pleaded guilty to possession. Another Salt Lake City mother kept a still going in the basement of her house while her husband was serving an eighteen-month term at McNeil Island for bootlegging.[44]

Many mothers turned to the business during the Depression years when federal aid was unavailable to help their indigent families. For others it was simply a wondrous opportunity to make money while women following the cultural patterns of their native countries. To have on hand the obligatory liqueur for guests, Greek women in Magna and elsewhere made *ouzo* from *chipoura,* the crushed grape skins left after the juice was extricated for wine. To make *mastiha,* the licorice-tasting liqueur, they combined *ouzo* with anise.[45] Italians used the crushed grape skins to make a second-grade, and therefore inferior, wine called *grappa*.

Bootlegging was commonly a family business. Children often left play and chores to deliver liquor: "I was fourteen years old and drove my dad's fancy Hupmobile to N—'s goat ranch in Butterfield Canyon. I'd load up and drive back to Magna. I'll never forget the time the feds raided our house and one of them pushed my mother out of the way. She bit his hand so hard, he had to [have] it bandaged up." In Spring Glen, Carbon County, "the appearance of an 8 year old boy on the Highway in the heat of the day garbed in a coat of manly proportions ... aroused the curiosity of agents, who, upon investigation, discovered two pints of whisky in the pockets of the coat."[46]

Agents overlooked the search and seizure restrictions of Prohibition law in their zeal to catch violators. In Salt Lake City, Sheriff Benjamin R. Harries wounded a fleeing confectioner who was fearful that invading officers were going to assault him. *To Fos* denounced the shooting of this "American citizen, of very short stature, quiet, a philanthropist, and well known in his business neighborhood." Fearful of agents, a seventy-eight-year-old man fell head first down an elevator shaft. A widow and her children who had moved into an alley house behind the Holy Trinity Greek Orthodox Church in Salt Lake City were terrorized by agents when, failing to find liquor in a neighbor's house, burst into her kitchen looking for contraband.[47]

Unconcerned about formalities, the Utah Supreme Court upheld the conviction of a Uintah County man who had contested his arrest without a signed warrant. In a unanimous decision the court held that the 4th and 5th Amendments of the U.S. Constitution on unreasonable search and seizure did not apply to state governments and state courts. The court did rule in favor of Bertha Jackson who brought suit against the Salt Lake County sheriff's office for "vigorously" searching her house, with a warrant, and causing her "severe nervous and emotional stress."[48]

Legal maneuvers, speakeasies, rum-running, fashionable cocktail parties, gang wars, and hypocrisy fused into the milieu of the dry years. From its inception Prohibition enforcement was a delusion. Although the liquor traffic was intense in almost every part of the state, the *Salt Lake Tribune* carried the caption "Utah Bone Dry, According to the Official Records." The reality was that during 1923-32, agents uncovered 448 distilleries and 702 stills in Utah along with thousands of pieces of distilling apparatus; over 47,000 gallons of spirits, malt liquor, wine, and cider; and 332,000 gallons of mash. Much more went undetected.[49]

While agents struggled to control the volume of domestic product, other law enforcement officials tried to stem the tide arriving from foreign countries. Representatives of the federal government and Canada attempted the impossible task of shutting off the supply of alcohol and drugs across the border. Trucks from throughout the country met Canadian ships and left with disguised loads. A Magna, Utah, family regularly drove a truck with a half load of lumber to the

Pacific Coast, set cases of whiskey and rum under the planks, and returned to Utah. Liquor brought by British ships to within twelve miles of shore was transported to lighter, faster craft to elude the United States Coast Guard, a small patrol that could not conduct adequate surveillance. Arrests were relatively few; the capture of a British rum schooner with the purported king of smugglers aboard made front-page news.[50]

While gang wars escalated in the East and Midwest—the 1929 Valentine's Day Massacre of seven O'Bannions by Al Capone's men was a grisly, ingenious performance—violence also erupted periodically in Utah. In Eureka near the Mammoth Mine, a bootlegger shot and killed a member of the pioneer McIntyre family. Halfway between West Jordan and Bingham Canyon in a barn where a still worked, a shooting left one of the bootleggers dead. Rivals shot at each other on a goat ranch near Lark, and in Lakepoint two still operators were killed over alcohol and slot-machine competition. Seventeen miles south of Price, near Mounds in Emery County, an agent shot and paralyzed a bootlegger who was protecting his still with a shotgun. The man died soon after. Two Salt Lake City revenue officers were wounded in Silver City when they discovered that the town's water line had been tapped, and then followed the pipe to an "effectively concealed" dugout. The three young distillers refused to come out of the dugout, thinking the officers were hijackers. In the midst of the confrontation, the boiler exploded and one of the young men came out shooting.[51]

The illegality of liquor and the determination of drinkers to get it by any means led to unprecedented corruption. Raids into neighborhoods were often shams: bribed officials telephoned still operators to give them time to dispose of their inventory. An area of West Jordan was under the protection of the sheriff and deputies were ordered not to enter it. In Summit County a deputy sheriff was indicted for allegedly furnishing a man with a still and conspiring with him to manufacture. Sheriff Amasa M. Hammon was charged with taking $100 from "Fats" Davis, owner of an Ogden speakeasy. This occurred in the same week that beer was again being legally sold in Wyoming and long lines of automobiles were crossing over the border from Utah as regular Sunday excursions.[52]

A federal grand jury in 1928 indicted deputy sheriffs, federal officers, "and reputed higher ups in [Salt Lake City] bootleg circles." In Clear Creek, Carbon County, the constable was arrested for serving "white mule" in his boardinghouse; and in Helper the mayor and all the councilmen except one asked for bribes from hotels, poolhalls, and candy stores in return for insurance against arrest. The owners notified Henry Ruggeri, the county attorney, who stripped the officials of their positions. In Ogden the mayor, a commissioner, the chief of police, a police captain, a patrolman, the sheriff, and two deputy sheriffs were arraigned in court, indicted for collaboration with an alcohol producer. The local Lions' Club passed a resolution in support of the officials.[53]

Citizens had a collective contempt for elected officials and, especially, for agents. Besides their solicitation of bribes, agents were often guilty of drunkenness and disorderly conduct. In Carbon County an agent was charged with being "too drunk to call the 'Black Mafia'" after making an arrest.[54] The Salt Lake City police chief suspended a patrolman caught in a speakeasy raid for intoxication.[55] A Salt Lake City federal agent with "a high-handed manner" was arrested in Helper for criminal assault on a woman he had kept captive for a period of five hours: "[He] held her nose and tried to force liquor down her throat after which he attacked her. [In his car were] two revolvers, a rifle, several pint flasks filled with moonshine, and an empty small keg."[56]

Agents carried on vendettas against bootleggers who tried to avoid paying bribes. Some kept confiscated liquor and openly defied the law: "The fed telephoned my dad to give him time to hide his whiskey, then walked in with his men, gave a quick look around, and after his men went out, motioned my father to get him a stiff drink."[57]

Bootleggers became bolder in their retaliation. A percentage of each fine was commonly paid to officers, on conviction—a policy that was particularly offensive to alcohol producers and a reason Helper dry agents became "unpopular with the foreign element." Producers in Bingham Canyon warned "Sheriff Corless ... not to destroy booze ... or [he] may come in contact with T.N.T." On Salt Lake City's west side, bootleggers fought with two undercover agents, leaving one with a battered face.[58]

On November 15, 1927, the *Salt Lake Tribune* reported: "War between police and bootleggers after nightfall, at the present time, has developed into more or less of a one-sided conflict, in which the rum dealers have the odds." Two years later the newspaper reported federal agents had been threatened with bodily harm so that precautionary measures had become necessary. Rumors of a similar nature surfaced throughout the era: "Members of a bootleg ring are believed to be planning a swift revenge, according to officers. Reports intimate that a group of racketeers had been brought to Salt Lake from a distant city to assist with the work."[59]

Agents especially feared going into Carbon County where scoffing at Prohibition was an amusement: a Helper baseball team was called the Bootleggers. The county had been described as "wide open" since early settlement days when cattle were rustled from southern Utah and northern Arizona through Nine Mile Canyon. The livestock were taken to Myton and Vernal for summer range and then on to Union Pacific railheads in Wyoming: "This brought into the county a bunch of hard riding fast shooting men who generally had money.... In addition these rustlers required liquor and entertainment and from somewhere these 'wide open' items always seemed available."[60] Carbon's wide-openness was accepted by almost everyone, even though W. F. Olsen, mayor of Price, angrily replied to a derogatory *Deseret News* editorial with a letter to the editor: "Our two marshalls [sic] are good Latter-day Saints even in keeping strictly the word of wisdom."[61]

Complaints about laxness in Carbon County did not abate. Letters to federal officials, the United States attorney general, and Governor George H. Dern resulted in a vast raid. Agents met in Scofield at 3:30 on an August afternoon in 1928 and spread out to Colton, Helper, Price, the surrounding coal camps, and Eureka in the Tintic Mining District. They succeeded in making numerous arrests.[62]

Other raids followed, and agents smiled for newspaper photographers in front of a pile of stills. But editors and readers were scornful of these raids: "Frequent accounts appear of the destruction of confiscated liquor, in which a great ceremony is made of the event. It is quite the fad to delegate the actual destruction to some dry organization, under the direction of the proper officers of the law. A public place in the streets is selected, due publicity given in advance and then the 'Roman holiday.' The assembled crowd looks on with varied audible expressions."[63]

The scorn was fueled constantly by an outward display of hypocrisy by lawmakers. George Zeese accompanied Carl R. Marcusen of Price, state Republican chairman and a candidate for governor, to the August 16, 1928, state GOP convention in Ogden. He said that "Whiskey was everywhere in the convention hall. What went on! It was almost impossible to believe. A big drinking party."[64] On another occasion when a well-known lobbyist dropped one of two quart bottles of pre-Prohibition Scotch whisky onto the marble floor of the Utah State Capitol building, he explained, before hurrying on, that it was medicine for the sick wife of a legislator.[65]

The "Era of the Big Lie," a writer characterized the period: "The drys lied to make prohibition look good. ... the wets lied to make it look bad; the government officials lied to make themselves look good and to frighten Congress into giving them more money to spend, and the politicians lied through force of habit."[66]

The foisting of Prohibition on the nation was catastrophic. The failure of the Volstead Act and the misery of the Depression brought a clamor for repeal of the 18th Amendment. Organizations sent resolutions to Governor Blood asking for a special session of the legislature to consider repeal. Yet Prohibitionists fought with valiant, impotent fervor to keep the amendment. At a mass meeting in the Salt Lake Tabernacle to rally against repeal, speakers pleaded for more money and men for enforcement. "Death is preferable to the iron collar of liquor," a Methodist minister proclaimed.[67]

Prohibition was repealed by the 21st Amendment that required ratification by thirty-six states. Utah won over Maine's bid to become the thirty-sixth state when Governor Blood's quick action in convening the legislature resulted in the overturn.[68] Yet Utah itself remained a dry state until 3.2 beer became legal in January 1934, and liquor continued to be bootlegged until the present, state-run monopoly was established in 1935. In the interim Wyoming whiskey from Kemmerer selling for $1.25 was a drinker's "good stuff."

Notes

1. *Deseret News,* July 31, 1917; *Salt Lake Tribune,* February 3, 1917. Studies of Prohibition in Utah include Brent Grant Thompson, "Utah's Struggle for Prohibition, 1908-1917" (M.A. thesis, University of Utah, 1979), and Larry Earl Nelson, "Problems of Prohibition Enforcement in Utah, 1917-1933" (M.S. thesis, University of Utah, 1970).

2. *Salt Lake Tribune,* July 1, 20, 1917.

3. *Deseret News,* August 1, 1917; *Kaysville Weekly Reflex,* August 2, 1917; *Richfield Reaper,* August 4, 1917; *Tooele Transcript,* August 3, 1917; *Salt Lake Tribune,* August 1, 1917; *Park Record,* August 3, 1917. For a personal account, see John Farnsworth Lund, "The Night before Doomsday," *Utah Historical Quarterly* 51 (1983), reprinted in this volume.

4. Larry Engelmann, *Intemperance: The Lost War against Liquor* (New York: Free Press, 1979), xi.

5. Mentioned in "Tales of Skill and Loss in Greek-American Recorded Humor," paper by Steve Frangos, Department of Anthropology, Indiana University.

6. *Utah Nippo* (Salt Lake City), February 8, 1919, January 10, 1923; *To Fos* (Salt Lake City), July 5, 1923. The author is indebted to Rev. K. Okuno, Nicherin Buddhist Temple, for researching back issues of *Utah Nippo.*

7. John S. H. Smith, "Localized Aspects of the Urban-Rural Conflict in the United States: Sanpete County, Utah, 1919-1929" (M.A. thesis, University of Utah, 1972), 69.

8. Interview with J. Bracken Lee, June 16, 1983; Rolla West Ms., 23, American West Center, University of Utah.

9. Nelson, "Problems of Prohibition Enforcement," 49, 104-16.

10. A Greek bootlegger of the era who, as many did, asked not to be identified.

11. Theodore Saloutos, *The Greeks in the United States* (Cambridge, MA: Harvard University Press, 1964), 48-56, gives a graphic picture of this dark period.

12. The author's husband remembers this scene at the wedding of his uncle in the mid-1920s.

13. Gary C. Kunz, "Provo in the Jazz Age," *Sunstone* 9 (January-February 1984): 34.

14. *Salt Lake Tribune,* March 8, 1929.

15. Smith, "Localized Aspects of the Urban-Rural Conflict," 69.

16. *Salt Lake Tribune,* November 15, 1930.

17. Raymond Sokolov, "White Lightning," *Natural History* 89 (1980): 86-90.

18. Frederick Lewis Allen, *Only Yesterday: An Informal History of the Twenties* (New York: Bantam Books, 1952), 224, states that appropriations in 1920 provided a force of only 1,520 federal agents.

19. Nelson, "Problems of Prohibition Enforcement," 108-109.

20. Statement of Emily Zeese, the author's mother.

21. West Ms., 24.

22. Interview with Joseph Hasalone, August 18, 1983.

23. Smith, "Localized Aspects of the Urban-Rural Conflict," 69-70.

24. *Salt Lake Tribune,* December 29, 1923.

25. The respondent asked not to be identified because "The U.P. was good to me."

26. *Salt Lake Tribune,* December 29, 1923.

27. For Warshaw's other bootlegging experiences in California, see his autobiography, *Life More Sweet than Bitter* (Salt Lake City, 1975), 157-59.

28. Smith, "Localized Aspects of the Urban-Rural Conflict," 69; interview with Robert Hernon.

29. *Salt Lake Tribune,* May 17, 1929.

30. Interview with Zelpha Vuksinick, April 2, 1980.

31. Kunz, "Provo in the Jazz Age," 35.

32. The godfather of the author's husband.

33. Interview with Ted A. Poulos, October 26, 1980.

34. *Bingham Bulletin,* September 22, 1932; *Salt Lake Tribune,* September 9, 1932.

35. *Salt Lake Tribune,* March 30, 1932, February 24, 1923; story related to author by Myra Varanakis.

36. See Larry R. Gerlach, *Blazing Crosses in Zion: The Ku Klux Klan in Utah* (Logan: Utah State University Press, 1982).

37. Interview with Mr. and Mrs. Andrew Dallas, June 26, 1972.

38. Reminiscence of George Zeese, the author's father.

39. *News Advocate,* April 29, 1920; Nelson, "Problems of Prohibition Enforcement," 117.

40. *Salt Lake Tribune,* June 11, 1930.

41. Lee interview.

42. *Salt Lake Tribune,* January 21, 1928.

43. Ibid.; Nelson, "Problems of Prohibition Enforcement," 129.

44. *News Advocate,* July 24, May 13, 1926; *Bingham Bulletin,* March 10, 1932; *Salt Lake Tribune,* February 17, 1933.

45. Interview with Mrs. John Klekas, May 10, 1979.

46. Interviews with Theodore Heleotes, September 3, 10, 1983; *News Advocate*, July 29, 1926.

47. *To Fos,* September 6, 1923; *Salt Lake Tribune,* November 29, 1923, February 20, 1933; interview with Steve Sargetakis, October 26, 1981.

48. *Salt Lake Tribune,* November 16, 1923; Nelson, "Problems of Prohibition Enforcement," 46.

49. *Salt Lake Tribune*, November 19, 1923; Nelson, "Problems of Prohibition Enforcement," appen. 1.

50. *Salt Lake Tribune,* November 26, 1923; *To Fos,* July 5, 1923.

51. *Salt Lake Tribune,* January 19, 1931; *Price News Advocate,* January 29, 1931; *Salt Lake Tribune,* January 11, 1931. Until mortuaries began sending obituaries to newspapers, families often neglected to insert death announcements. When relatives were involved in shootings, they were even more reluctant to inform newspapers. That, along with incomplete files for some newspapers, makes gathering details of shootings difficult. Accounts are often imprecise but vivid. Everett L. Cooley recalled a Boy Scout trek from West Jordan to Bingham and the awe of seeing the barn in which the shootings over the still took place.

52. *Salt Lake Tribune*, July 30, 1928; *Deseret News*, May 25, 19, 1933.

53. *Salt Lake Tribune,* April 24, 28, 1928; *Sun,* August 30, 1928; Zeese reminiscence; *Salt Lake Tribune,* January 25, 1923, April 6 and May 23, 1933; *Ogden Standard-Examiner,* April 5, 1933. Of the Helper officials, only Charles Bertolino was found innocent, and he became acting mayor.

54. *News Advocate,* April 15, 1927.

55. *Salt Lake Tribune,* February 12, 1931.

56. *News Advocate,* October 31, December 1, 1927.

57. Heleotes interviews.

58. *News Advocate,* April 27, 1922; *Bingham Press Bulletin,* August 9, 1918; *Salt Lake Tribune,* January 17, 1925.

59. *Salt Lake Tribune,* October 25, 1929, January 21, 1923.

60. West Ms., 17.

61. *Sun,* April 28, 1928.

62. Ibid., August 30, 1928.

63. *Salt Lake Tribune,* December 4, 1926.

64. Zeese reminiscence.

65. *Salt Lake Tribune,* February 25, 1931.

66. Herbert Asbury, quoted in Engelmann, *Intemperance*, 161.

67. *Salt Lake Tribune,* May 4, 16, April 6, 1933.

68. Ibid., February 21, 1933.

12.

The Night Before Doomsday

John Farnsworth Lund

It was a sad evening at the Martin apartment on 1st Avenue near Brigham Young's grave in Salt Lake. Mrs. Martin held a shredded handkerchief to puffed, red eyes. I didn't know until much later that her shiny hands with red palms, tissue-soft and cold, and the rosy cheeks which looked as if they were rouged for a party were the badges of an alcoholic. They were called "brandy blossoms." Nor did I understand the row upon row of bottled whisky, beer, and wine stacked in the kitchen cupboard. Mr. Martin spent most of his life in bed in a dark room off the kitchen.

The Martins' son, Claybourne, and I were fast friends and classmates at the Lafayette School on North Temple and State streets. This was the old school which burned down, on the upper grounds. Claybourne was a shy, thin, sensitive boy. Nearly everyone felt a little sorry for him, and even I felt the need to protect him. A few times I'd kept him out beyond the nine p.m. curfew whistle.

"Tomorrow's Doomsday," said Mrs. Martin.[1] "The government's takin' away our liberties. What's to become of us? We laid in what supply we could, but a workin' man can't get far enough ahead to last him very long."

This explained the store of liquor I'd seen in the cupboard. "Yes, ma'am," I whispered, feeling that I must make some answer.

"Claybourne's got to stay in tonight," she said to me. "He can't go no place with you."

"Yes, ma'am." Since I thought the Martins a mysterious family with dark secrets, and since I imagined I'd been taken into their confidence, I could not reveal these matters to anyone. Claybourne explained that tonight was the last time that liquor could be bought legally and that his parents were worried about being cut off from what amounted to their staff of life. It was very nearly the end of the world for them.

Their behavior was strange. They were known to be poor, but Mrs. Martin who was very pretty always had new clothes. It sounded like a picnic when she laughed. She wore high, cloth-topped, buttoned shoes that reached the tops of her calves. These came in black, grey, and tan and boasted high heels. She wore a variety of blouses and jackets that she sometimes changed two or three times a day. They pinched in at her tiny waist and were always of a bright color. Her hats came in all colors and shapes because a lady never appeared on Main Street without a hat. They made her hair look blacker and shinier than ever. She turned many a head including mine, but she spoke softly, her manner gentle and affectionate, and I loved her soft touch.

While the Martins awaited Doomsday, I counted the days until I'd be liberated to long pants. A guy's fourteenth birthday was supposed to be the magic time, but I must report that there was some fudging. However, the code was fairly well kept. A big reason for desiring the long ones was that a pretty girl of thirteen or fourteen avoided being linked with a kid in knee pants. With the casting off of knickers, one also gave up tops, marbles, kick-the-can, and other juvenile activities. With approaching manhood came more serious matters. A fellow had to have a watch, for any man worth his keep sported at least a dollar Ingersoll and a fancy fob. And he must have better shoes. Some went so far as to stop wearing the high-top kid shoes, switching to the new, low oxfords. I began to see that this manhood business was serious and could run into money.

I'd hoped that Claybourne would go downtown with me because it was rumored there would be big doings. My older brothers Cornelius (Curt) and Philo (Phike) were going to witness the celebration, but they did not include me in their plans. My younger brother Alton was too small. Any other time I would have tried to

Salt Lake City three months before Prohibition took effect. Notice how proudly the shop on the left sports a banner-advertisement for Budweiser beer stretching the length of the pediment. On top of the Tribune building a steeplejack hauls a rope up the flagpole. *Photo taken April 6, 1917, Shipler Collection, Utah State Historical Society, all rights reserved*

persuade my cousins Zack, Dick, or Herschel to join me, but tonight I had "loner" tendencies.

Our home stood at the corner of West Temple and North Temple on a dirt road that exploded with dust. The stream from City Creek Canyon ran uncovered down North Temple from Main Street to the Union Pacific Railroad yards. I walked to South Temple where the pavement began and saloons, betting houses, and cheap eating places dotted the streets.

From here to the railroad yards was a haven for Europeans who were brought in as cheap labor for the mines in Park City and Bingham Canyon. These people could not speak English and were preyed upon, abused, and even murdered, according to police reports. Armenians, Greeks, Turks, Serbs, and Italians made up this motley population. They were at the mercy of a few labor contractors who controlled nearly every job, exacting enormous cuts from wages of no more than ten or twelve cents an hour. Signs in mysterious foreign languages covered windows and doors. Rapid-fire talk and explosive laughter burst from the bars. Strong odors of liquor, spices, and sweat covered the neighborhood.

It was the triumphant day of the player piano, and these monstrous machines ground out mechanical versions of "When Irish Eyes Are Smiling," "End of a Perfect Day," "Everybody's Doing It," and the new sensation, "Alexander's Ragtime Band." Foreign saloons and other gathering places for minorities threaded the streets west and south to Pioneer Park and beyond. Second South and Fifth West was the heart of Greektown. I delivered newspapers in this district and was always treated kindly.

The small hotels and rooming houses were often surrounded by grass, flowers, and white picket fences, and eating and drinking was outdoors, weather permitting. Japanese lanterns and Christmas tree candles provided sufficient illumination. Small girls helped with the serving and bussing since this was the custom in the old countries. Extended families from the old to the very young all ate together. The music boomed and loud laughter filled the streets, but I never saw drunkenness or lewd behavior.

When my paper route took me inside the saloons and coffee houses, I made some observations. I almost never saw a woman because there were unwritten customs regarding them. There was often some form of gambling such as faro, cards, or dice. Some places featured a free lunch, although this was strictly policed. I learned that people everywhere seek their own social levels. They always go where they are welcome and comfortable.

One question remained unanswered. Why can't man settle down to serious, purposeful drinking with both feet on the floor? Spittoons stood at the foot of the bar, six feet apart. A rail extended the length of the bar about eight inches off the floor. The rail must have been magnetic, for it drew up one foot from every man in the place. I'm quite sure it's impossible to drink without one foot on the floor and the other on the rail.

This night heavily rouged women stalked customers along the crowded sidewalks, and weak, mean men offered stolen goods and the services of their women at bargain rates. I strolled past the Valley House, a Pony Express stop on the original trail at the southeast corner of South Temple and West Temple. It was a three-story building of adobe, recently stuccoed and painted red. Sandwiches, soft drinks, and gifts could be bought there, and the quaintness of the place attracted tourists. I continued along West Temple past the large Joseph William Taylor Mortuary, a few warehouses, and walk-up hotels to 200 South where I turned east.

A liquor auction offered bargains next to the Orpheum Theatre, which later became the Capitol Theater. An overhead electric sign extended across the street proclaimed the Orpheum vaudeville house the home of the world's best entertainment. W. C. Fields, Barbara Stanwyck, Frank Fay, William S. Hart, Fatty Arbuckle, and others equally famous displayed their acts at the Orpheum. When vaudeville died, the theatre remained empty for a time but reopened under the Capitol name. An electrician told me the name Capitol, with the same number of letters as Orpheum, was chosen because the sign would not have to be rewired.

Stocks of liquor were displayed all over town on tables set on the sidewalks. Peddlers tried to sell leftover supplies. A musician with a small piano mounted on wheels trudged the sidewalks, stopping when he found a friendly group. He stopped playing and moved on when the crowd stopped tossing coins.

The Salvation Army held forth in front of the Kenyon Hotel on the southeast corner of 200 South and Main. Their little band of cornet, bass drum, and trombone accompanied the singing of four or five army soldiers and lassies. The crowd this night paid little attention to them, and I noticed that very few coins were tossed onto the big drum.

Children and teenagers mixed in the crowds, and distraught women with children searched for husbands. A dozen families sat on curbs crying in abandonment. Very few policemen were visible, apparently deciding that arrests for drunkenness and fighting were useless. There was little they could do but let the celebration run its course.

I wanted to see the inside of a bar. A couple of kids about my age entered one on 200 South and I followed them in, but I was so roughly shoved out that I failed to work up enough nerve to try again.

Huge beer wagons lumbered over the streets, drawn by four large horses. They stopped at the larger saloons and hotels. The beds of these wagons hung below the axles, only a foot off the street to expedite the handling of big barrels. Some places lacked enough space at their bars. These had trap doors on the front sidewalk with steel covers. The barrels were let into the basement by chutes or block and tackle. A few had freight elevators. Beer was drawn from the barrels through copper tubing up to the bar. The tubing was encased in ice.

Ministers and members of the Anti-Saloon League patrolled the streets and watched what they mistakenly termed the death struggle of Demon Rum. They held small soapbox meetings, and one speaker pointed out how mankind was cursed with the love of his worst enemy. Great rejoicing and congratulatory back-slapping kept spirits high in these groups.

In front of a house near 200 East where a small crowd had gathered, I caught sight of the Martins as they wound their way to the porch. I looked in horror, but in my fascination I could not turn away. Several men hugged and kissed pretty Mrs. Martin and passed her around before letting her go inside. I was glad Claybourne was not with me. Mr. Martin walked with severe dignity, as stiff as a board. I tired suddenly of the whole scene and wanted to be home.

I went to 100 South and walked past the outdoor markets that lined the street solidly from Main to West Temple. Several of these had locked their doors early to avoid looting and vandalism. Broken glass from thousands of shattered bottles covered the sidewalks and gutters and I was afraid I'd scuff my new Scout shoes. As I approached our house, I heard a loud, forceful discussion at the front door between my father and Curt. It touched on such points as where Curt had been, how much he had drunk, and who the hell did he think he was? As I could add nothing to further the discussion, I slipped around to the back of the house where we boys kept a window unlocked and sprinted up to my bed. Apparently nobody had missed me. Through the night I heard Curt in the bathroom, his head hung over the toilet, bringing up grunts and low animal cries of distress from deep within him. It was the raucous, defiant end of an era.

Three days later I went to the Martins' apartment, but it was empty. I never saw them after that. Perhaps they had gone to a state where they could still buy liquor for a time.

Note

1. Doomsday for drinkers in Utah began at midnight on July 31, 1917. Statewide Prohibition went into effect on August 1, preceding the 18th Amendment by a year and a half. See Larry E. Nelson, "Utah Goes Dry," *Utah Historical Quarterly* 41 (Fall 1973).

13.

Utah's First Convict Labor Camp

Virgil Caleb Pierce

The Mormons who brought permanent settlement to Utah have always believed idleness a curse. Even convicts, it was thought, should not waste valuable time. But how to use their time to best advantage has been a lingering problem. To varying degrees inmates have been permitted to compete with the free labor and free enterprise system by working both inside and outside the prison walls. But their participation in private and public projects has caused controversy, even though nearly all penal institutions, both within Utah and without, have agreed that it is good that convicts work.

Hosea Stout recorded in his diary that in the pre-territorial era convict labor was sold to private individuals. During the territorial period convicts were permitted to labor outside the prison. But under federal law it was illegal to hire or contract prisoners for private work. With statehood in 1896 the new constitution made contract labor and outside projects unlawful except for public works. In 1909 the legislature enabled the state to receive additional convict participation, specifying that prisoners with terms of less than ten years could prepare and provide road-construction materials and help build them. A more extensive law in 1911 repealed most of the previous law to make even more extensive use of prisoner labor on state roads. Among other things, it removed any reference to length of terms in defining eligibility, and it provided for reduction of sentences for efficient work and good behavior. The law was also more detailed regarding the control and supervision of working prisoners.[1]

Utah governor William Spry was anxious to use inmates on a statewide road-building program. Before establishing Utah's first convict labor camp for that purpose, he and state warden Arthur Pratt visited Colorado where they were impressed by the state's low construction costs. They optimistically predicted that Utah would soon have the greatest road network in the country.[2]

It was decided to give convict labor its first tryout in Davis County which had been the first to apply for convicts. Officials saw the need for a road between Ogden and Salt Lake City. The sandy ridge along the mountainside made the existing road almost impassable. Warden Pratt had his men and equipment ready to commence operation on June 1, 1911, but because the county had not procured road machinery or designated its highways, Box Elder County preempted Davis with a road project already underway linking Hot Springs and Willard, bonded at $200,000. Besides being financially prepared, the county had a huge rock crusher and other heavy equipment in place.[3]

After Box Elder County was selected, an area to house the convicts was determined. The *Salt Lake Tribune* reported: "Yesterday afternoon a party of state officials and others came up from Salt Lake City to select a site for the establishment of a convict camp along the route of the state road now under course of construction from Hot Springs to this city [Brigham]. In the party were J. W. Jensen of the State Good Roads commission, Warden Pratt of the state penitentiary, State Engineer Caleb Tanner and a number of other officials and good road experts. The party reached this city in three automobiles and, joined by the local people, including E. W. Dunn of the Commercial club, Road Commissioner P. N. Pierce, Victor E. Madsen and others, they went to a point south of Willard where it was decided to establish the convict camp for about sixty prisoners who will help complete the state road to this city."[4]

The land for the camp was leased from a Willard farmer, Apollos Taylor, Sr., for fifty dollars. Just prior to the selection of the site, the State Board of Road Commissioners had authorized the purchase of $25,000 worth of equipment and materials for the roads and

A convict labor camp consisting of inmates from the state prison at Sugarhouse is busy building public roads. The inmates were placed on their honor not to escape, and only a few did. In exchange for volunteer cooperation, their sentences were reduced ten days for every day worked. The warden felt that the program built character. *Shipler Collection, Utah State Historical Society,*

construction of the camp. The equipment consisted of one concrete roller and a mixer, ten teams of horses, one stone crusher, ten wagons, a 60-horsepower engine, a road sprinkler, and other small pieces of equipment.[5]

On July 12 Governor Spry and S. W. Stewart of the Board of Corrections watched an advance delegation of fifteen convicts, many of them serving life sentences, leave the state prison at Sugarhouse, under guard of Charles Davies and W. D. Davis, with the road equipment and material for the stockade. They also took provisions for two weeks. Three four-horse teams driven by convicts led the procession through the prison gates, the guards on saddle horses. The party made camp that night eight miles south of Ogden and arrived at Willard early the next afternoon.[6]

A five-acre plot of ground was set aside, with a stockade in the center. The prisoners built a fence of barbed wire, with strands four inches apart, around four-by-four posts spaced every eight feet. Near the top of the posts an arm 2.5 feet long was spiked and projected over into the stockade, and on this three wires were strung to prevent prisoners from scaling the top. This enclosure covered an area 125 feet square and would comfortably hold sixty to seventy men. In all, the camp had twenty-three tents: the living areas, a bath, a barber shop, a kitchen, and a dining room, and there was a spring couch for each prisoner. A deadline was placed twenty feet from the perimeter of the stockade to indicate how close curious onlookers could approach. A water trench was dug to connect the camp with the Willard water system. Two strong electric spotlights were placed at the southeast and northeast corners and a large gate consisting of two swinging doors completed the enclosure.[7]

On July 17 an additional thirty-seven prisoners arrived with Warden Pratt, Assistant Warden Andrew C. Ure, and five guards in a special car of the Oregon Short Line and marched from the Willard train stop to camp. With the previous group of fifteen, a total of fifty-two inmates were now at the camp. Most of the new arrivals were serving long sentences, two for life.[8]

All were supplied with two khaki shirts each, trousers, a pair of high-top boots, and a hat—no striped clothing or balls and chains, which had long since been abandoned. In fact, they were given liberty of movement as they hauled crushed material onto the road for distances of two or three miles. They worked eight hours a day as rock-gatherers, blasters, cartmen, cooks, and general road workers. They operated everything but the engine on the rock crusher which was superintended by a Mr. Stevens of Willard. Two trusties did the blacksmithing and were constantly busy repairing machinery and shoeing horses, the latter also cared for by trusties who slept near the stable. A water trough was installed. The camp also possessed a large tent for the horses in bad weather. A commissary was located outside the barbed wire enclosure; a prisoner was detailed to check carefully every article that went in or out.[9]

While living at the camp, the prisoners enjoyed hospitable conditions. The meals, as reported by one writer, were "the best of food." The day he visited, the menu consisted of baked beans, luscious brown potatoes, big juicy slices of beef, a pudding "like mother makes," bread, butter, tea, coffee, and fresh fruit. "So far as eating is concerned," he concluded, "we wouldn't have the slightest objection to residing at the convict camp."[10] Many or possibly all of the vegetables were purchased from local farmers. Fred Woodyatt, a Willard resident, recalls that when he was a boy of about thirteen, a trusty would often come from the camp to his father's farm in a horse-drawn cart to pick up fresh vegetables.[11] Another man, Ace Taylor—now a resident of Bear River City and son of Appollos—who was in high school when he lived in Willard, recalls that his father also sold fresh vegetables to the camp as well as alfalfa for horse feed.[12]

After work the men could take baths, put on a clean change of clothes, and have their supper. They were then permitted to indulge in various kinds of sports and pastimes. The Brigham City newspaper reported that from the electric cars, passengers could occasionally witness the convicts wrestling, boxing, and jumping. One visitor to the camp saw baseballs, gloves, masks, and other sporting equipment hanging in the tents.[13] Ace Taylor remembers the men playing baseball in the field. "I never played ball with them," he said, "but on many occasions I kidded with them."[14] According to Helgar Packer, a Willard LDS bishop who, with his team of horses, had helped gather rock for the road, only one difference separated him and them: he could come and go as he pleased.[15] Governor Spry was boastful about the treatment of convicts: "I was delighted at what I saw during my recent visit to the camp. We have provided clean clothing, clean beds, clean food and surroundings, and have made the conditions as comfortable and agreeable as possible."[16] Other reports support his observation.[17]

There were six experienced guards stationed at the camp and road at all times. At night two of the guards patrolled the stockade; the prisoners were required to turn off their lights at 9:00. Charles Davies, chief guard, was under the jurisdiction of Warden Pratt and the Board of Corrections. It was his responsibility to keep the prisoners secured and to monitor their behavior. The State Road Commission engineered, supervised, and directed the actual work.[18]

The fourteen-foot-wide and eight-inch-deep road was the first in the county to be macadamized. The process involved collecting hillside rock and carting it from one-eighth to one-half mile to the crusher. The crushed rock was then hauled as far as three miles in two yard wagons, where it was spread along the roadway. A finer crushed rock was spread as the top layer; it was then sprinkled with water and rolled down. At times it was necessary to hire non-prisoners to haul rock from the mountainside to the crusher.[19]

At first it was thought that the convicts would build the road to Brigham City, but when their work terminated, the force had graded only one-fourth of a mile of earth road and had laid two and one-fourth miles of macadam road, stretching approximately from Hot Springs to Willard. The cost of the road per mile was $2,054.[20] Because of severe winter weather, on November 13, 1911, thirty-seven of the then forty-five prisoners were transported back to the penitentiary on the Denver and Rio Grande Railroad. They were soon moved south to Washington County to continue state road work in a milder climate. The eight remaining men were left to care for the horses and camp, thinking they would later complete the road between Hot Springs and Willard; but they never did. Nature would not grant them one more week of good weather to finish that stretch. Warden Pratt reported to the *Herald-Republican* upon their departure that he felt "highly elated over the outcome of the first venture in road making by convicts in the State of Utah."[21]

Each convict, before going to the road camp, had a personal interview with the warden, and each gave his word of honor that he would do good work and not escape. Pratt reported on many occasions that men in the state prison were anxious to work on the roads and that applications were received from nearly all of them. The warden was thoroughly converted to the idea of convict labor for public roads. He was convinced that being released from the grim and frowning walls of the prison and working outside encouraged the contentment and future well-being of the prisoners.[22] "Out in the open," he said, "prisoners can feel like men, sleep under the stars, have no steel bar in front of their eyes and be inspired with the idea of 'making good.'"[23] From all indications the warden sincerely thought that this was for the good of the men and not merely a cost-saving scheme for the state.

Ezra Knowlton, a state road engineer at one of the camps in Sanpete County in 1915, said that the warden felt nothing could be better, that Pratt seemed religiously converted to these "honor camps" and expected that the men who worked in them would grow and develop their manhood through this system of reformation.[24] The warden's heart-to-heart interviews must have done some good. One convict stated that the first time he felt any manhood was when he was placed on his honor by the warden.[25] According to Ace Taylor, the men at the Willard camp were honest and pleasant: "Father thought a lot of the ones he knew, and trusted them, even more than he trusted some of his neighbors."[26] Fred Woodyatt remembered them to be a "well behaved bunch of men," even though he did step a little faster past the camp while walking home from school.[27] Taylor and Woodyatt both indicated that the community, as far as they knew, did not resent the camp's presence. In fact, they claimed that farmers were happy to have a place to market their vegetables, as well as to have a good road built through their city. They remembered the camp as well kept and sanitary.

During the five months that the convicts worked on the roads in Box Elder County, not all kept their words of honor. Four men tried to escape and one succeeded. The first to take flight were Paul Van Houghton and Gus Dores on July 27, ten days after the camp was officially opened. They were gone for about seven hours before they were captured by Deputy Sheriff Joseph Saunders in north Ogden.

The men had been given permission to go two miles from the gravel pit. Because of the guard's confidence in them, they were permitted to take their lunch and have one hour for dinner. Another convict noticed their absence and went to the Utah Hot Springs to telephone the alarm. The men had an hour's start before pursuit began. At 8:30 that evening Saunders saw the men in a field and placed them under arrest. Warden Pratt commented: "Both men gave me their word that they would not try to escape if permitted to join the camp. Both had good records and Van Houghton was allowed to work at the fair grounds for 15 days prior to the time he was sent to the camp. They will lose considerable time by their foolish actions. I talked with each of the 52 men at the camp and explained to them if they obeyed the rules each would get a reduction of 10 days for every 30 days they worked."[28] Governor Spry, also quoted in the paper, said that he was grieved by the men's escape. He said that no ball and chain method was forthcoming but that the men would be dealt with. The governor also said that he was very pleased with the public's cooperation in the capture of the men. As a punishment the two were placed back in the penitentiary's "tombs."[29]

The next escape occurred the night of August 8 sometime between midnight and 1:00 a.m. Gus Johnson, serving a term of fifteen years, ten for attempted burglary and five for attempting to take the life of a fellow prisoner, climbed over the barbed wire fence. At noon the next day, Jewell Leavitt, a farmer and manager of the West Weber Cannery, discovered the escapee under the platform of the cannery building. He telephoned the local sheriff who sent his deputy to the scene. The escapee was taken without difficulty. The state had offered a $50 reward for his capture.[30]

The first convict to completely elude the guards was William Jones who left the encampment on November 6, believed headed for Brigham City along the mountainside. He was not to be found. His term of eighteen months for burglary would have expired five months later in April 1912, allowing time for accumulated good behavior.[31] This was the only successful escape during the experiment of the prison camp in Willard.

Other disciplinary problems were less serious. The *Box Elder News* reported an incident with two men who were returned to the penitentiary because they refused to work on the road. They endeavored to spread discontent among the other prisoners by trying to get them to refuse to work.[32]

Although there were more escapes among the road crew than at the prison, the warden still felt that the convict camps were a good thing: "The men appreciate the opportunity to get out for road work, and although there are occasional escapes, on the whole the record for trustworthiness is a good one. In this connection Utah stands ahead of most prisons of the United States. As the record now stands, there are only five men who escaped in the past five years who have not been recaptured. The escapes for the past five years number 18 in all. A representative prison in another state lost 57 men by escapes in only two years. From the prison proper we lost only one man in two years. He was a trusty."[33]

There was not a great deal of adverse publicity over the use of convicts on the public works. However, a rally held by the Socialist Party at Liberty Park, July 2, 1911, included a strong denouncement. About 500 people attended, with Alfred Sorensen presiding. The first of three speakers, E. S. Lund, told of a meeting between the governor and some Socialists who were concerned about unemployment. According to Lund the governor claimed that because the legislature had passed a public works law and failed to fund it, his hands were tied. But Lund concluded that the problem lay in "the use of convicts in public work" which was "a menace to the thousands now out of employment, men whose credit has been exhausted by their necessities. ... Let us make the state come to its senses. If the state sees fit to work convicts, it will have to feed you, and if it feeds you without asking you to work, I wouldn't kick about that."[34]

The second speaker, J. L. Donnelly, spoke briefly and called the governor a capitalist who did not care about the rights of laborers. He said that the solution to convict labor was to elect a Socialist governor. The final speaker, J. H. Walsh—although cut short by a band concert—delivered the longest speech, urging union workers to boycott the state fair because convicts had helped prepare the grounds and criticizing the governor for letting the prisoners labor on public works.[35]

Governor Spry replied to these criticisms at the end of July: "There has been some discussion regarding the men at work on the roads. This discussion has been of an adverse nature and without foundation, for the convicts are not taking work from any individual in any sense whatever. Every dollar that has been appropriated for good roads work will be spent with the public. These convicts are not in any sense competitors to the laboring man, as the work of the convict is largely separate from the appropriation for good roads. Nor are we paying the convicts any wage whatever. Their reward is a shortening of the time they have to serve."[36]

The use of convict labor proved to be financially successful during and after the Willard experiment. In 1911 it cost $2.25 to pay a free laborer for a day, while a prisoner cost an average of only 56 cents. The labor performed on the one project in Box Elder County amounted to 6,503 man-days, which would have totaled $14,632 in wages for non-prisoners, had they been employed, versus $3,609 for inmates—a savings of $11,023 or 25 percent of the fair market price. It must be kept in mind that outside labor was hired and that there were hidden costs involved in using prisoners. It is difficult to determine just how much money was saved, although officials rightly said that the amount was substantial.[37]

Arizona had used convict labor since 1909 and reported that it saved their state approximately the cost of wage labor. Colorado officials calculated the cost at 36 cents a day to use convict labor, whereas it would have cost them $2.50 a day for wage labor.[38]

Utah officials felt strongly that other benefits besides economic ones were derived from the use of convict labor. Warden George A. Storrs in 1918 said: "In conclusion about the road work, it might be pointed out that it is a success from three different angles: the value of roads to the traveling public, the savings to the taxpayers by working the prisoners there the same as on the prison farm, and the matter of giving the prisoners themselves an opportunity to show their worth in some measure, learn how to do a work that is helpful, and to get themselves into a mental state and a physical condition whereby they will be able to do the work secured for them upon their release from the prison, thus saving themselves from further transgression and the expense entailed in the matter of bringing the offenders to account."[39]

After the Willard camp experiment, and the Washington County work during the winter months of 1911-12, a camp was established in Davis County in 1912 where the state had intended to use convicts first. After 1911 most of the work was done on the more difficult and extensive side-hill cuts and on almost impassable sandy sections. Ezra Knowlton said the prisoners were easier to care for in regions where the work was more difficult and that the camps were better operated in less populated areas.[40] But the convict labor experiment had become solidly established in 1911 and would continue until about 1920. Thereafter the practice declined until mostly forgotten by the 1930s. The Depression and a movement toward vocational training for the prisoners were major reasons for the program's decline.[41] However, the convict labor law of 1911 is still on the books, and the state could reissue a call to prisoners to work on the roads today.

The opposition to convict labor arose because of its competition with wage labor. As time went on, other considerations induced the state to provide for vocational training to meet the needs of changing times. Today's experts see the road work as good for its day but irrelevant in the context of the modern, specialized training that prisoners can receive in nearly every imaginable skill, presumably better preparing them to meet society upon release.[42] It appears that convict labor was not only good for the state during a time of changing transportation needs but was an important step toward vocational training in Utah prisons.

Notes

1. Juanita Brooks, ed., *On the Mormon Frontier: The Diary of Hosea Stout, 1844-1861,* 2 vols. (Salt Lake City, 1964), 2:348. For legal background on convict labor, see Utah Territory, *The Compiled Laws of the Territory of Utah ...* (Salt Lake City, 1876). Under Title IV, Sec. 108, the directors of the penitentiary could require convicts to labor on public or private works, and under Sec. 125 the warden could hire out "any or all the convicts." It was possible for private individuals to lease the penitentiary and its labor force or to hire convicts for outside work as prescribed

in Sec. 123. Under Title XXII (2371), Sec. 105, prisoners in county jails could also be summoned to "public works or other works of the county." Later compilations of Utah laws included United States statutes, "Locally Applicable and Important," which prohibited *federal* prisoners from being hired out. (*The Compiled Laws of Utah* ... [Salt Lake City, 1888], Sec. 18.) However, territorial law continued to permit county prisoners to labor on public roads or buildings "for the benefit of the county," chap. 6, p. 304. For applicable laws following statehood in 1896, see State of Utah, *Constitution,* Article Ib; State of Utah, *Laws of the State of Utah* ... (Salt Lake City, 1911), chap. 76.

2. *Salt Lake Tribune,* May 9, 1911, 3.

3. State of Utah, Road Commission, Minutes of the State Road Commission, May 10, 1911, page 28, and June 10, 1911, p. 32, Utah State Archives, State Capitol, Salt Lake City; *Salt Lake Tribune,* June 20, 1911, 14, and May 9, 1911, 3; *Box Elder News* (Brigham City, Utah), June 15, 1911, 1, and September 14, 1911, 28.

4. *Salt Lake Tribune,* June 11, 1911, 3.

5. Box Elder County, Minutes of Box Elder County Board of Commissioners, Book H, 1911, p. 506, Box Elder County Courthouse, Brigham City; interview with Ace Taylor, Bear River City, July 31, 1966; *Deseret Evening News,* June 14, 1911, 5; *Salt Lake Tribune,* June 14, 1911, 16.

6. *Deseret Evening News,* July 13, 1911, 12.

7. State Of Utah, *Second Biennial Report of the State Road Commission* ... 1911 and 1912, bound as number 22 in *Public Documents* (Salt Lake City, 1913), 21; *Box Elder News,* June 15, 1911, 1; August 3, 1911, 1; September 14, 1911, 28, 29; August 17, 1911, 3; August 3, 1911, 1; *Deseret Evening News,* July 13, 1911, 12; interview with Ace Taylor. One tent within the stockade was set aside for Negroes only (referred to as "coons" in the article), according to the *Box Elder News,* August 17, 1911, 3.

8. *Salt Lake Tribune,* July 18, 1911, 11; *Box Elder News,* August 3, 1911, 3.

9. *Deseret Evening News,* July 13, 1911, 12; *Box Elder News,* August 17, 1911, 3.

10. *Herald-Republican,* November 13, 1911, 1.

11. Interview with Fred Woodyatt, Willard, July 31, 1966. He also noted that his father, an English gardener, took pride in growing excellent produce.

12. Interview with Ace Taylor.

13. *Box Elder News,* August 3, 1911, 1.

14. Interview with Ace Taylor.

15. *Box Elder News*, August 17, 1911, 3.

16. Ibid.

17. Ibid., August 3, 1911, 1, and June 15, 1911, 1; interviews with Ace Taylor and Fred Woodyatt.

18. *Box Elder News*, September 14, 1911, 28, and August 17, 1911, 3.

19. *Second Biennial Report of the State Road Commission,* 21; Lydia Walker Forsgren, ed., *History of Box Elder County* (n.p., [1939?]), 142; *Box Elder News,* September 14, 1911, 28.

20. *Deseret Evening News.,* July 13, 1911, 12; *Second Biennial Report of the State Road Commission,* 30.

21. *Herald-Republican,* November 13, 1911, 1.

22. *Box Elder News,* July 20, 1911, 3, and June 15, 1911, 1; *Deseret Evening News,* July 13, 1911, 12.

23. *Deseret Evening News,* December 18, 1915, 56.

24. Interview with Ezra Knowlton, Salt Lake City, August 4, 1966. He worked with Pratt on some of the first road projects where convicts were used.

25. *Box Elder News,* July 20, 1911, 3.

26. Interview with Ace Taylor.

27. Interview with Fred Woodyatt.

28. *Deseret Evening News,* July 28, 1911, 5.

29. Ibid., August 9, 1911, 10.

30. *Salt Lake Tribune,* August 9, 1911, 2; *Deseret Evening News,* August 9, 1911, 10.

31. *Box Elder News,* November 9, 1911, 1.

32. Ibid., September 14, 1911, 28.

33. *Deseret Evening News,* December 16, 1916, 45.

34. *Salt Lake Tribune,* July 3, 1911, 3.

35. Ibid.

36. *Deseret Evening News,* July 28, 1911, 5.

37. *Second Biennial Report of the State Road Commission,* 7-8. See also State of Utah, *Report of the State Board of Corrections* ... 1917-1918, bound as number 9 in *Public Documents* (Salt Lake City, 1919), 10-11.

38. *Public Roads* 2 (May 1919): 16; *Salt Lake Tribune,* May 9, 1911, 3.

39. *Report of the State Board of Corrections,* 11.

40. Interview with Ezra Knowlton.

41. Interview with Ernest Wright, executive director, Board of Corrections, August 4, 1966.

42. Ibid.

14.

Reclamation of Young Citizens

Reform of Utah's Juvenile Legal System, 1888-1910

Martha Sonntag Bradley

Utah's first reform school was created on March 8, 1888, by the territorial legislature. The intent was to provide "for the confinement, discipline, education, employment, and reformation of Juvenile offenders."[1] Over the next seven years reform-minded lawmakers would continue to rethink how the territory viewed children and those responsible for them, culminating in the 1905 establishment of a juvenile court system. Underlying this legislation was a belief that society could improve through progressive action.

In the first decades after the settlement of Utah, the care of neglected, abused, and delinquent children was addressed by Mormon church programs and agencies. Catholics and other denominational groups cared for their children. In the 1880s this tradition of in-house problem solving was supplemented and, in many cases, replaced by legislative decree.

The reform school was just one response to the increasing problems caused by urbanization and industrialization. The socio-economic changes due to the influx of a gentile (non-Mormon) population in the 1860s and 1870s with the founding of Fort Douglas and the development of the mining industry, along with the immigration of culturally diverse groups, upset established methods of control within families and neighborhoods. Earlier structures of authority and regulation showed signs of weakness that were reflected in increased crime among children. Not that this was just a problem of the city. However, urbanization and youth offenses did increase simultaneously and were indubitably related.

It seems that rapid population growth aggravated problems that already existed in urban areas. During the first two decades of the twentieth century, Utah's population would increase 69 percent. The populations of both Salt Lake City and Ogden would double in size; by 1920 half of all Utahns would live in cities. The move for reform recognized the emerging strains on Utah's society. As early as 1896, Utah would prohibit the employment of boys under fourteen and all females from working in mines and smelters. In the next two decades, boys under fourteen and girls under sixteen would be excluded from night work and limited to a fifty-four-hour work week of nine-hour days except in agriculture and domestic service. Finally in 1911 Utah would join seven other states in regulating children in street trades and prohibiting those under fourteen from occupations dangerous to their health or morals.

But in the late nineteenth century, children were prosecuted as young adults. Territorial law did not provide courts of summary jurisdiction. Yet children were not guaranteed the rights and privileges that their adult counterparts enjoyed. For instance, children could be seized without warrant or legal decree solely on the personal responsibility of the arresting officer. They were often thrust before the court without notification of the nature of their offense, assuming that the judge would give formal notice to the guardians and agents of the court (attorney, probation officers, sheriffs, etc.). Often the individual child's interest in the case was entirely disregarded.

The most fundamental flaw in the system was the punishment stage. By law all persons were equally liable, except for children under seven years of age if it could be determined that the latter did not know what they did was wrong. It was generally acknowledged that placement of children in adult jails would adversely affect their well-being. As a result, many judges ducked the issue entirely, leaving children unpunished or unrehabilitated. Other judges passed sen-

Ephraim G. Gowans, a physician and educator from Tooele, Utah, was one of the state's first probation officers for children. He believed that a caring and lenient approach to juvenile crime was the best policy, with an aim toward preventing future misdeeds. A bad home environment was to blame, according to Gowans—the absence of "a strong manly man and a loving womanly woman." *Utah State Historical Society, all rights reserved*

tences too severe considering the defendant's age. A consistent attitude towards children could not be developed, lacking official policy and procedures. Each case was treated individually.

Such problems prompted the establishment of the reform school. This bipartisan effort was backed by altruistic ideas about the potential for altering the life course of wayward youth by providing, first, for their confinement and, second, by attempting to discipline, educate, employ, and generally reform them. The redemptive rather than punitive function of the institution reflected the idealistic belief in affirmative action.

The bill was championed by legislator James H. Moyle, a Salt Lake City attorney who was later appointed chair of a committee to gather information across the United States. The committee left Utah on May 10, 1888, to inspect fourteen reform schools from Colorado to Washington, D.C. The institutions varied widely from prison-like facilities to "the Michigan plan" which, as recommended by the committee, patterned "the school on home life with a father and mother in a separate home with as many inmates as they could care for." Moyle recognized that the legislature had provided for only one building, "but the ideal was to make the [Ogden] school as near like a home as possible."[2]

Lawmakers had allotted $35,000 for land, buildings, and staff salaries. The school was built between Monroe and Jackson avenues and 19th and 20th streets in Ogden, and opened on October 31, 1889. By the end of the first year, suitable workshops, classrooms, and dormitories for 100 children were available for use. The sixty-acre site was reputed to be in the highest state of cultivation. The workshops were of prime importance, "for unless the reform school boy, upon his return to the busy world is able to earn an honest livelihood, he must, in order to exist, of necessity go back to his bad ways and evil associates, and subsist by vagrancy or dishonesty." The committee emphasized "the need of a good common school education and a practical training in some class of work that will enable [a boy] to confidently face the world, and say 'I am able to earn an honest living and I mean to do it.'" Such was the optimism of the day that the committee felt this education would make a boy's reformation "an assured fact."[3]

The school suffered a major setback on June 24, 1891, when the main building was partially destroyed by fire. The forty-nine boys were taken to the Ogden Military Academy and the six girls to the reform-farm barn until other accommodations could be found. According to a newspaper report, "None of the incorrigibles escaped, although one or two of the boys made a dash for liberty." Plans for rebuilding the school were discussed almost immediately.[4]

Progress at the school was initially good; public support and the opinion of the school superintendent indicate that "much good" was being accomplished. However, the school faced challenges. Throughout the early years, finances were a perpetual problem, as was the constant need for general repair and improvement of the buildings.

Although the school's administration was vested in a superintendent and seven-member board, ultimate authority was retained by the legislature. Still, the success or failure rested with the board, consisting of men from a variety of different backgrounds—lawyers, farmers, and educators. Five of the seven men were Latter-day Saint leaders who had no fewer than nine children each of their own. The biennial reports to the governor indicate that what bound this assortment of Republicans and Democrats together was their common commitment to the school. They were directed to report on the school's progress and to make a close accounting of all financial concerns. Outside of official committee work the group lobbied for continued financial aid. Periodically representatives from the legislature visited the school to study its progress or problems. Their findings were reported to the entire legislative body.

An obvious discrepancy existed between the philosophy of lawmaking and that of law enforcement about the purpose of the school. Under the statute, "[W]hen a boy or girl within the age of 18 years, shall, in any of the District Courts of the Territory, be found guilty of any crime, except murder, the court may, if in its opinion the accused is a proper subject therefore, instead of entering judgement, cause an order to be entered, that such boy or girl be sent to the Reform School."[5] This generous provision reserved judgment about a child's guilt or innocence and reflected the belief that these children could be redeemed and should be given a fresh start. Addressing this issue in 1896, Superintendent E. M. Allison said he was saddened by the fact that "where an inmate has been remanded to the school, the general idea has prevailed that the accused has received the judgement of the court to be committed to the Reform School instead of to some other place of punishment, and the original purpose of the law-givers that the child should not be punished at all, but removed from [the] surroundings which presumably led it into temptation, is entirely lost sight of."[6] His focus on environmental determinism, the potential for changed character through changed environs which was a common theme in progressive reform literature, was diametrically opposed to the use of the school for punishment. The latter concept placed a premium on the length of stay in the institution, rather than on the benefits and changes that might result.

The progressive notion about the school centered on its unique potential for correcting the evils of a society gone bad and on the chance to forge improved character. This was expressed in the committee's declaration of the school's purpose which emphasized the potential for improvement: "By reason of the youth of the offender [his offense] ought not to be punished, but ... the State ought to let the Reform School have control over the child, surround it with different attractions, give it a different idea of life than it has had, and in return for such control, the Reform School in effect promises ..., unless the child is confirmed in crime, or otherwise so morally depraved that reform is impossible[,] that whenever that child shall be discharged from the school, it shall as any patient from a hospital, or as any unfortunate from an asylum, [because they] have improved. ..."[7] Thus clearly stated, these objectives anticipated a sound moral foundation for the students that would in turn benefit the state.

The debate continued over the school's function, often focusing on the question, "Do reform schools reform?" Some idealistically justified the school by describing the regenerative powers of good health habits, the connection between mental and physical discipline, and, finally, the effect of positive environment on character. In 1896 Superintendent Allison described the cleansing process that students went through: "As a rule, inmates come to us with their elementary education entirely neglected, with no home training, and never having been taught any lessons of industry and honesty of purpose. They are confirmed truants. The quick transformation of such boys is wonderful. Regular habits in diet, sleep, exercise and in mental discipline works the reform. In a few months, boys have been known to make such rapid physical growth that parents and guardians have failed to recognize them at once. Taken from the streets of a city, half starved and poorly clad, with the tobacco, and, in many instances, the liquor habit firmly fixed and pervading their systems, and removal to clean apartments, provided with warm clothing, given plain but wholesome food, total abstinence from injurious habits, and the change affected is at once marked and surprising." He passionately concluded: "If these schools did no more than to develop the physical manhood by keeping them removed from the contaminating influences of a city life until they attained their majority, when they will be sufficiently able to control themselves, and will have been 'tided' over the dangerous period of life, [that] would in my opinion compensate the state for their maintenance."[8]

Despite a widening gap between theory and practice, the reform school had made a serious and dedicated attempt at the rehabilitation of 184 young citizens by the time Utah became a state. Almost from its inception the leaders of the institution had directed youth towards improvement in four areas of development: discipline, education, employment, and general reformation.

The modest staff in 1894 included Superintendent Isaac D. Haines, his wife (the school matron), and one instructor. Dr. J. S. Gordon, an Ogden physician, periodically visited the institution to attend to health problems. Discipline was considered basic to the efficient operation of the school, and a firm structure of rules and regulations directed daily life. Usually reform institutions adhered to one of two basic disciplines: strict military regimentation or corporal punishment. Superintendent Haines attempted to create a balance between the two, "administered in an intelligent and humane manner." By his order no punishment could be given at random or without his prior consent and supervision; it was considered by most a "painful duty."

In many ways the school's curriculum sought to imitate the functions of the family, providing structure and training in moral, religious, and civic areas. The moral well-being of each student was considered equal in importance to "book learning" to prepare for a productive life.

Education included traditional reading, writing, and mathematics but also stressed the development of skills in various kinds of industrial work. The basic purpose of what was often called the "industrial" school was to provide students with a means of securing a living. In the 1890s, for instance, an effort was made to establish the silk industry at the school. Tomizo Katsunuma, an expert on the subject, was consulted about the feasibility of the idea, but it never came to fruition.

The school had less than thirty females in its first six years, but these girls created problems for the administration. Nearly every girl had been charged with vagrancy or incorrigible conduct, but according to Superintendent David A. Curry the girls were actually offenders "against virtue" and their cases had been mislabeled to save families from disgrace. They were, for the most part, older than their male counterparts and likely to stir up trouble and promote immoral conduct among willing male delinquents. As a result, each report to the legislature had its accompanying plea for separate facilities.

The public support for the school reflected a general concern about young people and, in the reformation of youth, for the future of society. This philosophy was formed with a "view to reclaim youth, before it has become too far tainted with crime, and thus not only save to the state the expense of future criminal trials and detention, but also secure from the future labors of such youth, that support, which every re-claimed citizen as a special token of gratitude would naturally give the state."[9] The image of a caring society that reclaimed its wayward citizens justified the reformers' efforts.

At the same time that these ideals were expressed, an attempt was being made to modify laws accordingly. One objection to the 1853 statute was that it failed to define or provide punishment for a large class of offenses against public health and safety, including the safety of children. The laws were either vague or reticent on behavior that affected children.

Territorial laws were created for a different society—a sparsely settled place where a majority was involved in agriculture. Since that time, mining, manufacturing, and commerce had been introduced;

the population had increased tenfold; and the development of cities and contact with the outside world had changed social conditions. The territorial code was wholly inadequate for the new state of Utah.

One example of an improved statute was in the description of what constituted abuse or neglect. Territorial laws gave a general description of the responsibilities of guardians and parents to minor dependents in matters of physical care, education, and the necessity for stimulating their civic responsibility. But in dealing with the issue from a positive rather than negative point of view, it left matters unresolved.

The new state attempted to ensure the support and protection of children by clearly delineating the obligations of parents. Basically a parent or guardian was guilty of a misdemeanor if he or she willfully omitted, "without lawful excuse, to perform any duty imposed upon him by law to furnish necessary food, clothing, shelter, or attention for such child."[10]

As early as 1903 the legislature initiated action to protect the abused child, setting up "Children's Aid Societies" to care for those who needed to be removed from their homes. These foster-care units, like the settlement house movement, offered an environmental approach to social problems. The "place of safety," as the legislation described it, funded by municipal or county money, provided a way-station for troubled youths as protection from the influences of a bad home, to introduce them to new and more appropriate methods of living. The legislation's paternalism conveyed a conviction that government had the right to intervene into even the most private areas of its citizens' lives for the public good and the future of society.

The law addressed the issue of children who were willfully mistreated, neglected, abandoned, or exposed in a way that might have caused unnecessary suffering or serious injury to its health or morals. Certain forms of neglect were blatantly obvious, as in the case of a child found begging in the streets, sleeping at night in the open air along the roadside, or wandering about without a home or settled place to go to. These, as all abused children, could be apprehended without warrant and taken before the court for their own protection. Children found in the company of criminals, thieves, drunkards, vagrants, or other social malcontents, as well as those found in saloons, gambling halls, or brothels, could also be seized and brought before the court.

Evidence of abuse was also found in the conduct of the parents or guardians themselves. Children who failed to receive proper instruction or care because the "only surviving parent or guardian, is an habitual drunkard, or a person of notorious or scandalous conduct, or a reputed thief or prostitute or an habitual idler,"[11] or who were in the company of a "vicious or dissolute father or mother," could be apprehended. Often the reputation of the adult was enough to warrant action. Clearly the law set the well being of the child ahead of the custody rights of the parents.

With a new century came a general public awakening to the needs and rights of children as other facilities, similar to the state reform school, were established throughout Utah. Canyon Crest Boys Ranch, Uintah Training School, and the Lund Home for boys were all funded and maintained by private philanthropies. The December 1908 meeting of the Utah Federation of Women's Clubs included in its resolutions the objective of guaranteeing every child a good life.

The glaring inadequacies of the state's legal system was the battle cry for lobbyists who pushed for the creation of a juvenile court system. Success was met in 1905 when the court was created, not because of an overload of cases but because of an impulse to restructure the system, to create a viable social order that included children. Like the push to establish a reform school, the juvenile court represented an attempt at making sense out of the bewildering changes in the social order and to perhaps grasp control over society's new face.

In the early years of the court when the number of cases did not require a full-time judge or staff, judges served on a part-time basis for an annual salary of $1,000, sharing clerks and other officers with the city court. In cities of the first and second class, a commission consisting of the mayor, chief of police, and school superintendent was called for, with power to make court appointments.

The court had jurisdiction in all cases relating to the "custody, detention, guardianship of the person, probation, neglect, dependency, delinquency, examination, trial and care of children who are eighteen years of age and under." It had jurisdiction as well over adults accused of misdemeanors "relating to the custody, detention, guardianship, probation, neglect, dependency, delinquency, and care of children ...."[12] The juvenile court was therefore envisioned as having special jurisdiction over all cases relating to children.

A concomitant shift in attitude attended the new laws that clearly described procedures, rights, and practices in prosecuting youth. Utah minors had never been guaranteed equal constitutional rights with their adult counterparts, including trial by jury, notification of the nature of the accusation against them, or being delivered a warrant for their arrest.

Significantly the 1905 law was "not ... a criminal law, but ha[d] for its object the surrounding of such children with proper environments," and asserted for itself that it "violates no constitutional provisions [by] not providing for trial by jury, for arraignment and plea, a warrant, etc.; nor because of the manner of trial and examination, and the child, being required to be a witness."[13] Traditional criminal procedures would not apply in juvenile court.

This principle had been established by *Mull v. Brown* which stated that children could not be considered criminals. As different as this assumption was from that of modern legislation that guarantees children rights under all circumstances, the logic was consistent with the efforts to create a beneficial court, to clarify the law, and to establish reform facilities—all of which sprang from the belief that intervention was not only necessary and justifiable but a moral obligation.

In all matters relating to delinquent children and their disposition, the juvenile court exercised equity jurisdiction, adopting any procedure best suited to ascertain the truth in a particular case. The hearing was relatively simple, even informal. Young defendants were often compelled to testify concerning the allegations against them, with probation officers or other informed persons providing additional information. The judge evaluated the culpability of the suspect and determined the fitness of the person who had asserted rights of custody. Children were protected from intimidation by adults by a statute that provided for their exclusion "from the room or place where any child under 16 years of age is being tried, or having its case examined. ..."[14]

Throughout the territorial period minors were recognized as witnesses, which were defined by law as those who "can perceive, and, perceiving, can make known their perceptions to others."[15] The only restriction was on "children under ten years of age, who appear incapable of receiving just impressions of the facts respecting which they are examined, or of relating them truly."[16] However, common practice not only allowed children to testify but often compelled them to give information against their parents. They testified against their fathers in many of the cohabitation trials of the 1880s and 1890s, forced onto the stand by federal officials. Clearly the statements of a child would be cast with shades of love, aversion, or fear that would affect the veracity of the testimony.

By comparison, most orders, judgments, and decrees of the juvenile court truly attempted to adjust to the unique set of circumstances surrounding each individual case and were therefore subject to adaptation, amendment, modification, or suspension at any time until the child reached age twenty-one. Although the court could exercise a variety of options in dealing with children, each emphasized rehabilitation through an improved environment.

Ultimately the optimum situation was a good home with capable concerned parents or guardians to respond to the child's problems, along with a probation officer to carefully monitor, visit, and maintain a relationship with both the child and his or her parents. But many children created havoc at home, had no family, or in the opinion of the court had an undesirable home environment. In those cases the court looked for an alternate solution to the problem.

The first official, state-sponsored foster homes were instituted under the new provisions for juvenile justice. Commitment to state or private correctional institutions was usually reserved for crimes of a serious nature. The only alternative expressly forbidden by the state was the incarceration of a child; children could not be imprisoned with adults.

The probation officer was the pivotal figure in this new juvenile court system, and success or failure often depended on his intuition and good judgment. Probation officers were paid twice as much as judges although employed part time. They functioned in the court as the agent of the child. They did most of the legal legwork, including filing complaints, serving notices, and ensuring the appearance of the youth before the court. Responsible for the child both before and after the hearing, the probation officer was instructed to "exercise a friendly supervision and visitation over the child in accordance with the directions of the Court."[17]

Probation officers investigated all juvenile offenses. They prepared a detailed precursor of the modern "home study," consisting of an inquiry into the parentage of the child and a full examination of the circumstances surrounding the case. They submitted a written report to the judge. These reports attest to the variety of home situations that produced young criminals. Dr. Ephraim G. Gowans's visit to the home of one boy typified the problems encountered: "his mother upon the sick bed, told me that she wished me to take charge of him. She stated that he was absolutely incorrigible; that he would get several boys around him in a back room in the home and there smoke cigarettes and read dime novels; that he threatened her life whenever she corrected him; that he would not stay at home nights and was always running away."[18] These children, for whatever reasons, were beyond parental control.

Gowans, a physician and educator from Tooele, Utah, believed that young lives could be changed. Despite his busy schedule as town physician and instructor at the University of Utah, he devoted considerable time to the juvenile court system.

He described the basic methodology of the probation system. He would begin by "inquiring into the alleged delinquency and getting a knowledge, in an informal way, of all the facts relative thereto. In a great many cases the matter is found to be trivial; or the information was filed when the informant was angry, or an amicable settlement can be had without further proceedings."[19] In fact, twice as many cases were solved informally out of court as in. Gowans further maintained that these children were "undoubtedly benefitted by this, as we think, sane method of procedure."[20]

Children judged delinquent and placed under a probation officer's care were instructed to report daily, biweekly, or weekly, which, it was felt, kept a "restraining influence" around the child that tempered his or her misbehavior. The system sought both rehabilitation and the prevention of future crime. One officer said, "We feel that whatever we do in the way of prevention is far superior and more nearly truly philanthropy. The methods of dealing with younger boys must differ from those employed with the offenders who are 17 and 18 years of age. With the younger children, prevention is the keynote of our work."[21]

These informative reports indicate sincere interest in the child's welfare. In describing this important work, one officer centered on the relationships that were formed: "The labor and efforts of the Probation Officers cannot be shown by statistical tables because wherever they are they make their influence felt as the friends of the boys and girls. Hundreds of cases have been investigated in an unobtrusive way and quietly settled. Hundreds of others have been reminded of their little delinquents and in a friendly way made to feel that we were looking after them."[22]

The system's inherent reformist impulse was nowhere more apparent than in its concern with the causes of crime. Each report attempted to assess the "unfavorable and menacing elements in the child's environment" that prompted misbehavior, concluding that the chief cause of delinquency was an unsatisfactory home. This type of environment was described by Gowans as being "broken up by the entrance of one or more of three D's Death, Divorce, Desertion [or] ... not [being] presided over by a strong manly man and a loving womanly woman. They are homes in which either the father or mother or both, have some vicious habit. The viciousness may take the form of an uncontrollable temper which leaves no room for parental affection and solicitude, it may take the form of drunkenness with all of its damning sequellae, or simply the viciousness of indifference."[23] A second type of home had a parent who appeared to be incapable of effective parenting or affirmative action of any sort. This was attributed to the fact that people often had "absolutely no preparation for parenthood. They are passively good only. Being weak-willed they seem to be incapable of creating in the home that atmosphere of vigorous, wholesome morality, that mental attitude of no compromise with evil or lawbreaking which is absolutely necessary to the development of desirable citizenship."[24] It was felt that all other causes of delinquency could be precluded if the "unsatisfactory" home could be eliminated, which was this particular reforming officer's primary objective. Other causes of delinquency such as dance halls, theaters, and rooming houses were faulted because of the lack of control at home.

Each year a careful accounting of all cases was presented in the "Report of Operation of the Juvenile Courts," a document that enumerated the statistics of juvenile crime for the period. By comparing the reports over five years, it is possible to discern early patterns of problems. Fifty percent of all boys brought before the court were between the ages of thirteen and sixteen. Female delinquents were older, the majority between fifteen and seventeen years, and were usually accused of immoral conduct. One officer felt that this was the "age of vulnerability in girls. Many girls go wrong at this time because their mothers do not sufficiently understand the difficulties of the period in the girl's development, and have not established such confidence between themselves and their daughters as to be able to correctly advise them."[25]

Problems with truancy, curfew violation, and general incorrigibility implied laxity on the part of guardians who undoubtedly did not put limits on the behavior of the child. Thirty percent of all juvenile offenses, such as drunkenness, smoking, visiting saloons or pool halls, and crimes of violence, fighting, assault and battery, were committed exclusively by boys. Despite the disobedient and spirited nature of most delinquent girls, they were not culturally liberated; in 1900 there were still certain things that girls, no matter how wild they were, did not do.

The period from 1888 to 1910 formed a transition. The gears of society were shifting. The individualism of the nineteenth century was giving way to a new theory of law-like regularities in human experience and the ability to put in place predictable controls and programs. The new approach was more collectivist—supporting the weaker members, correcting, improving, and streamlining the mechanisms of society.

It is evident that the reform measures were not always successful. The actual cumulative benefits of the changes in the juvenile court system were minimal. In fact, in many ways the legislation institutionalized practices that restricted or blatantly denied the rights of children. But this was true in the country at large. The paternalism so typical of the era, the authoritarian absolutism that delegated for the masses the way to the good life, denied in the same way the civil rights of a major subgroup or class, that of children who had limited ability to vocalize, lobby, or demand representation. Not until the 1960s did the legal rights of children begin to approximate those of adults.

But certain aspects of the reform movement had an enduring effect on Utah society. Reform schools multiplied across the state. The juvenile court system continued. Today the court deals with young criminals in a professional and caring way, with a sophisticated staff of full-time judges, probation officers, and prosecuting attorneys. The tradition of protecting the youngest members of society remains. Its genesis is in the nineteenth century and the progressive movement when individuals first questioned the efficacy and fairness of laws relating to children.

Notes

1. Utah Territory, *Act of the Utah Territorial Legislature to Establish a Territorial Reform School, Statutes* (March 8, 1888), sec. 1.

2. *Mormon Democrat: The Religious and Political Memoirs of James Henry Moyle,* ed. Gene A. Sessions (Salt Lake City: Historical Department, Church of Jesus Christ of Latter-day Saints, 1975), 175-76. Moyle served three terms on the school's board of trustees and eventually became president of the board.

3. The committee's report was published in the *Ogden Semi-weekly Standard,* August 11, 1888.

4. *Salt Lake Tribune,* June 25, 1891.

5. Utah Territory, *Act ... to Establish a Territorial Reform School,* sec. 1.

6. Utah Territory, *Fourth Bi-ennial Report of the Trustees of the Territorial Reform School* (1896), 6.

7. Ibid., 7.

8. *First Annual Report of the Trustees of the State Industrial School ... 1896,* 11-12, bound in State of Utah, *Public Documents,* 1896. The new state legislature changed the name of the institution to the State Industrial School and made provisions to turn over the original building to the State School for the Deaf and Dumb and purchase the campus of the Ogden Military Academy in the northern part of the city for the Industrial School. Ibid., 5, 8.

9. Utah Territory, *Fourth Bi-ennial Report of the Trustees of the Territorial Reform School* (1896), and accompanying documents, December 31, 1895.

10. Utah, *Penal Code* (1896), 4224, p. 902, Special Collections, Law Library, University of Utah, Salt Lake City.

11. *Laws of the State of Utah* (1903), chap. 124, sec. 2.

12. *The Compiled Laws of the State of Utah* (1907), 720x1, p. 361.

13. Ibid.

14. *The Compiled Laws of the State of Utah* (1907), 720x32, p. 371.

15. *Compiled Laws of Utah* (1888), vol. 2, Title X, chap. 1, sec. 3876, s1154.

16. Ibid., sec. 3877, s1155.

17. "Probation Officer's Report to the Juvenile Court," 1907, Utah State Archives, Salt Lake City.

18. "General Complaint Register Record Book," February 9, 1908-April 17, 1908, Utah State Archives.

19. "Report to Juvenile Court Committee of the State of Utah," December 14, 1907, Utah State Archives.

20. Ibid.

21. Ibid.

22. Ibid.

23. "Probation Report," December 14, 1908, Utah State Archives.

24. Ibid.

25. "Probation Report," December 14, 1907.

Index

I

J

R

T

Y

Z

Contributors

THOMAS E. AUSTIN writes for *Utah Outdoors* and has authored three novels and contributed to several anthologies. At the time his essay was first published, he was the sheriff of Blanding, Utah. "Murder, Mayhem, and Mormons" appeared in 1987 (*Utah Historical Quarterly,* vol. 55, pp. 36-49).

MARTHA SONNTAG BRADLEY is an associate professor in the Graduate School of Architecture at the University of Utah. Her latest of seven books is *Four Zinas: A Story of Mothers and Daughters on the Mormon Frontier.* "Reclamation of Young Citizens" appeared in 1983 (UHQ, vol. 51, pp. 328-45).

DAVID L. BUHLER is a Salt Lake City Councilperson and Associate Commissioner of Higher Education for the state of Utah. He has been a Utah State Senator and member of the board of trustees for the University of Utah. "The Peculiar Case of James Lynch" appeared in 1992 (UHQ, vol. 60, pp. 101-23.

KENNETH L. CANNON II is an attorney in Salt Lake City and a former member of the Advisory Board of Editors for *Utah Historical Quarterly.* He is the author of an illustrated history of Utah County, *Provo & Orem: A Very Eligible Place.* "'Mountain Common Law'" appeared in 1983 (UHQ, vol. 51, pp. 308-27).

CRAIG L. FOSTER is a research librarian at the Family History Library in Salt Lake City and an executive officer of the Mormon History Association. "The Sensational Murder of James R. Hay" (for which he thanks Suzanne Foster, Marianne Sharp Long, Newell G. Bringhurst, and Elizabeth J. Hay Zobell for their assistance) appeared in 1997 (UHQ, vol. 65, pp. 25-48).

H. DEAN GARRETT is a professor of church history at Brigham Young University (currently on leave as president of the Calgary, Alberta, mission of the LDS church). He is the editor of *Regional Studies in Latter-day Saint History* and co-author of *A Commentary on the Doctrine and Covenants*. "The Controversial Death of Gobo Fango" appeared in 1989 (UHQ, vol. 57, pp. 264-72).

LARRY R. GERLACH is a professor of history at the University of Utah. He is the author of fifteen books on the American Revolution, baseball, the Ku Klux Klan, and Utah topics—most recently *The Men in Blue: Conversations with Umpires*. "Ogden's Horrible Tragedy" and "Justice Denied" appeared in 1981 and 1998 respectively (UHQ, vol. 49, pp. 157-72; vol. 66, pp. 355-64). The latter was first presented at a commemorative gathering in the Price, Utah, cemetery on April 4, 1998.

JOHN FARNSWORTH LUND, now deceased, was a retired businessman living in Salt Lake City at the time his essay was first published in 1983. "The Night Before Doomsday" appeared in UHQ, vol. 51, pp. 154-61.

JOHN S. MCCORMICK is a professor of history at Salt Lake Community College. His most recent of nine books is *The Gathering Place: An Illustrated History of Salt Lake City*. "Red Lights in Zion" appeared in 1982 (UHQ, vol. 50, pp. 168-81).

ROBERT S. MCPHERSON is a professor of social sciences at the College of Eastern Utah-San Juan Campus, a member of the Advisory Board of Editors for *Utah Historical Quarterly*, and author of *A History of San Juan County* and five other books. "Murder, Mayhem, and Mormons" appeared in 1987 (UHQ, vol. 55, pp. 36-49).

HELEN PAPANIKOLAS is a Fellow of the Utah State Historical Society and former member of the Board of State History. She is the author of seven books on Utah and western history, biography, and fiction including the novel, *The Time of the Little Black Bird*. "Bootlegging in Zion" appeared in 1985 (UHQ, vol. 53, pp. 268-91).

VIRGIL CALEB PIERCE was a teacher at Henry Perrine Baldwin High School on the island of Maui, Hawaii, at the time his essay was first published in 1974. "Utah's First Convict Labor Camp" appeared in UHQ, vol. 42, pp. 245-57.

JOHN S. H. SMITH is a professor of humanities and social sciences at Great Basin College in Elko, Nevada, and recipient of the 1998 Nevada Regents' Teaching Award. "Cigarette Prohibition in Utah" appeared in 1973 (UHQ, vol. 41, pp. 358-72).

MARY VAN WAGONER is an instructor in English at Salt Lake Community College and a member of the Lehi (Utah) Historical Preservation Commission. "Arthur Pratt: Utah Lawman" appeared in 1987 (UHQ, vol. 55, pp. 22-35).

RICHARD S. VAN WAGONER is a clinical audiologist in Salt Lake City, the Lehi City Historian, and a member of the Advisory Board of Editors for the *Utah Historical Quarterly*. He is the author of five books, most recently *Sidney Rigdon: A Portrait of Religious Excess*. "Arthur Pratt: Utah Lawman" appeared in 1987 (UHQ, vol. 55, pp. 22-35).

The articles in this anthology have been edited slightly for length.